PETRONIUS

Selections From The
Satyricon

PETRONIUS

Selections From The
Satyricon

**Introduction, Facing Vocabularies, Notes By
Gilbert Lawall**

Third Revised Edition - 1995

BOLCHAZY-CARDUCCI PUBLISHERS, INC.

Third Revised Edition 1995
Reprint 1997

Printed in the United States of America
1997

ISBN 0-86516-288-3

Bolchazy-Carducci Publishers, Inc.
1000 Brown Street
Wauconda, IL 60084

http://www.bolchazy.com

TABLE OF CONTENTS

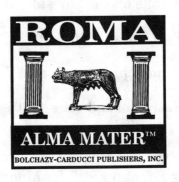

ROMA
ALMA MATER™
BOLCHAZY-CARDUCCI PUBLISHERS, INC.

INTRODUCTION

Petronius

Petronius, a member of Nero's court, earned the cognomen **Arbiter Ēlegantiae**, *Arbiter of Elegant Living*. He was a man of pleasure, wit, and style. When a charge of treason was trumped up against him, he killed himself by slowly bleeding to death (A.D. 66). Almost all we know about the man himself is contained in the following passage from Tacitus' *Annals* (16.18–19):

> His days were spent in sleep, his nights in duties and the pleasures of life. As industry had brought others to fame, so laziness brought him, and he was regarded not as a debauchee and spendthrift, as are most of those who squander their resources, but as a man of refined luxury. The more his words and deeds were unrestrained and displayed a certain neglect of his own best interests, the more they gave an appearance of simplicity and were received with goodwill. Yet when proconsul of Bithynia and then consul he showed himself vigorous and equal to his tasks. Then relapsing into his old vices, or merely imitating them, he was absorbed into the small group of men close to Nero as his arbiter of elegant living, with Nero thinking that nothing had charm or was conducive to delicate living unless Petronius had given it his stamp of approval. For this reason Tigellinus became jealous of Petronius as if he were a rival possessing greater knowledge of the science of pleasures. Therefore he addressed himself to the emperor's cruelty, which surpassed all the emperor's other passions, charging Petronius with complicity with Scaevinus, having first bribed one of Petronius' slaves to turn informer and then having removed any chance of his defending himself and having put the greater part of his household slaves in prison.
>
> It chanced that at that time the emperor had gone to Campania, and Petronius had progressed as far as Cumae when he was detained there. He did not brook any further delay, either of his fear or his hope, nor, however, did he take a headlong departure from life. Having cut his veins, he bound them up and opened them again as he pleased, and he talked with his friends, but not on serious matters or in order to seek glory for his steadfastness. Rather, as he listened, his friends were not talking about the immortality of the soul and the beliefs of philosophers but reciting frivolous poems and light verse. He awarded some of his slaves presents, others lashings. He partook of a banquet and indulged himself with sleep, so that his death, although forced upon

him, would seem natural. He did not flatter Nero or Tigellinus or any other powerful person even in his will, as most of those forced to commit suicide did. Rather, he wrote up the scandalous acts of the emperor with the names of his male and female prostitutes and the novelty of each one of his sexual crimes, and he sent the document to Nero under his own seal. He then broke his signet ring so that it would not be of use to mischief makers.

The *Satyricon*

To our surprise, Tacitus does not even mention Petronius' main claim to fame, his literary work, the *Satyricon*, in which he portrays and comments on the affluence, lust, greed, and luxury of life in the age of Nero. Only fragments of this work have been preserved. The following outline will serve to orient the selections from it that are contained in this book.

In the first preserved fragment of the work, Encolpius, the narrator, and his friend Ascyltos, both impoverished, vagrant young scholars and both with Greek names, are found outside a school of rhetoric in some town apparently in Campania. Encolpius is delivering a harangue against the contemporary style of rhetorical training that, he claims, makes fools out of its pupils by teaching them nothing of real life. Agamemnon responds that it is the parents who are to blame for not subjecting their sons to strict discipline and for pushing them too hastily along the path of ambition. While Encolpius is entranced by Agamemnon's ranting, Ascyltos slips away, and Encolpius soon follows when a mob of young students pours out of the school, mocking the speaker they have just heard.

Encolpius and Ascyltos both wander separately about the town, to which they have just come, in search of their lodgings, and they are both taken unwittingly by different obliging natives to a brothel. Escaping from there, they arrive at their own lodgings where they quarrel over the sexual favors of a pretty young boy named Giton, who is accompanying them on their wanderings.

The narrative is very fragmentary, and the first fully preserved episode takes place at evening time in a marketplace and involves Encolpius and Ascyltos in a squabble with natives over a stolen cloak (the first selection in this book).

When the pair return to their lodgings and find that Giton has prepared dinner for them, their tranquillity is suddenly interrupted by a knock on the door and a scene of wild debauchery in which a certain Quartilla, apparently a priestess of Priapus, the god of sexuality, punishes Encolpius and Ascyltos for having witnessed rites she was performing in the shrine of her god.

Next comes the longest fully preserved episode, that of the dinner party at the house of the nouveau riche freedman, Trimalchio. Selections from Encolpius' description of this dinner party make up the second part of this book and include the preliminaries and hors d'oeuvres, the conversation of the freedmen around the table, a joke that Trimalchio plays on his guests, two ghost stories, and Trimalchio's description of his rise from slavery to riches and his rehearsal of his funeral.

After another violent quarrel of Encolpius and Ascyltos over the pretty boy Giton, Ascyltos disappears from the narrative, but a new rascal has already joined the company of Encolpius and Giton, namely, Eumolpus, a bombastic and unpopular poet, a superb con man, and a cunning pederast who takes great interest in Giton, to the equally great chagrin of Encolpius. In the company of this interloper, Encolpius and Giton board a ship. While at sea, they are horrified to learn that they are on the ship of an old enemy, Lichas of Tarentum, and they frantically disguise themselves as branded slaves, hoping to avoid detection. Lichas and his companion Tryphaena, however, discover the ruse; a battle breaks out, but a truce is arranged by Tryphaena, who had been wronged by Giton on some earlier occasion but is still attracted to the pretty boy. Eumolpus, who helped arrange the truce, tries to lighten the atmosphere with snatches of poetry and mockery of the fickleness of women. He concludes with the prose-tale of the matron of Ephesus; this so-called Milesian tale is the next selection in this book and one of the most famous and influential episodes in the *Satyricon*.

A storm arises, and as the ship is sinking, Encolpius, Giton, and Eumolpus are forced to swim to shore, where they arrive in safety. Lichas, however, was not so lucky. Before cremating his washed-up hulk, Encolpius delivers a mock funeral oration in high rhetorical fashion on the theme of death. This brilliant and powerful patchwork of clichés is the next-to-the-last selection in this book.

The trio of Encolpius, Giton, and Eumolpus then set off on foot for Croton. Once there, Eumolpus passes as a millionaire who has lost his goods in a shipwreck, and he is treated like a king by sycophantic legacy-hunters. Meanwhile, Encolpius, apparently impotent and haunted by the angry Priapus, becomes involved with several women, who attempt, through means both natural and supernatural, to raise his fallen charger. The narrative becomes increasingly fragmentary. Encolpius is at last restored to his former self, and Eumolpus, fearing that the legacy-hunters may discover his ruse, writes his last will and testament, to which he adds a most unpleasant stipulation. The reading of this stipulation to the assembled Crotonites is contained in the last selection in this book.

There end the preserved fragments of the *Satyricon*.

The Title of the Work and Its Genre

Much about this literary work has been debated, including the identification of its author with the Petronius described in the passage from Tacitus above. The meaning of its title has also been debated, but most scholars now accept both the identification of the author of the work with the Petronius known from Tacitus and an explanation of the title as a Greek genitive plural, Σατυρικῶν, "Of Satyr-like Things," "Of Satyr-like Adventures," dependent on an implied **Librī**, Latin for *Books*, therefore, *Books of Satyr-like Adventures*. (Satyrs were Greek mythological creatures of the woods and pastures, ithyphallic, with bodies of men, legs of goats, and pointed ears, who played on Pan pipes and were famous for their sexual prowess—exactly what Encolpius tries repeatedly to display.) The fragments of the *Satyricon* that have been preserved are from books 14, 15, and 16, so the complete work would have been quite extensive.

Debate has also raged over whether the *Satyricon* is a comic romance, a satire, or a picaresque novel. It contains elements of all of these, including elements of Menippean satire in its mixture of poetry and prose. It contains echoes of other ancient literary forms as well, such as the Homeric theme of the wandering hero (Odysseus) pursued by the wrath of a god (Poseidon), a theme that is mocked and deflated in the *Satyricon* by the wanderings of Encolpius pursued by the wrath of Priapus. Petronius' elusiveness and originality have defied description for centuries, and the *Satyricon* resists being slipped into the strait jacket of any formal category of genre just as vigorously as it resists any single interpretation of its meaning. The *Satyricon* has, however, never ceased to delight its readers, and it remains one of the few works of ancient Roman literature that one reads simply for pleasure.

The Language of the Freedmen

One of the most intriguing features of the *Satyricon* is the language used by the uneducated or semi-educated freedmen in their speeches and conversation during the dinner party thrown by the freedman Trimalchio (the **cēna Trimalchiōnis**, Part II of this book). The language of these freedmen differs in rather obvious and important ways from the language used by Encolpius, the educated narrator of the whole work. In the language of the freedmen Petronius has included features typical of what is called *vulgar Latin*, described by Bret Boyce in his study of the language of the freedmen as "the language of the lower classes, in the case of Rome the *plebs*, which generally lacked access to a liberal education and formed the vast majority of the population of the Empire" (page 2). The term *vulgar Latin* is used with no pejorative connotations; the word *vulgar* here does not mean "obscene or indecent; offensive; coarse or bawdy" (*American Heritage Dictionary of the English Language*, see, **vulgar**, definition 4). Rather, it is used in its more strictly etymological sense, deriving from the Latin word **vulgus**, -ī, n., *the common people*, in the sense of definition 1 in the *American Heritage Dictionary*, "of or associated with the great masses of people as distinguished from the educated or cultivated classes; common." Between this vulgar Latin spoken by the common people and the elevated, stylized literary language of the grammar books and the standard Latin authors was a third level of Latin that Boyce describes as "'(cultivated) colloquial,' 'conversational,' or 'urbane' language"—"the everyday spoken language of the educated upper classes of society" (page 2). This is the language of the narrator Encolpius.

The vulgar Latin spoken by the freedmen finds many parallels in the language of the common people of the Roman empire as seen in their funerary inscriptions and in the graffiti on the walls of houses and buildings in Pompeii. It is of special interest to historical linguists in that many of its features prefigure developments that became characteristic of the Romance languages. Here are some examples.

1. Distinctions of gender are sometimes blurred in vulgar Latin with neuter words such as **vīnum** and **fātum** becoming masculine (**vīnus** and **fātus**); in all of the Romance languages except Romanian the neuter disappeared.

2. In vulgar Latin active forms of deponent verbs are sometimes found; for example, the active **loquis** is used instead of the standard deponent **loqueris**; the deponent forms disappeared as Latin transformed itself into the various Romance languages.

3. Vulgar Latin tended toward simplification by sometimes using the accusative case where other cases are called for in standard Latin; for example, the preposition **prae** is used with the accusative instead of the ablative. The language of the freedmen also contains examples of the use of the accusative case where the genitive, dative, and locative cases would be normal. Similarly, the archaic verb **frūnīscor**, *to enjoy*, was kept in use in the popular language and is used by the freedmen with the accusative case instead of the ablative. It is used by the freedmen as a substitute for the more elevated synonym **fruor**, which is regularly used with the ablative (as by the educated

character Eumolpus in his telling of the story of the matron of
Ephesus).

4. Instead of subordinating one thought to another by using subordinate clauses with their verbs in the subjunctive as in standard Latin, the popular language tended to set short, independent statements side by side. This is called *parataxis*, a Greek
term meaning "arranged side-by-side." Parataxis is seen in
many types of sentences in the popular language, such as in
indirect questions, where the question is left in its original indicative instead of being subordinated by use of the subjunctive; we thus find **nēmō cūrat, quid annōna mordet** (two
main clauses with their verbs in the indicative), *no one cares
how the price of grain pinches*, instead of **nēmō cūrat, quid
annōna mordeat** (indirect question subordinated with its verb
in the subjunctive).

5. Indirect statement is sometimes introduced in the vulgar Latin
of the freedmen with **quod** or **quia,** *that,* and has its verb in the
indicative instead of being expressed with the standard accusative and infinitive construction, thus **scīs . . . quod epulum dedī,** *you know that I gave a banquet,* instead of **scīs mē
epulum dedisse.** Sometimes in the vulgar language the direct
statement is left unchanged and is not even introduced with
quod or **quia** but is simply arranged paratactically against the
main verb, thus, **Scītis, magna nāvis magnam fortitūdinem
habet,** *You know, a great ship has great courage,* instead of **Scītis
quod/quia magna nāvis magnam fortitūdinem habet** or the
standard **Scītis magnam nāvem magnam fortitūdinem
habēre.**

In these and other ways vulgar Latin tended to be a simpler form of
Latin than the cultivated colloquial or the stylized literary language,
and it often prefigured developments that were to lead to the formation of the Romance languages.

The illiterate or semi-literate freedmen at the dinner seem to be
quite aware of the social, educational, and linguistic gap separating
them from the educated guests such as the narrator and his companions, who include a professor of rhetoric representing the highest level
of Roman education. One way in which some of the freedmen try to
bridge this gap is by using forms of language that they associate with
the language of the educated classes but by using them wrongly in a
vain attempt to appear more literate than they are. These wrong-
headed attempts to be correct appear as affectations and are called *hypercorrections* by the linguists. Thus, instead of simplifying the language by using active forms instead of the correct passive forms of deponent verbs (the leveling process described above as typical of vulgar

Latin), we find the freedmen occasionally doing just the opposite and using passive forms of regular active verbs but with an active sense, i.e., as if they were deponent verbs; for example, **somniātur** instead of **somniat**.

Another affectation or hypercorrection is seen in the use of subjunctive forms (the fancier forms!) in subordinate clauses that normally require the indicative; for example, **etiam sī magister . . . sit**, *even if the teacher should be*, instead of **etiam sī magister . . . est**, *even if the teacher is*, and **dōnec . . . pervenīrem**, *until I should come*, instead of **dōnec . . . pervēnī**, *until I came*.

These affectations or hypercorrections are part and parcel of the social climbing that is revealed in other aspects of the freedmen's speeches and character. In fact, Boyce has demonstrated a very close correlation between the language used by the freedmen and their distinctive and carefully differentiated characters and personalities.

The various features of vulgar Latin that appear in the selections contained in this book are gathered together in the Appendix in a systematic format with numerous examples (but not necessarily all examples of each feature). The various features of vulgar Latin are also identified in the facing vocabularies and the notes as they are encountered in the Latin passages, and references are there made to the appropriate page or pages of the Appendix. These features of vulgar Latin will cause little or no trouble in reading and translating the Latin, but recognizing them for what they are will add greatly to an enjoyment and appreciation of the scene at the banquet and the characterization of the freedmen that Petronius has given us.

The language of the freedmen is indeed rich and colorful. It contains many compound words, many diminutives, many new coinages, a number of hybrid words combining Greek and Latin elements, and some slang words taken directly from Greek. Both the names of the freedmen and their language have a Greek flavor, which is not surprising since the banquet takes place in some town in Campania, a meeting ground of Oscan, Greek, and Latin cultures. The language of the freedmen is also full of strong metaphors and lively proverbial phrases and wit. It also exploits effects and devices that were typical of Latin at all levels from the very beginning, such as alliteration, anaphora (the repetition of the same word at the beginning of successive clauses), and asyndeton (ommision of conjunctions or connective particles where they would be expected). Asyndeton is employed to make strong contrasts between phrases or clauses or to increase the pace and excitement of the story. Also present are colloquial repetitions of words (e.g., **modo modo**, and **vērō, vērō**) and distinctly colloquial oaths or asseverations, e.g., **Ita meōs frūnīscar, ut ego putō omnia illa ā diibus fierī**, freely transalted, *May I not enjoy my own kin, if I don't think all these things are happening at the will of the gods*. Moving from the rich and colorful language of the freedmen to Encolpius' polished, urbane recounting of the story of the matron of Ephesus and Encolpius' highly rhetorical funeral oration is like moving into a different world, thus giving us a clear picture of the linguistic stratification of Roman society that accompanied its social and economic stratification.

Using This Book

This book is designed to make the original, unadapted Latin of Petronius accessible to students as early as the second year of their study of Latin in high schools, colleges, and universities. Vocabulary is often a major stumbling block when reading unadapted Latin literature this early in the study of Latin, and this is especially true of Petronius, who uses many rare and unusual words. This impediment, however, is effectively removed by the running vocabularies that face each selection of the text in this book and gloss all but the most basic Latin words (see the list of assumed vocabulary below). When words occur a second time they are glossed again and marked in the running vocabulary with an asterisk, a third time with two asterisks, and a fourth time with three asterisks; subsequently they are dropped from the facing vocabulary lists. The basic, assumed vocabulary and all words marked with three asterisks may be found in the vocabulary at the end of the book.

Each vocabulary entry gives the essential information about the word in standard form and with standard dictionary spelling. When a variant colloquial or vulgar spelling of the word occurs in the passage, this is given as an indented subentry with an indication of its level of usage. Other colloquial or vulgar features of the language such as use of a noun in a masculine rather than a standard neuter form or use of a verb as active rather than deponent are also noted in subentries.

The main entries for words often contain in brackets important information on the derivation of the word. Compound verbs in which the spelling is different from that of the uncompounded elements are accompanied with brackets enclosing the uncompounded elements: for example, **concutiō [con- + quatiō, quatere,** *to shake; to strike*], **concutere, concussī, concussus,** *to shake out* (definitions of the most common verbs are not given in the information contained within the brackets). In order to understand the meaning of compound words such as this it is important to recognize the elements out of which they are made. Diminutives are identified: for example, **muliercula, -ae,** f. [dim. of **mulier, mulieris,** f., *woman*], *little woman*. Other important linguistic information is also given in brackets, such as the verbs from which adjectives are derived, as in the following entry: **ēmptīcius [emō, emere, ēmī, ēmptus,** *to buy*], **-a, -um,** *bought, purchased*. Greek loan words are also marked with appropriate information in brackets, as is the level of usage of colloquial and vulgar words and the rarity of some words (many of which are found only once in Petronius and nowhere else in extant Latin writings). All of these various pieces of information included in brackets deserve notice and contribute to a full understanding of the meaning and flavor of the words.

Some notes beneath the passages on the right-hand pages help the student to translate the passages by identifying uses of the cases and syntactical constructions (especially subordinate clauses with the sub-junctive) and by translating or providing partial translations of some phrases and clauses. Identification of constructions is especially important for students at the level for which this text is intended. There are fewer identifications of constructions in the last three sections of this book, leaving students more on their own.

Other notes beneath the passages on the right-hand pages call attention to passages in other authors that shed light on the customs or practices described by the narrator and the other speakers. Often a brief paraphrase is given of the passage from the other author, and citations are provided so that students may look up the comparative passage and read it for themselves. For easy reference, the titles of works are given as they are in the bilingual Loeb Library series, which is the most convenient series for students at this stage in their study of Latin to consult for comparative purposes.

The Assumed Vocabulary

The following basic words are not included in the running vocabularies, but are included at the end of the book. The reader should be familiar with these words before beginning the text.

A
ā or ab, prep. + abl., *from; by*
ac, conj., *and, and also, and even*
ad, prep. + acc., *to, toward; at, near*
agō, agere, ēgī, āctus, *to do; to drive*
alius, alia, aliud, *other, another*
    alius ... alius, *one ... another*
ambulō, -āre, -āvī, -ātūrus, *to walk*
amīcus, -ī, m. or amīca, -ae, f., *friend*
amō, -āre, -āvī, -ātus, *to love*
annus, -ī, m., *year*
aqua, -ae, f., *water*
atque, conj., *and, and also, and even*
audiō, -īre, -īvī, ītus, *to hear*

B
bene, adv., *well*
bonus, -a, -um, *good*

C
canis, canis, m./f., *dog*
caput, capitis, n., *head*
cēna, -ae, f., *dinner*
cēnō, -āre, -āvī, -ātus, *to dine*
centum, indecl. adj., *a hundred*
clāmō, -āre, -āvī, -ātūrus, *to shout*
crās, adv., *tomorrow*
cum, conj. + subjn. or indic., *when; since; although*
cum, prep. + abl., *with*

D
dē, prep. + abl., *down from; concerning*
decem, indecl. adj., *ten*
dēns, dentis, m., *tooth*
dīcō, dīcere, dīxī, dictus, *to say, tell*
diēs, diēī, m./f., *day*
digitus, -ī, m., *finger*
diū, adv., *for a long time*
dō, dare, dedī, datus, *to give*
dominus, -ī, m., *master*
dūcō, dūcere, dūxī, ductus, *to lead, take, bring*
dum, conj., *while*
duo, duae, duo, *two*

E
ē or **ex**, prep. + abl., *out of, from*
ego, meī, pron., *I*
eō, īre, iī, itūtus, irreg., *to go*
et, conj., *and*
　　et . . . et, conj., *both . . . and*

F
faciō, facere, fēcī, factus, *to make*
familia, -ae, f., *family*
fēmina, -ae, f., *woman*
ferō, ferre, tulī, lātus, irreg., *to bring, carry, bear*
fīlia, -ae, f., *daughter*
fīlius, -ī, m., *son*
fīō, fierī, factus sum, irreg., *to be made; to become; to happen*
forum, -ī, n., *marketplace*

frāter, frātris, m., *brother*

H

habeō, -ēre, -uī, -itus, *to have, hold; to consider*
hic, haec, hoc, dem. adj. and pron., *this; he, she, it*
hodiē, adv., *today*
homō, hominis, m., *man; human being*

I

iam, adv., *already, now*
īdem, eadem, idem, dem. adj. and pron., *the same*
ille, illa, illud, dem. adj. and pron., *that; he, she, it*
in, prep. + abl., *in; on*
in, prep. + acc., *into, onto*
ingēns, ingentis, *large, huge*
inter, prep. + acc., *between; among*
ipse, ipsa, ipsum, intens. adj. and pron., *himself, herself, itself*
is, ea, id, dem. adj. and pron., *this; that; he, she, it*
ita, adv., *thus, so*
itaque, adv., *and so, therefore*
iubeō, iubēre, iussī, iussus, *to order, command*

L

lēx, lēgis, f., *law; custom*
locus, -ī, m., *place*
longus, -a, -um, *long, tall*

M

magnus, -a, -um, *big, large, great*
maior, maior, maius, maiōris [compar. of **magnus, -a, -um**], *bigger, larger, greater*
male, adv., *badly*
mālō, mālle, māluī, irreg., *to prefer*
malus, -a, -um, *bad, evil*
manus, -ūs, f., *hand*
māter, mātris, f., *mother*
maximus, -a, -um [superl. of **magnus, -a, -um**], *biggest, largest, greatest*
melior, melior, melius, meliōris [compar. of **bonus, -a, -um**], *better*
meus, -a, -um, *my, mine*
mīlle, indecl. adj., *a thousand*
minimus, -a, -um [superl. of **parvus, -a, -um**], *smallest, very small*
minor, minor, minus, minōris [compar. of **parvus, -a, -um**], *smaller*

mittō, mittere, mīsī, missus, *to send*
mulier, mulieris, f., *woman*
multus, -a, -um, *much*
    multī, -ae, -a, *many*

N

nam, particle, *for*
nē, conj. + subjn., *in order that . . . not, so that . . . not*
nec, conj., *and not, neither*
    nec . . . nec, conj., *neither . . . nor*
nihil, n., indecl., *nothing*
nōlō, nōlle, nōluī, irreg., *to be unwilling; to refuse*
nōn, adv., *not*
nōn tantum . . . sed etiam, *not only . . . but also*
nōs, nostrī or **nostrum,** *we, us*
noster, nostra, nostrum, *our, ours*
novem, indecl. adj., *nine*
novus, -a, -um, *new*
nunc, adv., *now*

O

ō, interj., *oh!*
octō, indecl. adj., *eight*
omnis, -is, -e, *all, the whole, every*
optimus, -a, -um [superl. of **bonus, -a, -um**], *best, very good, excellent*

P

paene, adv., *almost*
pallium, -ī, n., *cloak*
parvus, -a, -um, *small, little*
pater, patris, m., *father*
pecūnia, -ae, f., *money*
peior, peior, peius, peiōris [compar. of **malus, -a, -um**], *worse*
pēs, pedis, m., *foot*
pessimus, -a, -um [superl. of **malus, -a, -um**], *worst, very bad*
pictūra, -ae, f., *picture*
pōnō, pōnere, posuī, positus, *to put, place*
possum, posse, potuī, *to be able; can*
postquam, conj., *after*
puer, puerī, m., *boy; slave*
pulcher, pulchra, pulchrum, *beautiful*
putō, -āre, -āvī, ātus, *to think*

Q

quam, adv., *than*
quattuor, indecl. adj., *four*
-que, enclitic conj., *and*
quī, quae, quod, rel. pron., *who, which, that;* rel. adj., *which;* interrog. adj., *what, which*
quia, conj., *because*
quīnque, indecl. adj., *five*
Quis . . . ? Quid . . . ? interrog. pron., *Who . . . ? What . . . ?*
quod, conj., *because*
quoque, adv., *also*

R

rēs, reī, f., *thing; matter*
rīdeō, rīdēre, rīsī, rīsus, *to laugh (at)*
rūsticus, -ī, m., *peasant*

S

sciō, scīre, scīvī, scītus, *to know*
scrībō, scrībere, scrīpsī, scrīptus, *to write*
sē, reflex, pron., *himself, herself, itself, themselves*
sed, conj., *but*
sedeō, sedēre, sēdī, sessūrus, *to sit*
septem, indecl. adj., *seven*
servus, -ī, m., *slave*
sex, indecl. adj., *six*
sī, conj., *if*
sīc, adv., *so, thus*
sine, prep. + abl., *without*
sōlus, -a, -um, *only, alone*
soror, sorōris, f., *sister*
spolium, -ī, n., *booty, spoil*
statua, -ae, f., *statue*
stō, stāre, stetī, statūrus, *to stand*
sum, esse, fuī, futūrus, irreg., *to be*
super, prep. + acc., *above, over, on*
suus, -a, -um, *his own, her own, its own, their own*

T

tempus, temporis, n., *time*
teneō, tenēre, tenuī, tentus, *to hold*
terra, -ae, f., *earth, ground*
timeō, timēre, timuī, *to fear*
tōtus, -a, -um, *all, the whole, the entire*
trēs, trēs, tria, *three*

tū, tuī, pron., *you* (sing.)
tunc, adv., *then*
tunica, -ae, f., *tunic*

U

ubi, adv., *where, when*
ūnus, -a, -um, *one, only*
ut, conj. + subjn., *in order to, so that;* + indic., *as, when*

V

veniō, venīre, vēnī, ventūrus, *to come*
via, -ae, f., *road*
videō, vidēre, vīdī, vīsus, *to see*
    videor, vidērī, vīsus sum, *to seem, appear*
vir, virī, m., *man; husband*
vīta, -ae, f., *life*
volō, velle, voluī, *to be willing; to wish*
vōs, vostrī or vostrum, pron., *you* (pl.)

Acknowledgments

Material for this book was first assembled by the following students in a seminar on Petronius conducted at the University of Massachusetts at Amherst in the fall of 1974: Patricia Moore, Diane Steen, Janet Gillies, and Isabel Kangas. The material was edited by Gilbert Lawall in the summer of 1975 and published in its first edition that year. The text used was that of Konrad Müller: *Petronii Arbitri Satyricon* (Munich: Ernst Heimeran Verlag, 1961). In the second edition (1980) some changes were made on the basis of Martin S. Smith's 1975 edition with commentary: *Petronii Arbitri Cena Trimalchionis* (Oxford: Clarendon Press, 1975). The third, revised edition (1995) brings the book into the world of computerized desktop publishing with improved typeface and layout. The Latin text is based partly on those of Müller and Smith but follows neither in all readings.

The following editions (listed in chronological order) were especially useful in preparing the vocabularies and notes, and the author of the present book gratefully acknowledges his debt to the material in these editions, from which he has drawn extensively:

Ludwig Friedlaender, ed. *Petronii Cena Trimalchionis.* Leipzig: Verlag von S. Hirzel, 1891.

E. P. Crowell, ed. *Petronii Cena Trimalchionis: A Brief Introduction and Notes.* Rev. ed. Amherst, Mass.: Latin Department, Amherst College, 1901.

William E. Waters, ed. *Petronius: Cena Trimalchionis: Edited with*

Introduction and Commentary. Boston: Benjamin H. Sanborn & Co., 1902.

W. D. Lowe, ed. *Petronii Cena Trimalchionis: Edited with Critical and Explanatory Notes and Translated into English Prose.* Cambridge: Deighton Bell and Co., 1905.

W. B. Sedgwick. *The Cena Trimachionis of Petronius together with Seneca's Apocolocyntosis and a Selection of Pompeian Inscriptions.* 2d ed. Oxford: Clarendon Press, 1950.

Evan T. Sage and Brady B. Gilleland. *Petronius: The Satiricon.* New York: Appleton-Century-Crofts, 1969.

Enzo V. Marmorale, ed. *Petronii Arbitri Cena Trimalchionis: Testo Critico e Commento.* 2d ed. Florence: "La Nuova Italia" Editrice, 1961.

Martin S. Smith, ed. *Petronii Arbitri Cena Trimalchionis.* Oxford: Clarendon Press, 1975.

The Lewis and Short *Latin Dictionary* (1879) and the *Oxford Latin Dictionary* (1982) served as the ultimate authority for most of the vocabulary items.

The Appendix on language and style owes much to Martin S. Smith (above) and to Bret Boyce, *The Language of the Freedmen in Petronius' Cena Trimalchionis* (Leiden: E. J. Brill, 1991). For further information and for bibliography on these matters, consult Boyce. See also Mario Pei, *The Story of Latin and the Romance Languages* (New York: Harper & Row, 1976).

Further Reading

It is highly recommended that the student read the preserved parts of the novel in English translation (Arrowsmith or Sullivan) before translating the selections in this book.

The following standard books on Petronius contain discussions of the main topics of Petronian scholarship and extensive bibliographies (listed in chronological order):

J. P. Sullivan. *The 'Satyricon' of Petronius: A Literary Study.* London: Faber and Faber Limited, 1968.

Philip B. Corbett. *Petronius.* New York: Twayne Publishers, 1970.

P. G. Walsh. *The Roman Novel: The Satyricon of Petronius and the Metamorphoses of Apuleius.* Cambridge: Cambridge University Press, 1970.

Niall W. Slater. *Reading Petronius.* Baltimore: The Johns Hopkins University Press, 1990.

For brief, up-to-date summaries of scholarship on Petronius, see the chapters on Petronius in E. J. Kenney and W. V. Clausen, eds., *The Cambridge History of Classical Literature: II Latin Literature* (Cambridge: Cambridge University Press, 1982) and in Gian Biagio Conte, *Latin Literature: A History*, trans. Joseph B. Solodow, rev. Don Fowler and Glenn W. Most (Baltimore: The Johns Hopkins University Press, 1994), and see Gareth Schmeling, "Quid attinet veritatem per interpretem quaerere? Interpretes and the Satyricon," *Ramus: Critical Studies in Greek and Roman Literature* 23.1&2 (1995): 144–168.

For background reading on Roman daily life, highly recommended for understanding what is going on at the banquet of Trimalchio and what is said by the freedmen at the banquet, consult the following standard books (listed in chronological order):

Jérôme Carcopino. *Daily Life in Ancient Rome: The People and the City at the Height of the Empire.* Trans. E. O. Lorimer. Ed. Henry T. Rowell. New Haven: Yale University Press, 1940.

F. R. Cowell. *Life in Ancient Rome.* New York: G. Putnam's Sons, 1961.

Ugo Enrico Paoli. *Rome: Its People, Life and Customs.* Trans. R. D. Macnaghten. White Plains, N.Y.: Longman, 1963.

J. P. V. D. Balsdon. *Life and Leisure in Ancient Rome.* New York: McGraw-Hill Book Company, 1969.

Jo-Ann Shelton. *As the Romans Did: A Sourcebook in Roman Social History.* New York: Oxford University Press, 1988.

Michael Grant and Rachel Kitzinger, eds., *Civilization of the Ancient Mediterranean: Greece and Rome.* 3 vols. New York: Charles Scribner's Sons, 1988.

SELECTIONS
FROM THE
SATYRICON

1 dēficiō [dē- + faciō], dēficere, dēfēcī, dēfectus, *to leave, cease, fail, end.*
2 notō, -āre, -āvī, -ātus, *to note, observe.*
   frequentia, -ae, f., *crowd, multitude.*
   vēnālis, -is, -e, *for sale.*
   quidem, particle, *indeed, it is true, to be sure.*
3 pretiōsus, -a, -um, *valuable, expensive.*
   tamen, adv., *yet, nevertheless.*
   fidēs, fideī, f., *trust; trustworthiness.*
   obscūritās, obscūritātis, f., *darkness.*
4 facillimē, superl. adv., *most easily.*
   tegō, tegere, tēxī, tēctus, *to cover, hide, conceal.*
   ergō, particle, *therefore.*
   rapiō, rapere, rapuī, raptus, *to seize, carry off, steal.*
   latrōcinium, -ī, n., *robbery; act of violent robbery.*
5 dēferō, dēferre, dētulī, dēlātus, irreg., *to carry, bring (down).*
   ūtor, ūtī, ūsus sum + abl., *to use, make use of.*
   occāsiō, occāsiōnis, f., *opportunity, occasion.*
   opportūnus, -a, -um, *convenient, timely.*
6 coepī, coepisse, coeptus [pf. tenses only], *to begin.*
   quīdam, quaedam, quoddam, indef. adj., *a certain.*
   angulus, -ī, m., *angle, corner.*
   lacinia, -ae, f., *edge, border* (of a garment).
   extrēmus, -a, -um, *outermost.*
7 concutiō [con- + quatiō, *to shake; to strike*], concutere, concussī, concussus, *to shake out.*
   quī, qua, quod, indef. adj. [used after sī, nisi, num, and nē], *any.*
   forte, adv., *by chance* [fors, fortis, f.]
   ēmptor, ēmptōris, m., *buyer.*
   splendor, splendōris, m., *brightness, brilliance, splendor.*
   vestis, vestis, vestium, f., *garment.*
8 addūcō, addūcere, addūxī, adductus, *to bring in/to, draw, attract.*
   moror, -ārī, -ātus sum, *to delay.*
   *quīdam, quaedam, quoddam, indef. adj., *a certain.*
   familiāris, -is, -e, *familiar.*
   oculus, -ī, m., *eye.*
9 muliercula, -ae, f. [dim. of mulier, mulieris, f., *woman*], *little woman.*
   comes, comitis, m./f., *companion.*
   propius, compar. adv., *more/rather closely.*
   accēdō [ad- + cēdō, *to go*], accēdere, accessī, accessus, *to approach.*
   dīligentius, compar. adv., *more/rather attentively.*
10 cōnsīderō, -āre, -āvī, -ātus, *to look at, inspect.*
   *coepī, coepisse, coeptus [pf. tenses only], *to begin.*

I.

A SCENE AT THE MARKETPLACE

*Encolpius and his comrade Ascyltos had a tunic (**tunica**), in the hem of which they had sewn their money. They hid the tunic in some deserted place, and a peasant (**rūsticus**) found it and carried it off without discovering that it concealed a small fortune. Apparently Encolpius observed the peasant's finding of the tunic, but Ascyltos charged him with stealing the money.*

*We find Encolpius and Ascyltos in the market place (**forum**) at the end of the day. They have with them a valuable cloak (**pallium**), which they had stolen, perhaps to compensate for the loss of their tunic with its treasure; they now decide to try to sell it. Unexpected complications arise.*

[12–15] Veniēbāmus in forum dēficiente iam diē, in quō 1
notāvimus frequentiam rērum vēnālium, nōn quidem 2
pretiōsārum sed tamen quārum fidem male ambulantem ob- 3
scūritās temporis facillimē tegeret. Cum ergō et ipsī raptum la- 4
trōciniō pallium dētulissēmus, ūtī occāsiōne opportūnissimā 5
coepimus atque in quōdam angulō laciniam extrēmam 6
concutere, sī quem forte ēmptōrem splendor vestis posset 7
addūcere. Nec diū morātus rūsticus quīdam familiāris oculīs 8
meīs cum mulierculā comite propius accessit ac dīligentius 9
cōnsīderāre pallium coepit. 10

---

1 **dēficiente ... diē**: ablative absolute.
3 **quārum fidem ... obscūritās temporis ... tegeret**: a relative clause of characteristic expressing result; imperfect subjunctive in secondary sequence.
fidem male ambulantem: *their scarcely walking (= stumbling) trustworthiness = their shoddiness.*
4 **Cum ... dētulissēmus**: pluperfect subjunctive in a causal clause in secondary sequence.
5 **ūtī ... coepimus**: Petronius often uses the verb **coepī** with an infinitive instead of a simple verb in the perfect tense, thus **ūtī ... coepimus**, *we began to make use of* = **ūsī sumus**, *we made use of.*
occāsiōne opportūnissimā: ablative with **ūtī** (infinitive of **ūtor**).
7 **sī ... forte ... posset**: imperfect subjunctive expressing possibility, *if by chance the ... might. ...*
sī quem ... ēmptōrem: *if ... any buyer.*
8 **Nec diū morātus**: adjectival, modifying **rūsticus**, but translate as adverbial, *And without much delay. ..., And soon. ...*

3

11   **invicem**, adv., *in turn*.
    Ascyltos, -ī, m. [Greek word meaning "not pulled about, undis-
    turbed"], *Ascyltos (companion of the narrator, Encolpius)*.
    Forms: dat., **Ascyltō**; acc., **Ascylton**; abl., **Ascylte or Ascyltō**.
    iniciō [in- + iaciō, *to throw*], **inicere, iniēcī, iniectus**, *to throw,
    cast*.
    contemplātiō, contemplātiōnis, f., *glance*.
    super, prep. + acc., *above, over*.
    umerus, -ī, m., *shoulder*.
12   **subitō**, adv., *suddenly*.
    exanimātus, -a, -um, *out of breath, terrified, paralyzed*.
    conticēscō [con- + taceō], **conticēscere, conticuī**, *to become quiet*.
    nē . . . quidem, *not . . . even*.
13   **aliquī, aliqua, aliquod**, indef. adj., *some, any*.
    mōtus, -ūs, m., *movement, agitation*.
    cōnspiciō [con- + speciō, *to see*], **cōnspicere, cōnspexī, cōnspec-
    tus**, *to catch sight of, see*.
14   **tunicula, -ae**, f. [dim. of **tunica, -ae**, f., *tunic*], *little tunic*.
    sōlitūdō, sōlitūdinis, f., *deserted place*.
    inveniō, invenīre, invēnī, inventus, *to find*.
    plānē, adv., *clearly, plainly, openly*.
15   ***fidēs, fideī**, f., *trust; trustworthiness, credibility*.
    ***oculus, -ī**, m., *eye*.
    quis, qua/quae, quid, indef. pron. [used after **sī, nisi, num**, and
    nē], *anyone, anything*.
    temere, adv., *blindly, rashly, without reason*.
    prius, compar. adv., *before, sooner, first*.
16   **tamquam**, conj., *just as (if)*.
    ***ēmptor, ēmptōris**, m., *buyer*.
    ***propius**, compar. adv., *more/rather closely*.
    ***accēdō [ad- + cēdō**, *to go*], **accēdere, accessī, accessus**, *to ap-
    proach*.
    dētrahō, dētrahere, dētrāxī, dētractus, *to draw/pull off*.
    ***umerus, -ī**, m., *shoulder*.
    ***lacinia, -ae**, f., *edge, border* (of a garment).
17   ***dīligentius**, compar. adv., *more/rather attentively*.
    temptō, -āre, -āvī, -ātus, *to handle, feel, test*.
    lūsus, -ūs, m., *play, game*.
    fortūna, -ae, f., *fortune, good luck*.
    mīrābilis, -is, -e, *wonderful, marvelous*.
    adhūc, adv., *until now, still, yet*.
18   ***nē . . . quidem**, *not . . . even*.
    sūtūra, -ae, f., *seam*.
    afferō [ad- + ferō], **afferre, attulī, allātus**, irreg. + dat., *to bring
    (to)*.

Ascyltos recognizes the peasant and notices that he has the lost tunic.

Invicem Ascyltos iniēcit contemplātiōnem super umerōs rūs- 11
ticī ac subitō exanimātus conticuit. Ac nē ipse quidem sine 12
aliquō mōtū hominem cōnspexī, nam vidēbātur ille mihi esse quī 13
tuniculam in sōlitūdine invēnerat. Plānē is ipse erat. Sed cum 14
Ascyltos timēret fidem oculōrum, nē quid temere faceret, prius 15
tamquam ēmptor propius accessit dētrāxitque umerīs laciniam 16
et dīligentius temptāvit. Ō lūsum fortūnae mīrābilem! Nam ad- 17
hūc nē sūtūrae quidem attulerat rūsticus cūriōsās manūs, sed 18
tamquam mendīcī spolium etiam fastīdiōsē vēnditābat. 19

---

cūriōsus, -a, -um, *careful, curious, inquisitive.*
19 *tamquam, conj., *just as (if).*
mendīcus, -ī, m., *beggar.*
etiam, particle, *still; also; even; actually.*
fastīdiōsē, adv., *disdainfully, scornfully.*
vēnditō, -āre, -āvī, -ātus, *to seek to sell, offer for sale.*

---

12 nē . . . quidem: emphasizing the enclosed word, *not even* (I) *my-self.* . . .
14 in sōlitūdine: some deserted place where the tunic had been lost or accidentally left behind. Apparently Encolpius saw the peasant find it (cf. familiāris oculīs meīs, 8). The part of the book in which this event was narrated has been lost.
   cum . . . timēret: imperfect subjunctive in a causal clause in secondary sequence.
15 nē . . . faceret: negative purpose clause in secondary sequence.
   prius: translate *first*, rather than *before.*
16 umerīs: ablative of separation with dētrāxit.
17 lūsum . . . mīrābilem: accusative of exclamation.
19 vēnditābat: *he was trying to sell* (it); the imperfect is conative, expressing an attempt to carry out the action of the verb.

20 **dēpositum, -ī,** n., *deposit, cache.*
    inviolātus, -a, -um, *unhurt, undisturbed.*
    persōna, -ae, f., *person.*
21 **vēndēns, vēndentis,** m., *seller.*
    contemptus, -a, -um, *despicable, contemptible.*
    sēdūcō, sēdūcere, sēdūxī, sēductus, *to lead away, draw aside.*
    paululum, dim. adv., *a little bit.*
    turba, -ae, f., *crowd.*
22 **inquit,** *(he/she) says, said.*
    redeō, redīre, rediī, reditūrus, irreg., *to come back, return.*
    thēsaurus, -ī, m. [Greek loan word], *treasure.*
23 **queror, querī, questus sum,** *to complain, lament.*
    ***tunicula, -ae,** f. [dim. of **tunica, -ae,** f., *tunic*], *little tunic.*
    ***adhūc,** adv., *until now, still, yet.*
    appāreō [ad- + **pareō,** *to obey*], **-ēre, -uī, -itūrus,** *to appear.*
    intāctus, -a, -um, *untouched, intact.*
    aureus, ī, m., *gold coin.*
24 **plēnus, -a, -um** + gen. or abl., *full* (of).
    ***ergō,** particle, *therefore.*
    iūs, iūris, n., *law; right; authority.*
    vindicō, -āre, -āvī, -ātus, *to claim, recover.*
25 **exhilarātus, -a, -um,** *delighted.*
    praeda, -ae, f., *booty.*
26 ***fortūna, -ae,** f., *fortune, good luck.*
    turpis, -is, -e, *ugly, base.*
    suspīciō, suspīciōnis, f., *suspicion.*
    dīmittō [dis- + **mittō**], **dīmittere, dīmīsī, dīmissus,** *to send away, dismiss, release.*
27 **negō, -āre, -āvī, -ātus,** *to say not, deny.*
    circu[m]itus, -ūs, m., *circling, indirect route, roundabout way.*
    ***plānē,** adv., *clearly, plainly, openly.*
    ***iūs, iūris,** n., *law; right; authority.*
    cīvīlis, -is, -e, *civil.*
    dīmicō [dis- + **micō,** *to dart, flash*], **-āre, -āvī, -ātūrus,** *to fight, struggle, contest.*
28 **aliēnus, -a, -um,** *of another.*
    reddō, reddere, reddidī, redditus, *to give back, return.*
    interdictum, -ī, n., *interdiction* (an order or injunction of a **praetor,** a judicial magistrate, to prohibit, **interdīcere,** some act in a dispute over property).

Ascyltos confers with Encolpius as to how to recover the tunic.

Ascyltos postquam dēpositum esse inviolātum vīdit et per- 20
sōnam vēndentis contemptam, sēdūxit mē paululum ā turbā et, 21
"Scīs," inquit, "frāter, rediisse ad nōs thēsaurum dē quō 22
querēbar? Illa est tunicula adhūc, ut appāret, intāctīs aureīs 23
plēna. Quid ergō facimus aut quō iūre rem nostram vindicā- 24
mus?" Exhilarātus ego nōn tantum quia praedam vidēbam, sed 25
etiam quod fortūna mē ā turpissimā suspīciōne dīmīserat, 26
negāvī circuitū agendum, sed plānē iūre cīvīlī dīmicandum, ut sī 27
nōllet aliēnam rem dominō reddere, ad interdictum venīret. 28

---

22 **rediisse**: perfect infinitive in indirect statement (subject is **thē-saurum**).
23 **ut appāret**: ut + indicative = *as*.
    intāctīs aureīs: ablative with **plēna** (24).
24 **facimus . . . vindicāmus**: indicatives where one would expect deliberative subjunctives, *What are we to do . . . how are we to recover . . . ?*
    rem: i.e., their tunic.
25 **Exhilarātus ego**: the main verb, of which these words are the subject, is **negāvī** (27).
26 **ā turpissimā suspīciōne**: Ascyltos suspected that Encolpius had stolen the money. This suspicion is now proven false.
27 **negāvī . . . agendum (esse) sed . . . dīmicandum (esse)**: gerundives with **esse** (implied) to express necessity, *I said that it (the matter) should not be handled . . . but (said) that it should be contested. . . .*
    ut . . . venīret: purpose clause with imperfect subjunctive in secondary sequence, *so that if he should refuse . . . (the matter) would come. . . .*
    sī nōllet: the future indicative of the implied future-more-vivid condition (**sī nōlet . . . veniet**, *if he refuses . . . [the matter] will come*) becomes an imperfect subjunctive when the condition is stated in the purpose clause in secondary sequence.

29   **contrā**, adv., *on the other hand.*
     aiō, defective verb used mainly in present and imperfect indicative, *to say.*
30   **nōscō, nōscere, nōvī, nōtus**, *to become acquainted with;* pf., *to know.*
     **fidēs, fideī, f., *trust.*
     **plānē, adv., *clearly, plainly, openly.*
     placeō, -ēre, -uī + dat., *to please.*
31   **emō, emere, ēmī, ēmptus**, *to buy.*
     quamvīs, rel. adv. + subjn. or indic., *even though, although.*
     agnōscō [ad- + gnōscō, *to become acquainted with*], **agnōscere, agnōvī, agnitus**, *to recognize.*
     parvus, -a, -um, *small, little.*
     aes, aeris, n., *copper, money.*
     recuperō, -āre, -āvī, -ātus, *to get back, recover.*
32   **potius . . . quam**, *rather . . . than.*
     *thēsaurus, -ī, m. [Greek loan word], *treasure.*
     ambiguus, -a, -um, *doubtful.*
     līs, lītis, f., *dispute, lawsuit.*
     dēscendō, dēscendere, dēscendī, dēscēnsūrus, *to go down, descend.*
34   **rēgnō, -āre, -āvī, -ātūrus**, *to rule, reign.*
35   **paupertās, paupertātis**, f., *poverty.*
     vincō, vincere, vīcī, victus, *to conquer; to be victorious, win.*
     nūllus, -a, -um, *no.*
36   **Cynicus, -a, -um**, *Cynic* (referring to a philosophic sect; see note below text).
     trādūcō [trāns- + dūcō], **trādūcere, trādūxī, trāductus**, *to lead across; to spend, pass* (time).
     pēra, -ae, f., *bag, pouch.*
37   **numquam**, adv., *never.*
     nummus, -ī, m., *piece of money, coin;* pl., *money, cash.*
     vēndō, vēndere, vēndidī, vēnditus, *to sell.*
     verbum, -ī, n., *word.*
     soleō, solēre, solitus sum, *to be accustomed.*
38   ****ergō**, particle, *therefore.*
     iūdicium, -ī, n., *judgment, trial, court of justice.*
     nisi, conj., *unless, except.*
     pūblicus, -a, -um, *public.*
     mercēs, mercēdis, f., *pay, reward, bribe; an article put up for sale, commodity.*

Ascyltos argues against recourse to the law, recommends that they buy the tunic, and condemns the corrupt legal system.

Contrā Ascyltos lēgēs timēbat et, "Quis," aiēbat, "hōc locō 29
nōs nōvit aut quis habēbit dīcentibus fidem? Mihi plānē placet 30
emere, quamvīs nostrum sit, quod agnōscimus, et parvō aere re- 31
cuperāre potius thēsaurum quam in ambiguam lītem dēscen- 32
dere: 33

"Quid faciunt lēgēs, ubi sōla pecūnia rēgnat 34
  aut ubi paupertās vincere nūlla potest? 35
Ipsī quī Cynicā trādūcunt tempora pērā 36
  nōn numquam nummīs vēndere verba solent. 37
Ergō iūdicium nihil est nisi pūblica mercēs, 38
  atque eques in causā quī sedet ēmpta probat." 39

---

39 **eques, equitis,** m., *horseman, horse-soldier; knight* (member of the
equitēs, who held a position in Roman society between the senatorial class and the plebs and who controlled the juries).
eques, here = **iūdex,** *judge.*
causa, -ae, f., *lawsuit.*
ēmpta, -ōrum, n. pl. [p.p.p. of **emō, emere, ēmī, ēmptus,** *to buy*],
things that have been bought.
probō, -āre, -āvī, -ātus, *to test, examine, give official approval to.*

---

30 **dīcentibus:** supply **nōbīs,** *in us* (when we) *speak* (in court).
34 Elegiac couplets, consisting of a dactylic hexameter followed by a
pentameter:

$- \smile\smile \mid - \smile\smile \mid - \smile\smile \mid - \smile\smile \mid - \smile\smile \mid - \times$
$- \smile\smile \mid - \smile\smile \mid - \parallel - \smile\smile \mid - \smile\smile \mid \times$

35 **paupertās ... nūlla:** abstract for concrete, = *no poor person.*
36 **Cynicā ... pērā:** ablative of attendant circumstances, *who spend
their time* (**trādūcant tempora**) *with the Cynic pouch.* The Cynics
were a sect of philosophers who preached extreme frugality and
carried a small pouch (**pēra**) that supposedly contained all their
worldly possessions. Their detractors charged them with
hypocrisy, and Ascyltos here implies that they were willing to
sell their words, i.e., to lie and perjure themselves for bribes.
37 **nōn numquam:** litotes = **saepe.**
39 **ēmpta probat:** i.e., passes judgment on cases he has already made
up his mind about due to bribery; the cases are therefore **ēmpta,**
things that have been bought.

40 **praeter,** prep. + acc., *except for.*
   dipondius, -ī, m., *coin* (worth two **assēs**; the **as,** gen., **assis,** was the basic unit of Roman coinage).
   lupīnus, -ī, m., *lupine* (a plant of which the round, flat seeds are edible).
   dēstinō, -āre, -āvī, -ātus, *to fix, resolve, intend.*
41 **mercor, -ārī, -ātus sum,** *to buy, purchase.*
   interim, adv., *in the meantime, meanwhile.*
   ***praeda, -ae,** f., *booty.*
   discēdō, discēdere, discessī, discessūrus, *to go away, depart.*
42 **vel,** particle, *even.*
   addīcō, addīcere, addīxī, addictus, *to sell.*
   ***placeō, -ēre, -uī** + dat., *to please.*
   pretium, -ī, n., *reward, return.*
43 **compendium, -ī,** n., *profit, gain.*
   levis, -is, -e, *light.*
   iactūra, -ae, f., *a throwing away, loss.*
   cum prīmum, *when first, as soon as.*
   ****ergō,** particle, *therefore.*
   explicō, explicāre, explicuī, explicitus, *to unfold.*
44 **merx, mercis,** f., *goods, merchandise.*
   operiō, operīre, operuī, opertus, *to cover.*
45 **īnspiciō [in- + speciō, *to see*], īnspicere, īnspexī, īnspectus,** *to look at, examine.*
   ****dīligentius,** compar. adv., *more/rather attentively.*
   signum, -ī, n., *mark, sign, embroidered figure.*
   ***iniciō [in- + iaciō, *to throw*], inicere, iniēcī, iniectus** + acc. and dat., *to throw onto.*
   uterque, utraque, utrumque, *each of two, both.*
   ****lacinia, -ae,** f., *edge, border* (of a garment).
46 **vōciferātiō, vōciferātiōnis,** f., *loud cry, outcry.*
   latrō, latrōnis, m., *thief.*
   ***contrā,** adv., *on the other hand.*
47 **perturbātus, -a, -um,** *disturbed, upset.*
   scissus, -a, -um, *torn.*
   sordidus, -a, -um, *dirty.*

They decide to sell their stolen cloak to get money to buy the tunic, but an un-expected complication arises.

Sed praeter ūnum dipondium, quō lupīnōs dēstināverāmus 40
mercārī, nihil ad manum erat. Itaque nē interim praeda dis- 41
cēderet, vel minōris pallium addīcere placuit, ut pretium maiōris 42
compendiī levior faceret iactūra. Cum prīmum ergō explicuimus 43
mercem, mulier opertō capite, quae cum rūsticō steterat, 44
īnspectīs dīligentius signīs iniēcit utramque laciniae manum 45
magnāque vōciferātiōne latrōnēs clāmāvit. Contrā nōs 46
perturbātī, nē vidērēmur nihil agere, et ipsī scissam et sordidam 47
tenēre coepimus tunicam atque eādem invidiā prōclāmāre nostra 48
esse spolia quae illī possidērent. 49

---

48 **coepī, coepisse, coeptus** [pf. tenses only], *to begin.*
   invidia, -ae, f., *ill-will, indignation.*
   prōclāmō, -āre, -āvī, -ātus, *to cry out, shout.*
49 **possideō, possidēre, possēdī, possessus,** *to hold, possess.*

---

41 **nē . . . discēderet**: purpose clause in secondary sequence.
42 **minōris**: genitive of price, *for less.*
   ut . . . faceret iactūra: result clause in secondary sequence, *so that a lighter loss* (i.e., selling the cloak for less than they had hoped) *would produce a return of greater profit* (by allowing them to buy back the tunic and recover the treasure sewn in its hem).
43 **Cum . . . explicuimus**: **cum** temporal + indicative defines the exact time at which the actions of the main verbs (**iniēcit**, 45, and **clāmāvit**, 46) took place.
44 **mercem**: i.e., the **pallium**.
   opertō capite: ablative of description, *with. . . .*
45 **īnspectīs dīligentius signīs**: ablative absolute.
   iniēcit . . . manum: the phrase is reminiscent of a formal legal procedure, the **manūs iniectiō**, the laying of one's hand in court on an object one claims to own.
   laciniae: dative with the compound verb, **iniēcit**.
46 **nōs**: nominative; **contrā** is an adverb, not a preposition.

50   *nūllus, -a, -um, *no.*
     genus, generis, n., *birth; kind; way.*
     pār, paris, *equal.*
     *causa, -ae, f., *lawsuit, cause.*
     cōciō, cōciōnis, m., *tradesman.*
     clāmor, clāmōris, m., *shouting.*
51   cōnfluō, cōnfluere, cōnflūxī, *to flow together, run together.*
     īnsānia, -ae, f., *madness.*
     prō, prep. + abl., *for, on behalf of.*
     pars, partis, partium, f., *part; side.*
52   *vindicō, -āre, -āvī, -ātus, *to claim, recover.*
     *pretiōsus, -a, -um, *valuable, expensive, costly.*
     *vestis, vestis, vestium, f., *garment.*
     *prō, prep. + abl., *for, on behalf of.*
     pannūcius, -a, -um, *ragged, tattered.*
53   **nē . . . quidem, *not . . . even.*
     centō, centōnis, m., *patchwork.*
     dignus, -a, -um + abl., *worthy* (of).
     hinc, adv., *from here, next.*
     repente, adv., *suddenly.*
     rīsus, -ūs, m., *laughter.*
54   discutiō [dis- + quatiō, *to shake; to strike*], discutere, discussī,
        discussus, *to strike apart, shatter; to dispel.*
     silentium, -ī, n., *silence.*
     *inquit, *(he/she) says, said.*
55   quisque, quaeque, quidque/quicque, indef. pron., *each one, every
        one.*
     cārus, -a, -um, *dear.*
     *reddō, reddere, reddidī, redditus, *to give back, return.*
56   recipiō [re- + capiō], recipere, recēpī, receptus, *to get back.*
     etsī, conj. + indic., *even if, although.*
     **placeō, -ēre, -uī + dat., *to please.*
     permūtātiō, permūtātiōnis, f., *exchange.*
57   advocō, -āre, -āvī, -ātus, *to summon.*
     *tamen, adv., *yet, nevertheless.*
     nocturnus, -ī, m., *night watchman* (the **nocturnī** were a commis-
        sion of three men who oversaw public safety at nighttime).
     flāgitō, -āre, -āvī, -ātus, *to demand.*
     utī, = ut.
     *uterque, utraque, utrumque, *each of two, both.*
        utraque, n. pl., *both things* (the tunic and the cloak).

Tradesmen and police intervene in the dispute.

    Sed nūllō genere pār erat causa, et cōciōnēs, quī ad clāmōrem 50
cōnflūxerant, nostram rīdēbant īnsāniam, quod prō illā parte 51
vindicārī vidēbant pretiōsissimam vestem, prō hāc pannūciam 52
nē centōnibus quidem bonīs dignam. Hinc Ascyltos repente rī- 53
sum discussit, quī silentiō factō, "Vidēmus," inquit, "suam 54
cuique rem esse cārissimam; reddant nōbīs tunicam nostram et 55
pallium suum recipiant." Etsī rūsticō mulierīque placēbat per- 56
mūtātiō, advocātī tamen nocturnī flāgitābant utī apud sē utraque 57
dēpōnerentur ac posterō diē iūdex querellam īnspiceret. 58

---

58   **dēpōnō, dēpōnere, dēposuī, dēpositus,** *to put down, deposit.*
        posterus, -a, -um, *next, following.*
        iūdex, iūdicis, m., *judge.*
        querella, -ae, f., *complaint, accusation.*
        *īnspiciō [in- + speciō, *to see*], **īnspicere, īnspexī, īnspectus,** *to look at, examine.*

---

52   **pannūciam:** supply **vestem.**
54   **quī:** = **et is.**
        silentiō factō: ablative absolute.
55   **reddant . . . recipiant:** hortatory subjunctives expressing commands.
57   **advocātī:** perfect passive participle modifying **nocturnī.**
        utī . . . dēpōnerentur . . . īnspiceret: indirect commands with imperfect subjunctives in secondary sequence introduced by **flāgitābant.**

59   **neque enim,** *for . . . not.*
    tantum, adv., *only.*
    contrōversia, -ae, f., *debate, controversy.*
    in contrōversiam esse, *to be disputed.*
60   **longē,** adv., *far, by far.*
    quod, (the fact) *that.*
    **uterque, utraque, utrumque, *each of two, both.*
    *pars, partis, partium, f., *part; side.*
    scīlicet, particle, *of course, certainly, evidently.*
    *latrōcinium, -ī, n., *robbery, theft.*
61   ***suspīciō, suspīciōnis,** f., *suspicion.*
    sequester, sequestrī, m., *depositary* (a third party to whom a disputed object is entrusted until the dispute is settled).
    ***placeō, -ēre, -uī + dat., *to please.*
    nesciō quis, *I don't know who = someone.*
62   ***cōciō, cōciōnis,** m., *tradesman.*
    calvus, -a, -um, *bald.*
    tūberōsus, -a, -um, *full of lumps/bumps* [**tūber, tūberis,** n.].
    frōns, frontis, frontium, f., *forehead.*
    *soleō, solēre, solitus sum, *to be accustomed.*
    aliquandō, adv., *once, formerly.*
63   ***etiam,** particle, *still; also; even; actually.*
    **causa, -ae, f., *lawsuit, cause.*
      causās agere, *to plead ' cases.*
    invādō, invādere, invāsī, invāsus, *to attack, rush upon.*
    exhibeō [ex- + habeō], -ēre, -uī, -itus, *to hold forth, produce, present for inspection.*
    crāstinus, -a, -um, *of tomorrow.*
      crāstinus diēs, *tomorrow.*
64   **affirmō [ad- + firmō,** *to make strong*], **-āre, -āvī, -ātus,** *to assert, affirm.*
    cēterum, adv., *for the rest, moreover.*
    *appāreō [ad- + pāreō, *to obey*], **-ēre, -uī, -itūrus,** *to appear.*
    quaerō, quaerere, quaesīvī or **quasiī, quaesītus,** *to seek.*
    *nisi, conj., *unless, except.*
65   **semel,** adv., *once.*
    *dēpōnō, dēpōnere, dēposuī, dēpositus, *to put down, deposit.*
    **vestis, vestis, vestium, f., *garment.*
    praedō, praedōnis, m., *robber, thief.*
    strangulō, -āre, -āvī, -ātus, *to strangle; to keep a tight hold on.*
    metus, -ūs, m., *fear.*
66   **crīmen, crīminis,** n., *crime.*
    cōnstitūtum, -ī, n., *agreement, appointment.*
      ad cōnstitūtum, *at the appointed time.*
    ***plānē, adv., *clearly, plainly, openly.*

The cloak will be kept to be presented as evidence at a trial to take place the next day.

Neque enim rēs tantum, quae vidērentur, in contrōversiam   59
esse, sed longē aliud, quod in utrāque parte scīlicet latrōnciniī   60
suspīciō habērētur. Iam sequestrī placēbant, et nesciō quis ex   61
cōciōnibus, calvus, tūberōsissimae frontis, quī solēbat aliquandō   62
etiam causās agere, invāserat pallium exhibitūrumque crāstinō   63
diē affirmābat. Cēterum appārēbat nihil aliud quaerī nisi ut   64
semel dēposita vestis inter praedōnēs strangulārētur et nōs metū   65
crīminis nōn venīrēmus ad cōnstitūtum. Idem plānē et nōs   66
volēbāmus. Itaque utrīusque partis vōtum cāsus adiūvit.   67

---

67   ***uterque, utraque utrumque,** *each of two, both.*
pars, partis, partium, f., *part; side.*
vōtum, -ī, n., *wish, desire.*
cāsus, -ūs, m., *chance, accident.*
adiūvō, adiūvāre, adiūvī, adiūtus, *to help.*

---

59   **rēs** (*acc. pl.*) . . . **esse** . . . **aliud**: indirect statement. The verb upon
which the indirect statement depends (*they said*) is omitted be-
cause it can be inferred from the previous sentence.
quae vidērentur: subjunctive in a dependent clause in indirect
statement, *which were apparent.*
60   **quod . . . habērētur**: subjunctive in a relative clause in indirect
statement.
61   **nesciō quis ex cōciōnibus**: partitive use of **ex** + abl., *someone of the
tradesmen.*
62   **tūberōsissimae frontis**: genitive of description, *with. . . .*
63   **(sē) exhibitūrum**: indirect statement after **affirmābat,** *he kept as-
serting that he would. . . .*
64   **nihil aliud quaerī**: infinitive clause serving as subject of **appārēbat,** *that nothing else was being sought appeared = it appeared that. . . .*
ut . . . strangulārētur . . . venīrēmus: substantive clause of result
serving as a second subject of **appārēbat**; imperfect subjunctive
in secondary sequence.

68   **indignor, -ārī, -ātus sum,** *to take offense at, resent* + **quod** clause.
     enim, particle, *for.*
     ***centō, centōnis,** m., *patchwork.*
     ***exhibeō [ex- + habeō], -ēre, -uī, -itus,** *to hold forth, produce, present for inspection.*
69   **postulō, -āre, -āvī, -ātus,** *to ask, demand.*
     faciēs, faciēī, f., *face.*
     līberātus, -a, -um, *freed from* + abl.
70   ***querella, -ae,** f., *complaint, accusation.*
     ****dēpōnō, dēpōnere, dēposuī, dēpositus,** *to put down, deposit.*
     ***līs, lītis,** f., *dispute, lawsuit.*
71   ***recuperō, -āre, -āvī, -ātus,** *to get back, recover.*
     ****thēsaurus, -ī,** m. [Greek loan word], *treasure.*
     dēversōrium, -ī, n., *inn, lodging.*
     praeceps, praecipitis, *headlong.*
72   **abeō, abīre, abiī, abitūrus,** irreg., *to go away, depart.*
     praeclūdō [prae- + claudō, *to shut*], **praeclūdere, praeclūsī, praeclūsus,** *to shut, close.*
     forēs, forium, f. pl., *two leaves of a door.*
     acūmen, acūminis, n., *sharpness, shrewdness.*
     nōn minus . . . quam, *no less . . . than.*
     ****cōciō, cōciōnis,** m., *tradesman.*
73   **calumnior, -ārī, -ātus sum,** *to accuse falsely, blame unjustly.*
     calumniantium, present participle, gen. pl., *of those who were accusing* (us), i.e., the **rūsticus** and his female companion.
     *****coepī, coepisse, coeptus** [pf. tenses only], *to begin.*
     calliditās, calliditātis, f., *shrewdness, cunning, slyness.*
74   ****reddō, reddere, reddidī, redditus,** *to give back, return.*
75   **cupiō, cupere, cupīvī** or **cupiī, cupītus,** *to desire, want.*
     statim, adv., *immediately.*
76   **victōria, -ae,** f., *victory.*
     mī, = mihi.
     parātus, -a, -um, *prepared, ready to hand, available* (i.e., *easy*).

Ascyltos and Encolpius recover their tunic and return to their lodgings.

Indignātus enim rūsticus, quod nōs centōnem exhibendum   68
postulārēmus, mīsit in faciem Ascyltī tunicam et līberātōs   69
querellā iussit pallium dēpōnere, quod sōlum lītem faciēbat. Et   70
recuperātō, ut putābāmus, thēsaurō in dēversōrium praecipitēs   71
abīmus praeclūsīsque foribus rīdēre acūmen nōn minus cō-   72
ciōnum quam calumniantium coepimus, quod nōbīs ingentī cal-   73
liditāte pecūniam reddidissent.   74

    Nōlō quod cupiō statim tenēre,   75
    nec victōria mī placet parāta.   76

---

68 **quod . . . postulārēmus**: the subjunctive implies that the reason
given is attributed to the **rūsticus** and is not necessarily vouched
for by the speaker.
exhibendum: supply **esse**, *that the patchwork* (i.e., the ragged tunic)
must be exhibited.
70 **querellā**: ablative of separation with **līberātōs**.
71 **recuperātō . . . thēsaurō**: ablative absolute.
ut putābāmus: **ut** + indicative = *as.*
72 **praeclūsīs . . . foribus**: ablative absolute.
73 **quod . . . reddidissent**: the subjunctive implies that the reason
given is attributed to the other party.
ingentī calliditāte: ablative of manner, *with* (what they thought to
be their) *immense cleverness.*
75 Hendecasyllabic verses:

    – – – ∪ – ∪ – ∪ – ∪̆

1   **tertius, -a, -um,** *third.*
    tot, indecl. adj., *so many.*
    vulnus, vulneris, n., *wound.*
    cōnfodiō, cōnfodere, cōnfōdī, cōnfossus, *to dig up; to pierce, stab.*
2   **fuga, -ae,** f., *flight.*
    magis . . . quam, *more . . . than.*
    quiēs, quiētis, f., *rest, quiet* (i.e., staying where we were).
    maestus, -a, -um, *sad, dejected.*
    dēlīberō, -āre, -āvī, -ātus, *to consult, deliberate.*
3   **quīnam, quaenam, quodnam,** interrog. adj., *what.*
    *****genus, generis,** n., *birth; kind; way.*
     quōnam genere, = **quōmodo,** *in what way, how.*
    praesēns, praesentis, *present, imminent.*
    ēvītō, -āre, -āvī, -ātus, *to avoid.*
    procella, -ae, f., *violent storm.*
4   **Agamemnōn, Agamemnonis,** m. [Greek name], *Agamemnon* (a
    rhētor, *professor of rhetoric,* who bears the name of the ancient
    king of Mycenae who led the Greeks against Troy).
    interpellō, -āre, -āvī, -ātus, *to interrupt.*
    trepidō, -āre, -āvī, -ātus, *to tremble; to be nervous/anxious.*
5   ******inquit,** *(he/she) says, said.*
    nesciō, -īre, -īvī, -ītus, *not to know; to be ignorant.*
    apud quem, *with whom, at whose house.*

II.

TRIMALCHIO'S DINNER

1. Preliminaries and Hors d'oeuvres

Encolpius and Ascyltos are invited to dinner at Trimalchio's and go first to the baths.

[26–33] Vēnerat iam tertius diēs, sed tot vulneribus cōnfossīs   1
fuga magis placēbat quam quiēs. Itaque cum maestī dēlīberārē-   2
mus quōnam genere praesentem ēvītārēmus procellam, ūnus   3
servus Agamemnonis interpellāvit trepidantēs et, "Quid? Vōs,   4
inquit, "nescītis, hodiē apud quem fīat?   5

(paragraph continued on page 21)

---

1 **tot vulneribus cōnfossīs** . . . **placēbat**: supply **nōbīs** with **cōnfos-sīs**, dative with **placēbat**, *pleased us, pierced with.* . . . The previous episode has been lost, and it is not known what kinds of wounds (physical or emotional) are being referred to.

2 **cum** . . . **dēlīberārēmus**: circumstantial clause with imperfect subjunctive in secondary sequence.

3 **quōnam genere** . . . **ēvītārēmus**: indirect question with deliberative subjunctive in secondary sequence: *how we were to avoid.* . . .

   praesentem . . . **procellam**: apparently referring to the impending banquet, which the narrator Encolpius and his friend Ascyltos shudder at the thought of attending.

   ūnus: almost = indefinite article, *a*; the normal Latin would be **ūnus ē servīs** (see p. 248).

4 **Agamemnonis**: Agamemnon, the professor of rhetoric, has been invited to dinner by Trimalchio, and he is going to take his friends Ascyltos and Encolpius along with him. Such uninvited companions were called **umbrae**, *shadows, shades;* see Horace, *Satires* 2.8.21–22, where Maecenas is said to have brought Vibidius and Servilius Balatro along to a dinner party thrown by the rich Nasidienus.

   trepidantēs: supply **nōs** (acc. pl.).

   Vōs: redundant; personal pronouns are used in Petronius more frequently than normal.

5 **fīat**: subjunctive in an indirect question, *at whose house it happens to-day* = *who will be our host today.*

6 **Trimalchiō, Trimalchiōnis,** m. [**tri-,** *three times* + a Semitic base meaning *prince,* cf. the Semitic names Malchus and Malachi, or, though less likely + Greek *malakos,* "soft, effeminate"; in either case, compare the name Malchio, which appears in Martial 3.82.32], *Trimalchio* (the full name Petronius gives him is **Gaius Pompeius Tramalchiō Maecēnātiānus: Trimalchiō** was his name as a slave in Asia Minor; he is to be imagined as having taken **Gaius Pompeius,** his **praenōmen** and **nōmen,** from the master who manumitted him; his **cognōmen, Maecēnātiānus,** would have been taken from an earlier master and has literary allusions to Gaius Maecenas, the diplomatic agent and cultural minister of the emperor Augustus; this historical Maecenas was a wealthy, eccentric, and effeminate patron of the arts—see Seneca, *Epistle* 114.4–8).

lautus, -a, -um [**lavō, lavāre, lāvī, lautus,** *to wash*], *elegant, luxurious; neat, smart.*

hōrologium, -ī, n. [Greek loan word], *sundial; water clock.*

trīclīnium, -ī, n., *dining room.*

7 **būcinātor, būcinātōris,** m. [**būcina, -ae,** f., *curved trumpet*], *trumpeter.*

subōrnō, -āre, -āvī, -ātus, *to fit out, equip; to dress up* (in uniform).

subinde, adv., *repeatedly, constantly.*

quantum, -ī, n., interrog. pron., *how much?*

8 **perdō, perdere, perdidī, perditus,** *to destroy; to lose.*

amiciō, amicīre, amicuī, amictus, *to wrap around, clothe* (used of outer garments); pass. used reflexively, *to clothe oneself.*

dīligenter, adv., *carefully.*

oblīvīscor, oblīvīscī, oblītus sum + gen., *to forget.*

  oblītus, -a, -um + gen., *forgetful* (of).

9 **mala, -ōrum,** n. pl., *evils, troubles.*

Gītōn, Gītōnis, m. [Greek word meaning "neighbor, borderer"], *Giton* (a pretty, adolescent boy, Encolpius' darling). Forms: acc., **Gītōna** or **Gītōnem;** abl., **Gītōne.**

libentissimē, superl. adv., *very willingly.*

servīlis, -is, -e, *servile, of a slave.*

officium, -ī, n., *duty.*

tueor, tuērī, tuitus sum, *to guard, maintain, see to.*

10 **balineum, -ī,** n., *bath; baths* (i.e., a public bathing establishment or a set of rooms for bathing in a private home).

  balneum, syncopated colloquial variant of **balineum** (see p. 241).

sequor, sequī, secūtus sum, *to follow.*

"Trimalchiō, lautissimus homō hōrologium in trīclīniō et   6
būcinātōrem habet subōrnātum, ut subinde sciat quantum dē   7
vītā perdiderit." Amicimur ergō dīligenter oblītī omnium   8
malōrum, et Gītōna libentissimē servīle officium tuentem iubē- 9
mus in balneum sequī.   10

---

6 **homō:** *fellow.*
  hōrologium: for clocks in the Roman world, see Paoli, pp. 82–84.
7 **ut . . . sciat:** purpose clause in primary sequence after **habet.**
  Martial (8.67.1) and Juvenal (10.216) mention slaves announcing
  the hour of the day to their masters—a common practice in the
  Roman world with no convenient, portable timepieces such as
  wristwatches.
  quantum dē vītā: informal use of prepositional phrase instead of
  partitive genitive (**quantum vītae**) (see p. 248).
  quantum . . . perdiderit: perfect subjunctive in indirect question:
  how much. . . .
8 **oblītī omnium malōrum:** the troubles referred to in the phrase **tot
  vulneribus cōnfossīs** (1).
9 **Gītōna:** Giton will now serve as Encolpius' and Ascyltos' slave
  since they have no actual slave. They will thus be able to maintain their dignity, and they will have someone to watch their
  clothes in the baths (a usual task for a slave), so that no one will
  steal them.
  servīle officium tuentem: *seeing to the duty of. . . .* = *playing the role
  of. . . .* The slave who would accompany his master to the baths
  and to dinner was called a **pedisequus,** *foot-follower.*
10 **in balneum:** Romans generally bathed before dinner. Here the
  bath is actually the beginning of the dinner (see below, lines 23–
  24). Pliny (*Letters* 3.1.8–9) describes the well-ordered daily activ-
  ity of an elderly gentleman named Spurinna, who would go to
  the baths at mid-afternoon in winter or a little earlier in summer,
  exercise by walking in the sunshine without his clothes and by
  playing a long and energetic game of ball, lie down to rest for a
  while before dinner while listening to someone reading, and then
  take dinner with his friends. While at the baths, his friends could
  do as he did or not as they pleased. Pliny praises Spurrina's
  quiet, modest, and well-ordered activities. Note how Trimalchio
  keeps to the usual pattern of bathing and exercising before dinner but differs in some respects from Pliny's praiseworthy ideal.

11   *interim, adv., *in the meantime, meanwhile.*
     vestiō, -īre, -īvī, -ītus, *to clothe.*
     errō, -āre, -āvī, -ātūrus, *to wander.*
     immō, particle, *nay, on the contrary, rather.*
     iocor, -ārī, -ātus sum, *to joke, jest.*
     magis, compar. adv., *more; rather.*
12   circulus, -ī, m., *circle, group of people* (here of people exercising in
     the gymnasium).
     **accēdō [ad- + cēdō, *to go*], accēdere, accessī, accessus + dat., *to
     approach.*
     *subitō, adv., *suddenly.*
     senex, senis, m., *old man.*
     *calvus, -a, -um, *bald.*
13   *vestiō, -īre, -īvī, -ītus, *to clothe.*
     russeus, -a, -um, *reddish.*
     capillātus, -a, -um, *having long hair* [capillus, -ī, m.].
     lūdō, lūdere, lūsī, lūsūrus, *to play.*
     pila, -ae, f., *ball.*
     tam . . . quam (15), = tantum . . . quantum, *as much as.*
14   quamquam, conj., *although.*
     opera, -ae, f., *work; service, attention.*
     *pretium, -ī, n., *worth, value, reward.*
         operae pretium, *a reward for trouble, worthwhile.*
     spectāculum, -ī, n., *sight.*
15   pater familiae, *father of the family, head of the household.*
     soleātus, -a, -um, *wearing sandals* [solea, -ae, f.].
     *pila, -ae, f., *ball.*
     prasinus, -a, -um, *green.*
     exerceō, -ēre, -uī, -itus, *to exercise;* pass. used reflexively, *to exer-
     cise oneself.*
16   amplius, compar. adv., *more, longer, further, again.*
     repetō, repetere, repetīvī, repetītus, *to seek again, fetch back.*
     contingō, contingere, contigī, contāctus, *to touch.*
17   follis, follis, follium, m., *bag.*
     *plēnus, -a, -um + gen. or abl., *full* (of).
     sufficiō [sub- + faciō], sufficere, suffēcī, suffectus, *to give, sup-
     ply.*
     *lūdō, lūdere, lūsī, lūsūrus, *to play.*

An old, bald man is playing ball in the gymnasium that is part of the bathing establishment.

Nōs interim vestītī errāre coepimus, immō iocārī magis et 11
circulīs accēdere, cum subitō vidēmus senem calvum, tunicā 12
vestītum russeā, inter puerōs capillātōs lūdentem pilā. Nec tam 13
puerī nōs, quamquam erat operae pretium, ad spectāculum dūx- 14
erant, quam ipse pater familiae, quī soleātus pilā prasinā exer- 15
cēbātur. Nec amplius eam repetēbat quae terram contigerat, sed 16
follem plēnum habēbat servus sufficiēbatque lūdentibus. 17

(paragraph continued on page 25)

11 **vestītī**: i.e., not undressed for the bath.
errāre: i.e., to wander around in the gymnasium.
12 **cum . . . vidēmus**: the **cum inversum** construction, in which the preceding main clause takes the place of what would normally be a **cum** circumstantial clause with the subjunctive and the **cum** clause with the indicative contains the main statement of the sentence, *we suddenly saw an old man*. This construction is met frequently in Petronius and highlights the statement in the **cum** clause.
13 **puerōs capillātōs**: long-haired, effeminate slave boys were highly prized by their masters. Trimalchio himself began his career as such a slave (see line 54).
lūdentem pilā: abl. of instrument; Trimalchio is playing ball with two other players in a triangle (the game called **trigōn**); there was a separate part of the gymnasium for such games, called the **sphaeristērium [sphaera, -ae, f., Greek loan word, *ball*]. For playing ball before dinner, see the reference to Spurinna in the note on line 10; Maecenas, Augustus' minister of culture, was fond of this game (Horace, *Satires* 1.5.48–49 and 2.6.49).
tam . . . quam: translate with **ipse pater familiae** (15).
14 **quamquam erat operae pretium**: i.e., although the long-haired boys were worth looking at.
15 **soleātus**: an eccentricity because sandals were normally worn only in the house.
16 **eam**: supply **pilam**.
17 **follem plēnum**: supply **pilārum**.
sufficiēbat: supply **pilās**.

18 *notō, -āre, -āvī, -ātus, *to note, observe.*
    **etiam, particle, *still; also; even; actually.*
    spadō, spadōnis, m., *castrated person, eunuch.*
    dīversus, -a, -um, *opposite.*
    ***pars, partis, partium, f., *part; side.*

19 *circulus, -ī, m., *circle, group of people.*
    alter, altera, alterum, *the one, the other* (of two).
    matella, -ae, f., *chamber-pot* (usually made of clay or bronze, not silver).
    argenteus, -a, -um, *of silver.*

20 numerō, -āre, -āvī, -ātus, *to count.*
    **pila, -ae, f., *ball.*
    *quidem, particle, *indeed, it is true, to be sure.*
    expellō, expellere, expulī, expulsus, *to drive/push away; to throw.*

21 vibrō, -āre, -āvī, -ātus, *to move rapidly back and forth.*
    dēcidō [de- + cadō, *to fall*], dēcidere, dēcidī, *to fall down.*

Notāvimus etiam rēs novās. Nam duo spadōnēs in dīversā parte   18
circulī stābant, quōrum alter matellam tenēbat argenteam, alter   19
numerābat pilās, nōn quidem eās quae inter manūs expellentēs   20
vibrābant, sed eās quae in terram dēcidēbant.   21

---

18   **duo spadōnēs**: castrated slaves brought high prices. The religious
     basis of castration is explored by Catullus, who in poem 63
     describes how the legendary Attis fled from Greece to Asia
     Minor and castrated himself to become a votary of the great
     mother goddess Cybele, whose emasculated priests were called
     Galli. Emasculation guaranteed the purity of the goddess's
     votaries. Eunuchs were employed by eastern potentates such as
     Darius (Livy 9.17.16) and in wealthy and imperial households in
     the Roman world. Augustus' minister of culture, Maecenas, was
     attended in public by two eunuchs (Seneca, *Epistulae morales*
     114.6), and the emperor Claudius especially esteemed the
     eunuch Posides among his freedmen (Suetonius, *Claudius* 28).
     Maecenas may have been Petronius' model for having two eu-
     nuchs accompany Trimalchio here.
20   **nōn quidem eās**: usually points were scored by how many throws
     were caught, but here the missed balls are counted and not
     reused (a conspicuous extravagance!).
     manūs expellentēs: *the hands* (that were) *throwing* (them).

22 mīror, -ārī, -ātus sum, *to wonder at.*
    lautitia, -ae, f., *elegance, splendor* (cf. line 6, **lautissimus**).
    accurrō [ad- + currō], accurrere, accurrī, accursūrus, *to rush up.*
    Menelāus, -ī, m. [Greek name], *Menelaus* (an assistant to the pro-
       fessor of rhetoric, Agamemnon; he bears the name of Helen's
       husband, who went to Troy to fetch back his wife after she was
       abducted by Paris).
23 ***inquit, *(he/she) says, said.*
    *apud quem, *with whom, at whose house.*
    cubitum, -ī, n., *elbow.*
    **quidem, particle, *indeed, it is true, to be sure.*
    prīncipium, -ī, n., *beginning.*
24 etiamnum, particle, *still, even now.*
    loquor, loquī, locūtus sum, *to speak.*
25 concrepō, concrepere, concrepuī, *to make a noise; to snap* (the fin-
       gers).
    *signum, -ī, n., *sign.*
    *matella, -ae, f., *chamber-pot.*
    *spadō, spadōnis, m., *castrated person, eunuch.*
26 **lūdō, lūdere, lūsī, lūsūrus, *to play.*
    subiciō [sub- + iaciō, *to throw*], subicere, subiēcī, subiectus, *to
       put under; to furnish, supply.*
    exonerō, -āre, -āvī, -ātus, *to free from a burden* [onus, oneris, n.],
       unload, empty.
    vēsīca, -ae, f., *bladder.*
    poscō, poscere, poposcī, *to ask for, demand.*
27 *paululum, dim. adv., *a little bit.*
    adspergō [ad- + spargō, *to sprinkle*], adspergere, adspersī,
       adspersus, *to sprinkle.*
    tergeō, tergēre, tersī, tersus, *to wipe, wipe dry.*

The old man turns out to be none other than Trimalchio himself.

Cum hās ergō mīrārēmur lautitiās, accurrit Menelāus et, "Hic   22
est," inquit, "apud quem cubitum pōnitis, et quidem iam prīn-   23
cipium cēnae vidētis." Etiamnum loquēbātur Menelāus, cum   24
Trimalchiō digitōs concrepuit, ad quod signum matellam spadō   25
lūdentī subiēcit. Exonerātā ille vēsīcā aquam poposcit ad   26
manūs, digitōsque paululum adspersōs in capite puerī tersit.   27

---

22   **Cum . . . mīrārēmur:** circumstantial clause with imperfect subjunctive in secondary sequence.
hās . . . lautitiās: i.e., this elegant way of playing ball.
accurrit Menelāus: Menelaus runs up to tell Encolpius and Ascyltos that the bald old man is their host for dinner so that they
won't jeer too openly at his eccentricities.

23   **cubitum pōnitis:** to place one's elbow = to recline at dinner,
propped with the left elbow on a pillow. **pōnitis:** the present
tense is used where we would expect a future; while this is
common in vulgar Latin, it occurs here even in the words of an
educated speaker (see p. 248).
prīncipium cēnae: it was usual to exercise and bathe before dinner
and to go directly from the bathing establishment to the house to
which one was invited to dinner. Menelaus highlights this
practice by describing the activities in the baths as actually the
beginning of the dinner.

26   **lūdentī:** supply **eī,** dative with **subiēcit;** the eunuch supplied the
chamber pot to Trimalchio while he was still playing ball.
Exonerātā . . . vēsīcā: ablative absolute, *after emptying. . . .*
ad manūs: ad + acc. to express purpose, *for* (washing his) *hands.*

28   **longum est** + infin., *it is* (too) *long a task* (to).
     singulī, -ae, -a, *single, separate.*
        singula, *single things, details.*
     excipiō [ex- + capiō], excipere, excēpī, exceptus, *to take/pick out; to catch;* here, *to notice, mention.*
     intrō, -āre, -āvī, -ātus, *to enter.*
     ***balineum, -ī,** n., *bath; baths* (i.e., a public bathing establishment or a set of rooms for bathing in a private home).
        balneum, syncopated colloquial variant (see p. 241).
29   **sūdor, sūdōris,** m., *sweat.*
     calefaciō, calefacere, calefēcī, calefactus, *to make warm/hot.*
        calfactī, syncopated colloquial variant of **calefactī** (see p. 241).
     mōmentum, -ī, n., *moment.*
     frīgida (aqua), *cold (water).*
     exeō, exīre, exiī, exitus, irreg., *to go out.*
30   **unguentum, -ī,** n., *ointment, perfume.*
     perfundō, perfundere, perfūdī, perfūsus, *to pour over, wet, moisten.*
     ***tergeō, tergēre, tersī, tersus,** *to wipe, wipe dry.*
     linteum, -ī, n., *linen cloth.*
31   **lāna, -ae,** f., *wool.*
     mollis, -is, -e, *soft.*
     ****interim,** adv., *in the meantime, meanwhile.*
     iātralīptēs, -ae, m. [Greek loan word], *healer with ointments and rubbing, masseur.*
     cōnspectus, -ūs, m., *sight, view, presence.*
32   **Falernum (vīnum),** *Falernian (wine)* (excellent wine from the Falernian area of Campania).
     pōtō, -āre, -āvī, -ātus, *to drink.*
     plūrimus, -a, -um [superl. of **multus, -a, -um**], *the most, the greater part of something* (supply **vīnum**).
     rixor, -ārī, -ātus sum, *to quarrel, fight.*

     effundō [ex- + fundō, *to pour*], **effundere, effūdī, effūsus,** *to pour out.*
33   **propīn,** n. [vulgar, see p. 247; Greek infinitive used as a noun], *drink taken before a meal; drink to someone's health, toast.*

They all bathe. Trimalchio is rubbed down with exceedingly soft woolen cloaks.

Longum erat singula excipere. Itaque intrāvimus balneum, 28
et sūdōre calfactī mōmentō temporis ad frīgidam exīmus. Iam 29
Trimalchiō unguentō perfūsus tergēbātur, nōn linteīs, sed palliīs 30
ex lānā mollissimā factīs. Trēs interim iātralīptae in cōnspectū 31
eius Falernum pōtābant, et cum plūrimum rixantēs effunderent, 32
Trimalchiō hoc suum propīn esse dīcēbat. 33

---

28 **Longum erat**: *It was.* . . . (and so we didn't attempt it) = *It would have been.* . . .
29 **sūdōre calfactī** . . . **ad frīgidam**: there were usually three separate rooms in the baths with different temperatures of water: hot (the **calidārium**), warm (the **tepidārium**), and cold (the **frīgidārium**). Sometimes there was also a small, heated sweat-bath (**Lacōnicum** = *Spartan*) in addition to the **calidārium**. Here the guests enter the hot bath (referred to simply as **balneum**), work up a sweat in the **Lacōnicum**, and go directly to the **frīgidārium**.
exīmus: = **exiimus**, perfect tense (contracted form).
30 **palliīs**: not *cloaks* but simply large rectangles of soft woolen cloth.
31 **iātralīptae**: masseurs of this sort fomed a distinct and respected class in the ancient health-care profession (see Pliny, *Letters* 10.5).
32 **cum . . . effunderent**: circumstantial clause with imperfect subjunctive in secondary sequence.
plūrimum: supply **vīnī**.
rixantēs: *while.* . . .
33 **suum propīn**: *a toast to himself* (**suum**).

34   *hinc, adv., *from here, next.*
     involvō, involvere, involvī, involūtus, *to roll up, wrap up, cover.*
     coccinus, -a, -um [Greek loan word], *scarlet.*
     gausapa, -ae, f., *woolen cloth* (shaggy on one side and felted on the
        other); *heavy cloak* (made of such material and used by travelers
        and soldiers; here used as a bathrobe).
     lectīca, -ae, f., *litter.*
     impōnō [in- + pōnō], impōnere, imposuī, impositus, *to place
        upon.*
35   praecēdō, praecēdere, praecessī, praecessus, *to go before, precede.*
     phalerātus, -a, -um, *decorated with metal discs* [phalerae, -ārum, f.
        pl., Greek loan word] (on chest and forehead; usually a sign of
        military achievements).
     cursor, cursōris, m., *runner; footman* (who runs ahead of a litter or
        carriage to clear the way).
     chīramaxium, -ī, n. [Greek loan word found only here in Latin,
        see p. 246], *wagon drawn by hand.*
36   dēliciae, -ārum, f. pl., *beloved, favorite, pet.*
     vehō, vehere, vexī, vectus, *to bear, carry.*
     puer, puerī, m., *boy; homosexual pet; young male slave.*
     vetulus, -a, -um [dim. of vetus], *little old.*
     lippus, -a, -um, *bleary-eyed, half-blind.*
37   dēfōrmis, -is, -e, *ugly.*
     auferō [ab- + ferō], auferre, abstulī, ablātus, *to carry off, carry
        away.*
38   symphōniacus, -ī, m. [Greek loan word], *singing boy.*
     tibia, -ae, f., *pipe.*
     ***accēdō [ad- + cēdō, *to go*], accēdere, accessī, accessus, *to ap-
        proach.*
     **tamquam, conj., *just as (if).*
     auris, auris, aurium, f., *ear.*
39   aliquis, aliquis, aliquid, indef. pron., *someone, anyone, something,
        anything.*
     sēcrētō, adv., *secretly.*
     iter, itineris, n., *journey.*
     cantō, -āre, -āvī, -ātus, *to sing, play.*

Dressed in scarlet and placed in his litter, Trimalchio is carried home in an outlandish procession.

Hinc involūtus coccinā gausapā lectīcae impositus est   34
praecēdentibus phalerātīs cursōribus quattuor et chīramaxiō, in   35
quō dēliciae eius vehēbantur, puer vetulus, lippus, dominō Tri-   36
malchiōne dēfōrmior. Cum ergō auferrētur, ad caput eius cum   37
minimīs symphōniacus tibiīs accessit et tamquam in aurem   38
aliquid sēcrētō dīceret, tōtō itinere cantāvit.   39

---

34 **lectīcae**: dative with the compound verb **impositus est.** The litter carried by four or eight slaves was the usual means of transportation for influential and wealthy men.

35 **praecēdentibus . . . cursōribus . . . et chīramaxiō**: ablative absolute, *preceded by. . . .*
   phalerātīs cursōribus: Nero was accompanied on his travels by an escort of footmen decorated with **phalerae** (Suetonius, *Nero* 30).

36 **dēliciae**: the boy is named Croesus after the king of Lydia famous for his vast wealth. The noun **dēliciae** is used only in the plural but with a singular sense (*pet*); it takes a plural verb.
   puer: in apposition to **dēliciae.**

37 **Cum . . . auferrētur**: circumstantial clause with imperfect subjunctive in secondary sequence. Trimalchio is the subject.
   Cum ergō: *Well then, when. . . .* The particle **ergō** resumes the narrative from line 34 after the digression on Trimalchio's footmen and pet slave.

38 **symphōniacus**: such musicians are mentioned several times by Cicero in connection with notables of his day (see, for example, *In Pisonem* 83 and *Pro Milone* 55).
   tamquam . . . dīceret: contrary to fact with the imperfect subjunctive, *as if he were. . . .*

39 **tōtō itinere**: ablative of the route followed.

40   *sequor, sequī, secūtus sum, *to follow.*
admīrātiō, admīrātiōnis, f., *admiration, wonder.*
satur, satura, saturum + abl., *full* (of), *satisfied* (with), *filled* (with).

41   iānua, -ae, f., *door.*
perveniō, pervenīre, pervēnī, perventūrus, *to come to, arrive.*
postis, postis, postium, m., *door-post.*
libellus, -ī, m. [dim. of liber, librī, m., *book*], *little book; notice, plac-
ard.*
īnscrīptiō, īnscrīptiōnis, f., *inscription.*

42   fīgō, fīgere, fīxī, fīxus, *to fix, fasten.*
quisquis, quisquis, quidquid/quicquid, indef. adj., *any . . . that,
whatever.*
dominicus, -a, -um, *of/belonging to the master* [dominus, -ī, m.].
iussus, -ūs, m., *order.*
forās, adv., *out of doors* (implying motion).
*exeō, exīre, exiī, exitus, irreg., *to go out.*

43   accipiō [ad- + capiō], accipere, accēpī, acceptus, *to receive.*
plāga, -ae, f., *strike, blow* (of a whip).
aditus, -ūs, m., *entrance, doorway.*
autem, particle, *moreover, furthermore.*
ōstiārius, -ī, m., *door-keeper* (who guards the ōstium, -ī, n., *doorway,* and was often referred to as the iānitor).

44   prasinātus, -a, -um [Greek root], *wearing a green garment.*
cerasinus, -a, -um [Greek loan word found only in Petronius, see
p. 246], *cherry-colored.*
succingō [sub- + cingō, *to encircle*], succingere, succīnxī, succīnctus, *to tuck up, gird about.*
cingulum, -ī, n., *belt.*
lānx, lancis, f., *plate, dish.*
*argenteus, -a, -um, *of silver.*

45   pīsum, -ī, n., *pea;* here used collectively, *peas.*
pūrgō, -āre, -āvī, -ātus, *to make clean, wash* (here used of shelling
the peas).
līmen, līminis, n., *threshold, door, entrance.*
*autem, particle, *moreover, furthermore.*
cavea, -ae, f., *hollow place; cage.*
pendeō, pendēre, pependī, *to hang.*
aureus, -a, -um, *of gold.*

46   pīca, -ae, f., *magpie.*
varius, -a, -um, *diverse, different, many-colored.*
*intrō, -āre, -āvī, -ātus, *to enter.*
salūtō, -āre, -āvī, -ātus, *to greet.*

At the doorway: a threatening sign, a doorkeeper shelling peas, a magpie greeting the guests.

Sequimur nōs admīrātiōne iam saturī et cum Agamemnone 40
ad iānuam pervenīmus, in cuius poste libellus erat cum hāc īn- 41
scrīptiōne fīxus: "Quisquis servus sine dominicō iussū forās ex- 42
ierit, accipiet plāgās centum." In aditū autem ipsō stābat ōs- 43
tiārius prasinātus, cerasinō succīnctus cingulō, atque in lance ar- 44
genteā pīsum pūrgābat. Super līmen autem cavea pendēbat au- 45
rea, in quā pīca varia intrantēs salūtābat. 46

---

42 **Quisquis servus**: *Whatever slave* = *If any slave.*
    exierit, accipiet: future more vivid condition (with future perfect
    and future indicative), *if any slave goes* (lit., *will have gone*) *out, he
    will receive.*
46 **pīca . . . salūtābat**: Pliny describes talking magpies and other talk-
    ing birds in his *Natural History* (10.117–124); Martial (7.87.6)
    mentions a **pīca salūtātrīx**, a magpie that says **Salvē!** *Hello!*

47   ***cēterum**, adv., *for the rest, moreover.*

    stupeō, -ēre, -uī, *to be struck dumb; to be amazed at.*

    resupīnō, -āre, -āvī, -ātus, *to throw on one's back; to fall on one's back.*

    crūs, crūris, n., *leg.*

48   **frangō, frangere, frēgī, frāctus,** *to break.*

    sinistra -ae, f., *left hand.*

    *enim, particle, *for.*

    **intrō, -āre, -āvī, -ātus, *to enter.*

    *longē, adv., *far.*

    *ōstiārius, -ī, m., *door-keeper* (who guards the **ōstium, -ī,** n., *doorway,* and was often referred to as the **iānitor**).

49   **cella, -ae,** f., *room.*

    catēna, -ae, f., *chain.*

    vinciō, vincīre, vīnxī, vīnctus, *to bind, fasten.*

    pariēs, parietis, m., *wall.*

    pingō, pingere, pīnxī, pictus, *to paint, represent.*

    super, adv., *above.*

50   **quadrātus, -a, -um,** *squared, square-cut* (here of large capital letters).

    littera, -ae, f., *letter.*

    caveō, cavēre, cāvī, cautus, *to beware.*

    collēga, -ae, m., *companion.*

    ***quidem, particle, *indeed, it is true, to be sure.*

51   ****autem,** particle, *moreover, furthermore.*

    colligō [con- + **legō,** *to gather*], **colligere, collēgī, collēctus,** *to gather, collect.*

    spīritus, -ūs, m., *air; breath.*

    dēsistō, dēsistere, dēstitī + infin, *to stop, cease* (doing something).

    *pariēs, parietis, m., *wall.*

52   **persequor, persequī, persecūtus sum,** *to follow;* here, *to go over, examine, explore.*

Amazement and shock

Cēterum ego dum omnia stupeō, paene resupīnātus crūra   47
mea frēgī. Ad sinistram enim intrantibus nōn longē ab ōstiāriī   48
cellā canis ingēns, catēnā vīnctus, in pariete erat pictus superque   49
quadrātā litterā scrīptum "Cavē canem." Et collēgae quidem   50
meī rīsērunt, ego autem collēctō spīritū nōn dēstitī tōtum pari-   51
etem persequī.   52

---

47 **dum . . . stupeō**: **dum** regularly takes the present indicative for a
continuous past action when the main verb is in the perfect tense,
while I was. . . .
paene: with **resupīnātus** and **frēgī**, *I almost fell on my back and
(almost). . . .*
48 **intrantibus**: dative, *with respect to those entering* (the house) = *as you
entered*.
ōstiāriī cellā: the door-keeper had a small room at the entrance to
the house.
49 **canis . . . pictus**: pictures of dogs (painted or in mosaic) with the
inscription **CAVE CANEM** were frequent at the front entrances
of houses, as in the house of the tragic poet in Pompeii. Another
entrance to Trimalchio's house is guarded by a real dog.
50 **quadrātā litterā**: collective singular; translate as plural.
collēgae meī: i.e., Agamemnon, Menelaus, Ascyltos, and Giton.
51 **collēctō spīritū**: ablative absolute, *when I. . . .*
tōtum parietem persequī: the wall that Encolpius is now examining is no longer that of the entrance hall with the picture of the
dog, but rather that of the **porticus** which comes after the entrance hall and before the **ātrium**. The pictures that Encolpius is
here examining are described in the next passage.

53   ***autem, particle, *moreover, furthermore.*
      vēnālīcium, -ī, n., *slave-market.*
      titulus, -ī, m., *label, tag* (hung around the necks of slaves for sale
          and stating nationality, age, price, etc.).
      *pingō, pingere, pīnxī, pictus, *to paint, represent.*
54   *capillātus, -a, -um, *having long hair* [capillus, -ī, m.].
      cādūceum, -ī, n. or caduceus, -ī, m. [Greek loan word], *caduceus*
          (winged staff with serpents twining around it carried by the god
          Mercury).
      Minerva, -ae, f., *Minerva* (Roman goddess equated with the Greek
          goddess Athena, virgin daughter of Zeus and patroness of
          handicrafts, skill, and wisdom).
      ***intrō, -āre, -āvī, -ātus, *to enter.*
55   **hinc, adv., *from here, next.*
      quemadmodum, adv., *in what mannter, how.*
      ratiōcinor, -ārī, -ātus sum, *to reckon, compute, calculate.*
      discō, discere, didicī, *to learn.*
      deinque, = dein + -que.
          dein or deinde, adv., *afterward, then, next.*
      dispēnsātor, dispēnsātōris, m. [dis- + pēnsō, -āre, *to weigh/pay
          out*], *household superintendent, manager, steward.*
56   *dīligenter, adv., *carefully.*
      *cūriōsus, -a, -um, *careful, diligent; very careful, fussy.*
      pictor, pictōris, m., *painter.*
      *īnscrīptiō, īnscrīptiōnis, f., *inscription.*
57   ***reddō, reddere, reddidī, redditus, *to give back; to represent.*
      *dēficiō [dē- + faciō], dēficere, dēfēcī, dēfectus, *to leave, cease,
          fail, end.*
      vērō, adv., *but, however.*
      porticus, -ūs, f., *porticus* (walkway covered by a roof supported
          by columns).
      levō, -āre, -āvī, -ātus, *to raise.*
      mentum, -ī, n., *chin.*
58   tribūnal, tribūnālis, n., *tribunal* (raised platform on which the
          magistrate's chair was placed).
      excelsus, -a, -um, *lofty, elevated, high.*
      Mercurius, -ī, m., *Mercury* (Roman god of merchants and com-
          merce, equated with the Greek Hermes).
      *rapiō, rapere, rapuī, raptus, *to seize, carry off.*
      praestō, adv., *ready, at hand, nearby.*
      Fortūna, -ae, f., *Fortuna* (goddess of good luck).
59   cornū, -ūs, n., *horn.*
      abundāns, abundantis, *overflowing.*
      Parcae, -ārum, f. pl., *Parcae* (the Fates, three goddesses who spin
          the destinies of men).

Trimalchio's career: from the slave-market to riches

Erat autem vēnālīcium cum titulīs pictum, et ipse Trimalchiō 53
capillātus cādūceum tenēbat Minervāque dūcente Rōmam intrā- 54
bat. Hinc quemadmodum ratiōcinārī didicisset deinque dispēn- 55
sātor factus esset, omnia dīligenter cūriōsus pictor cum īnscrīp- 56
tiōne reddiderat. In dēficiente vērō iam porticū levātum mentō 57
in tribūnal excelsum Mercurius rapiēbat. Praestō erat Fortūna 58
cum cornū abundantī et trēs Parcae aurea pēnsa torquentēs. 59

---

aureus, -a, -um, of gold.
pēnsum, -ī, n., *wool weighed out* [pendō, pendere, pependī, pēn-
sus, *to hang, weigh*] *for the day's spinning;* here, *threads.*
torqueō, torquēre, torsī, tortus, *to twist, wind, spin.*

---

54 capillātus: see line 13 and note.
   cādūceum tenēbat Minervāque dūcente: Trimalchio, sold as a
   long-haired slave, carries the staff of Mercury, the patron god of
   commerce, and enters Rome as if in a kind of triumphal procession under the guidance of Minerva, goddess of handicrafts,
   skill, and wisdom. The picture thus alludes to Trimalchio's success as a skillful businessman. For an illustration, see the fron-
   tispiece in W. B. Sedgwick's *The Cena Trimalchionis of Petronius*
   (Oxford, 1925).
55 didicisset . . . factus esset: pluperfect subjunctives in indirect
   questions introduced by quemadmodum, *how he had. . . .*
   dispēnsātor: by learning arithmetic, Trimalchio rose to the position of chief steward or cashier in the household of his master in
   Rome.
57 In dēficiente . . . porticū: *At the end of the. . . .*
   levātum mentō: supply Trimalchiōnem; translate, *Mercury was
   carrying Trimalchio raised up by his chin* or *raising Trimalchio by his
   chin, Mercury was carrying him.*
58 tribūnal excelsum: the raised platform with magistrate's seat
   where Trimalchio sat in his office of sēvir Augustālis (see line
   72), the highest (and only) magistracy he attained after his manumission.
   Fortūna: symbolizing the immense fortune Trimalchio made in
   shipping.
59 aurea: the Fates could only have spun golden threads for this millionaire.

60 **notō, -āre, -āvī, -ātus, *to note, observe.*
   ***etiam, particle, *still; also; even; actually.*
   *porticus, -ūs, f., *porticus* (walkway covered by a roof supported
      by columns).
   grex, gregis, m., *flock.*
   *cursor, cursōris, m., *runner; footman.*
   magister, magistrī, m., *master, teacher, trainer.*
61 *exerceō, -ēre, -uī, -itus, *to exercise.*
   praetereā, adv., *besides, moreover.*
   grandis, -is, -e, *large.*
   armārium, -ī, n., *cabinet.*
   *angulus, -ī, m., *angle, corner.*
62 aedicula, -ae, f., *niche* (a shrine for the image of a god; here, the
      larārium, shrine holding the household gods).
   Larēs, Larum, m. pl., *household gods.*
   **argenteus, -a, -um, *of silver.*
   Venus, Veneris, f., *Venus* (Roman goddess of love, equated with
      the Greek Aphrodite).
   **signum, -ī, n., *sign, image, statue.*
   marmoreus, -a, -um, *of marble.*
63 pyxis, pyxidis, f. [Greek loan word], *pyxis* (small covered vase or
      box).
   **aureus, -a, -um, *of gold.*
   pusillus, -a, -um, dim. adj., *very small.*
   barba, -ae, f., *beard.*
   condō, condere, condidī, conditus, *to put/lay away* (for safe keep-
      ing).

65 interrogō, -āre, -āvī, -ātus, *to ask, question.*
   ātriēnsis, ātriēnsis, ātriēnsium, m., *overseer of the ātrium* (the
      main room in a Roman house), *steward.*
   medium, -ī, n., *middle part, center.*
      in mediō, *available, on view.*
66 Īlias, Īliadis, f., the *Iliad* (of Homer). Form: acc., Īliada.
   Odyssēa [here, Odyssīa], -ae, f., the *Odyssey* (of Homer). Form:
      acc., Odyssīan.
   Laenās, Laenātis, m., *Laenas.*
   gladiātōrius, -a, -um [gladius, -ī, m., *sword*], *gladiatorial.*
67 mūnus, mūneris, n., *duty; gift; gladiatorial show.*
   licet, -ēre, -uit, impersonal, *it is permitted.*
   *cōnsīderō, -āre, -āvī, -ātus, *to look at, inspect.*

The **larārium** *and Trimalchio's beard*

Notāvī etiam in porticū gregem cursōrum cum magistrō sē   60
exercentem. Praettereā grande armārium in angulō vīdī, in cuius   61
aediculā erant Larēs argenteī positī Venerisque signum mar-   62
moreum et pyxis aurea nōn pusilla, in quā barbam ipsīus condi-   63
tam esse dīcēbant.   64

---

62   **aediculā**: such shrines, often with miniature columns to either side and a triangular temple pediment above, are found in houses in Pompeii, such as the house of the Vettii.

    Venerisque signum: the goddess of sexual love is an appropriate patronness for Trimalchio's household because his rise as a long-haired slave in the house of his master was due in part to his being the sexual plaything of both his master and his mistress. Also, his success as a businessman was due in part to his wife's sacrifice of her jewelry to finance a shipping venture.

63   **barbam**: the shavings of a boy's first beard were generally kept and dedicated to a god. Suetonius tells how Nero first shaved his beard at a public gymnnastic contest amid an elaborate sacrifice of bulls, placed the shavings in a golden **pyxis** decorated with pearls, and dedicated it in the Capitol (*Nero* 12).

    ipsīus: *of the master*; the word **ipse**, (the man) *himself*, is often used to refer to the master of the household, the **dominus**, from the practice of slaves referring to their master as **ipse**.

The Iliad, *the* Odyssey, *and a famous gladiatorial show*

Interrogāre ergō atriēnsem coepī, quās in mediō pictūrās   65
habērent. "Īliada et Odyssīan," inquit, "ac Laenātis gladiātōrium   66
mūnus." Nōn licēbat multa iam cōnsīderāre.   67

---

66   **Laenātis**: Laenas is unknown except for this passage; he is probably to be thought of as the magistrate who gave the gladiatorial show, which, in Trimalchio's uneducated judgment, is important enough to be set beside the *Iliad* and the *Odyssey*.

68   *trīclīnium, -ī, n., *dining room.*
     *perveniō, pervenīre, pervēnī, perventūrus, *to come to, arrive.*
     prīmus, -a, -um, *first.*
69   prōcūrātor, prōcūrātōris, m., *manager, steward, bookkeeper.*
     ratiō, ratiōnis, f., *account.*
     *accipiō [ad- + capiō], accipere, accēpī, acceptus, *to receive; to deal with, handle.*
     praecipuē, adv., *chiefly, most of all.*
     *mīror, -ārī, -ātus sum, *to wonder; to marvel at.*
70   *postis, postis, postium, m., *door-post.*
     fascēs, fascium, m. pl., *fasces* (a ceremonial bundle of wooden rods, **virgae**, carried by lictors in front of magistrates as a symbol of their authority).
     secūris, secūris secūrium, f., *axe; executioner's axe* (carried in the **fascēs** and symbolizing the magistrate's power to execute criminals).
     *fīgō, fīgere, fīxī, fīxus, *to fix, fasten.*
     īmus, -a, -um, *lowest.*
71   quasi, conj., *as if.*
     embolum, -ī, n. [Greek loan word found only here in Latin, see p. 246], *beak of a ship.*
     nāvis, nāvis, nāvium, f., *ship.*
     aēneus, -a, -um, *of bronze.*
     fīniō, -īre, -īvī, -ītus, *to end, terminate.*
72   C., abbrev. of **Gaius**, *Gaius.*
     Pompeius, -ī, m., *Pompeius, Pompey.*
     sēvir, sēvirī, m., *sevir* (a member of a board of six men; in provincial towns, one of the **sēvirī Augustālēs**, six citizens, usually freedmen, annually appointed, upon payment of a fee, to maintain the cult of Rome and of Augustus and succeeding emperors).
     Augustālis, -is, -e, *of the emperor Augustus.*
     Cinnamus, -ī, m., *Cinnamus* (a steward in Trimalchio's household).
73   *dispēnsātor, dispēnsātōris, m. [dis- + pēnsō, -āre, *to weigh/pay out*], *household superintendent, manager, steward.*

Trimalchio's dining room

Nōs iam ad trīclīnium pervēnerāmus, in cuius parte prīmā 68
prōcūrātor ratiōnēs accipiēbat. Et quod praecipuē mīrātus sum, 69
in postibus fascēs erant cum secūribus fīxī, quōrum īmam 70
partem quasi embolum nāvis aēneum fīniēbat, in quō erat 71
scrīptum: "C. Pompeiō Trimalchiōnī, sēvirō Augustālī, Cinna- 72
mus dispēnsātor." 73

(paragraph continued on page 43)

---

69 **ratiōnēs accipiēbat**: as the chief bookkeeper, he was receiving and
handling accounts from other slaves in charge of particular
activities of the household.

70 **fascēs . . . cum secūribus fīxī**: a flattering memento given to Trimalchio by Cinnamus, his **dispēnsātor**. As a **sēvir**, Trimalchio
would have a right to lictors bearing **fascēs**, as long as he was in
office, but not the **secūrēs**. Cinnamus has flattered him by including the **secūrēs**, which belong only to the highest magistrates.

quōrum īmam partem quasi embolum nāvis aēneum fīniēbat: a
kind of bronze beak of a ship ended the lower part of the bundle
of **fascēs** and **secūrēs**. The whole display here is reminiscent of
the trophies of war normally displayed by Romans in the
vestibules of their homes. The beak of a ship would normally
symbolize a victory won by a nobleman in a naval battle; for the
freedman Trimalchio it symbolizes his successful shipping ventures.

72 The words **hoc** and **dēdicat** must be supplied in the inscription.

74   **sub**, prep. + abl., *under*.

     *****titulus, -ī**, m., *label, tag, notice*.

     lucerna, -ae, f., *oil-lamp*.

     bilychnis, -is, -e [rare hybrid compound with Greek root, see p. 247], *having two wicks/lights*.

     camera, -ae, f., *arched/vaulted ceiling*.

     *****pendeō, pendēre, pependī**, *to hang*.

75   **tabula, -ae**, f., *tablet*.

     ******postis, postis, postium**, m., *door-post*.

     dēfīgō, dēfīgere, dēfīxī, dēfīxus, *to fix, fasten*.

     *****alter, altera, alterum**, *the one, the other* (of two).

76   **meminī, meminisse** [perfect forms with present sense], *to remember*.

     īnscrīptum, -ī, n., *inscription*.

     prīdiē, adv. + acc., *on the day before*.

     kalendae, -ārum, f. pl., *kalends* (the first day of each month).

77   **Iānuārius, -a, -um**, *of January*.

     *****C.**, abbrev. of **Gaius**, *Gaius*.

     *****forās**, adv., *out of doors* (implying motion); vulgar use here of the accusative form **forās** in the sense of the locative **forīs**, *out of doors, abroad* (place where) (see p. 247).

     ******alter, altera, alterum**, *the one, the other* (of two).

     lūna, -ae, f., *moon*.

     cursus, -ūs, m., *course*.

     stella, -ae, f., *star; planet; heavenly body*.

78   **imāgō, imāginis**, f., *image*.

     ******pingō, pingere, pīnxī, pictus**, *to paint, represent*.

     bonus, -a, -um, *good;* here, *lucky*.

     incommodus, -a, -um, *inconvenient, unsuitable, unlucky*.

79   **distinguō, distinguere, distīnxī, distīnctus**, *to distinguish*.

     bulla, -ae, f., *bubble; locket hung around the neck of Roman boys; knob, stud, marker*.

     *******notō, -āre, -āvī, -ātus**, *to note, mark*.

Sub eōdem titulō et lucerna bilychnis dē camerā pendēbat, erant 74
et duae tabulae in utrōque poste dēfīxae, quārum altera, sī bene 75
meminī, hoc habēbat īnscrīptum: "III. et prīdiē kalendās 76
Iānuāriās C. noster forās cēnat," altera lūnae cursum stel- 77
lārumque septem imāginēs pictās; et quī diēs bonī quīque in- 78
commodī essent, distinguente bullā notābantur. 79

---

74 **Sub eōdem titulō:** i.e., the **lucerna** had the same dedicatory inscription as the bundle of **fascēs** and **secūrēs**.

76 **III.:** = **tertiō** or **ante diem tertium,** *on the third day before.*
III. et prīdiē kalendās Iānuāriās: the Romans counted back from
fixed dates in the month; the third day before and the day before
the kalends of January would be December 30 and 31. Note that
in counting back from the kalends, the kalends itself is counted.

77 **C. noster:** i.e., Trimalchio; only free men were entitled to a
praenōmen, and its use here in abbreviated form reminds everyone of Trimalchio's present status. Freedmen felt flattered
when addressed by their first names.
cēnat: colloquial use of present tense for the future (see p. 248).
stellārum . . . septem imāginēs: the earth, the five other then-
known planets, and the sun. Trimalchio is an astrology buff.
Among those who held that the earth was the center of the cos-
mos, the Egyptians and Plato held that the celestial bodies were
in the following order: earth, moon, sun, Venus, Mercury, Mars,
Jupiter, and Saturn. The Chaldeans and Cicero placed them in
this order: earth, moon, Mercury, Venus, sun, Mars, Jupiter, and
Saturn.

79 **distinguente bullā:** probably with white markers for lucky days
and black for unlucky.

80　repleō, replēre, replēvī, replētus, *to fill up.*
voluptās, voluptātis, f., *pleasure.*
cōnor, -ārī, -ātus sum, *to attempt, try.*
exclāmō, -āre, -āvī, -ātus, *to shout out.*
81　suprā, prep. + acc., *above, over.*
*officium, -ī, n., *duty, task.*
dexter, dextra, dextrum, *right.*
82　dubium, -ī, n., *doubt; hesitation.*
paulisper, adv., *for a short time.*
*trepidō, -āre, -āvī, -ātus, *to tremble; to be nervous/anxious.*
contrā, prep. + acc., *against, contrary to.*
praeceptum, -ī, n., *rule, precept.*
83　*aliquis, aliquis, aliquid, indef. pron., *someone, anyone, something, anything.*
nostrum, gen. of nōs.
*līmen, līminis, n., *threshold, door, entrance.*
trānseō, trānsīre, trānsiī, trānsitus, irreg., *to go over/across, cross.*

84　**cēterum, adv., *for the rest, moreover.*
pariter, adv., *equally, at the same time, together.*
moveō, movēre, mōvī, mōtus, *to move.*
*dexter, dextra, dextrum, *right.*
gressus, -ūs, m., *step.*
85　dēspoliātus, -a, -um, *robbed; despoiled of his clothes, naked.*
prōcumbō, prōcumbere, prōcubuī, prōcubitūrus, *to fall forward; to prostrate oneself before* + dat.
rogō, -āre, -āvī, -ātus, *to ask.*
poena, -ae, f., *punishment.*
86　ēripiō [ex- + rapiō], ēripere, ēripuī, ēreptus, *to snatch, take away, deliver from.*
peccātum, -ī, n., *error, mistake, sin.*
propter, prep. + acc., *because of, on account of.*
87　perīclitor, -ārī, -ātus sum, *to be in danger.*
subdūcō, subdūcere, subdūxī, subductus, *to take away, steal.*
**enim, particle, *for.*
vestīmentum, -ī, n., *clothing;* pl., *clothes.*
**dispēnsātor, dispēnsātōris, m. [dis- + pēnsō, -āre, *to weigh/pay out*], *household superintendent, manager, steward.*
88　**balineum, -ī, n., *bath; baths* (i.e., a public bathing establishment or a set of rooms for bathing in a private home).
balneō: syncopated colloquial variant of balineō (see p. 241).
vix, adv., *scarcely.*
mīlia, mīlium, n. pl., *thousands.*
sēsterius, -ī, m., *sesterce* (small silver coin).

A warning at the entrance to the dining room

Hīs replētī voluptātibus cum cōnārēmur intrāre, exclāmāvit 80
ūnus ex puerīs quī suprā hoc officium erat positus: "Dextrō 81
pede." Sine dubiō paulisper trepidāvimus, nē contrā praecep- 82
tum aliquis nostrum līmen trānsīret. 83

---

80 **cum cōnārēmur**: circumstantial clause with imperfect subjunctive
in secondary sequence.
81 **ūnus ex puerīs**: the usual partitive construction with numbers, *one
of the slaves.*
Dextrō pede: it was thought to be an unlucky omen to start with
the left foot or to stumble at the threshold. Vitruvius remarks
that the steps ascending to temples should be uneven in number
so that when one begins to ascend with the right foot one will
place one's right foot on the top of the temple steps (*De architec-
tura* 3.4.4).
82 **nē . . . trānsīret**: negative purpose clause, with imperfect subjunctive in secondary sequence.
83 **aliquis nostrum**: the usual partitive construction with indefinite
pronouns, *anyone of us.*

They save a slave from punishment.

Cēterum ut pariter mōvimus dextrōs gressūs, servus nōbīs 84
dēspoliātus prōcubuit ad pedēs ac rogāre coepit, ut sē poenae 85
ēriperēmus: nec magnum esse peccātum suum, propter quod 86
perīclitārētur; subducta enim sibi vestīmenta dispēnsātōris in 87
balneō, quae vix fuissent decem mīlium sēsteriōrum. 88

(paragraph continued on page 47)

---

84 **ut . . . mōvimus**: ut with indicative = *as, when.*
85 **dēspoliātus**: stripped for a flogging.
ut . . . ēriperēmus: indirect command with imperfect subjunctive
in secondary sequence.
poenae: dative of separation, *from punishment.*
86 **nec magnum esse . . . subducta (esse)**: indirect statement.
propter quod perīclitārētur: subjunctive in a relative clause in indirect statement.
87 **subducta (esse) . . . sibi**: dative of separation, *were stolen from him.*
For theft of clothes from the baths, see Plautus, *The Rope* 382–385,

and Catullus 33.1.

90   **quae . . . fuissent**: pluperfect subjunctive in a relative clause in indirect statement.

decem mīlium sēstertiōrum: genitive of price, (garments) *worth ten thousand sesterces*, or genitive of description, *ten-thousand sesterce-*(garments), a high price to mention, but not without precedent (see Martial 4.61.4–5).

89   **referō, referre, rettulī, relātus**, irreg., *to bear/carry/bring back*.
**dexter, dextra, dextrum, *right*.
***dispēnsātor, dispēnsātōris, m. [dis- + pēnsō, -āre, *to weigh/pay out*], *household superintendent, manager, steward*.
oecārium, -ī, n. [Greek loan word], *little room*.
*aureus, -ī, m., *gold coin*.
90   ***numerō, -āre, -āvī, -ātus**, *to count*.
dēprecor, -ārī, -ātus sum, *to beg*.
remittō, remittere, remīsī, remissus, *to send/take back; to slacken, relax; to dismiss*.
*poena, -ae, f., *punishment*.
91   **superbus, -a, -um**, *haughty, proud*.
sufferō [sub- + ferō], **sufferre, sustulī, sublātus**, irreg., *to lift up*.
vultus, -ūs, m., *face*.
*tam . . . quam (92), = **tantum . . . quantum**, *as much as*.
*iactūra, -ae, f., *a throwing away, loss*.
*moveō, movēre, mōvī, mōtus, *to move*.
92   **neglegentia, -ae**, f., *negligence*.
nēquissimus, -a, -um [superl. of **nēquam**, indecl. adj., *worthless*], *most/very worthless*.
*vestīmentum, -ī, n., *clothing*; pl., *clothes*.
cubitōrius, -a, -um [cubō, cubāre, cubuī, cubitūrus, *to lie down*], *worn while lying at the table*.
93   ***perdō, perdere, perdidī, perditus**, *to destroy; to lose*.
nātālis, nātālis, nātālium, m., *birthday*.
cliēns, clientis, m., *client*.
**quīdam, quaedam, quoddam, indef. adj., *a certain*.
dōnō, -āre, -āvī, -ātus, *to give*.
94   **Tyrius, -a, -um**, *Tyrian* (i.e., dyed with expensive purple dye from Tyre in Phoenicia).
*dubium, -ī, n., *doubt*.
*semel, adv., *once*.
lavō, lavāre, lāvī, lavātus or **lautus** or **lōtus**, *to wash*.
*dōnō, -āre, -āvī, -ātus, *to give; to excuse; to forgive, let off*.

Rettulimus ergō dextrōs pedēs dispēnsātōremque in oecāriō au-   89
reōs numerantem dēprecātī sumus, ut servō remitteret poenam.   90
Superbus ille sustulit vultum et, "Nōn tam iactūra mē movet,"   91
inquit, "quam neglegentia nēquissimī servī. Vestīmenta mea cu-   92
bitōria perdidit, quae mihi nātālī meō cliēns quīdam dōnāverat,   93
Tyria sine dubiō, sed iam semel lōta. Quid ergō est? Dōnō vōbīs   94
eum."   95

---

90 **ut . . . remitteret**: indirect command with imperfect subjunctive in
    secondary sequence.

92 **cubitōria**: word found only here; such clothes were usually called
    cēnātōria.

93 **cliēns**: wealthy and powerful Romans helped the less fortunate in
    exchange for favors and political support. The former were pa-
    trons (**patrōnī**), the latter their clients (**clientēs**). Even Trimal-
    chio's slaves have their clients.

94 **Tyria**: Tyrian purple dye was an expensive luxury; Nero forbade
    its use and even had a matron wearing a purple garment at one
    of his recitals dragged out and stripped on the spot (Suetonius,
    Nero 32).

    iam semel lōta: Suetonius mentions Nero's extravagant habit of
    never wearing the same garment twice (*Nero* 30). Once washed,
    the steward's expensive garment is of no value to him.

    Quid ergō est: *So, what am I to do?* or *What does it matter?* or *What of
    it?*

    vōbīs: *for your sake* or *as a favor to you.*

96   obligō, -āre, -āvī, -ātus, *to bind, oblige.*
tam, adv., *as, so, such.*
*grandis, -is, -e, *large.*
beneficium, -ī, n., *kindness, favor.*
**trīclīnium, -ī, n., *dining room.*
97   occurrō [ob- + currō], occurrere, occurrī, occursūrus + dat., *to run to meet.*
**prō, prep. + abl., *for, on behalf of*
*rogō, -āre, -āvī, -ātus, *to ask.*
*stupeō, -ēre, -uī, *to be amazed, be astonished.*
98   spissus, -a, -um, *thick, frequent.*
bāsium, -ī, n., *kiss* (usually that of a lover; ōsculum is the usual term for a kiss given in fulfillment of a duty or obligation).
impingō [in- + pangō, *to fix*], impingere, impēgī, impactus, *to fasten, fix on.*
grātia, -ae, f., *favor, regard.*
grātiās agere + dat., *to give thanks* (to), *thank.*
hūmānitās, hūmānitātis, f., *humanity; kindness.*
99   ad summam, *in short, to be brief.*
*statim, adv., *immediately.*
*aiō, defective verb used mainly in present and imperfect indicative, *to say.*
*beneficium, -ī, n., *kindness, favor.*
100   vīnum, -ī, n., *wine.*
*dominicus, -a, -um, *of/belonging to the master* [dominus, -ī, m.].
ministrātor, ministrātōris, m., *attendant, waiter* (at table).
*grātia, -ae, f., *favor; gratitude.*

The slave's gratitude

Obligātī tam grandī beneficiō cum intrāssēmus trīclīnium,   96
occurrit nōbīs ille īdem servus, prō quō rogāverāmus, et stupen-   97
tibus spississima bāsia impēgit grātiās agēns hūmānitātī nostrae.   98
"Ad summam, statim sciētis," ait, "cui dederitis beneficium.   99
Vīnum dominicum ministrātōris grātia est."   100

---

96 **tam grandī:** = **tantō.**
    intrāssēmus: = **intrāvissēmus,** pluperfect subjunctive in circum-
    stantial clause in secondary sequence.
97 **stupentibus bāsia impēgit:** supply **nōbīs,** *fixed kisses on us* (who
    were) *dumbfounded* = *to our amazement.*
98 **impēgit:** instead of the more usual and less vigorous **impressit.**
99 **Ad summam:** a common colloquial expression.
    cui dederitis: perfect subjunctive in indirect question in primary
    sequence.
    Vīnum dominicum ministrātōris grātia est: proverbial: The but-
    ler's favor is the master's wine. The waiter will show his grati-
    tude to a favored guest by serving him the same wine as he
    serves the master, while the other guests will get an inferior vin-
    tage. Pliny comments on a host at a dinner party who served
    three grades of wine, the best for himself and his close friends,
    the next grade for his lesser friends, and the poorest for the
    freedmen (*Letters* 2.6).

101 **tandem**, adv., *finally.*

discumbō, discumbere, discubuī, discubitūrus, *to recline at table.*

Alexandrīnus, -a, -um, *Alexandrian, from Alexandria* (a city in Egypt).

102 **nivātus, -a, -um**, *cooled with snow* [**nix, nivis**, f.].

īnfundō, īnfundere, īnfūdī, īnfūsus, *to pour in/on.*

īnsequor, īnsequī, īnsecūtus sum, *to follow.*

103 **parōnychium, -ī**, n. [Greek loan word], *whitlaw* (medical term for an inflammation around a fingernail or toenail); *hangnail.*

subtīlitās, subtīlitātis, f., *exactness.*

tollō, tollere, sustulī, sublātus, *to lift; to take away, remove.*

*****nē . . . quidem**, *not even.*

104 ***tam**, adv., *as, so, such.*

molestus, -a, -um, *troublesome, annoying.*

taceō, -ēre, -uī, *to be silent.*

****officium, -ī**, n., *duty, task.*

obiter, adv., *along the way; at the same time.*

***cantō, -āre, -āvī, -ātus**, *to sing.*

105 **experior, experīrī, expertus sum**, *to test.*

an, particle, *whether.*

familia, -ae, f., *family; the slaves of a household.*

****cantō, -āre, -āvī, -ātus**, *to sing.*

pōtiō, pōtiōnis, f., *drink.*

***poscō, poscere, poposcī**, *to ask for.*

106 ***parātus, -a, -um**, *prepared, ready.*

minus, compar. adv., *less.*

acidus, -a, -um, *harsh, shrill.*

canticum, -ī, n., *song.*

***excipiō [ex- + capiō], excipere, excēpī, exceptus**, *to take up, catch up, receive;* here, *to answer.*

107 **quisquis, quisquis, quidquid/quicquid**, indef. pron., *whoever, whatever.*

****aliquis, aliquis, aliquid**, indef. pron., *someone, anyone, something, anything.*

****rogō, -āre, -āvī, -ātus**, *to ask.*

pantomīmus, -ī, m. [Greek loan word], *pantomime* (a performer/dancer who acted out stories in dumb show to the accompaniment of instrumental music and choral singing).

chorus, -ī, m. [Greek loan word], *chorus.*

108 ***pater familiae**, *father of a family, head of a household.*

*****trīclīnium, -ī**, n., *dining room.*

crēdō, crēdere, crēdidī, crēditus, *to believe, think.*

Before dinner begins, slaves attend the guests.

Tandem ergō discubuimus puerīs Alexandrīnīs aquam in   101
manūs nivātam īnfundentibus aliīsque īnsequentibus ad pedēs   102
ac parōnychia cum ingentī subtīlitāte tollentibus. Ac nē in hōc   103
quidem tam molestō tacēbant officiō, sed obiter cantābant. Ego   104
experīrī voluī an tōta familia cantāret, itaque pōtiōnem poposcī.   105
Parātissimus puer nōn minus mē acidō canticō excēpit, et   106
quisquis aliquid rogātus erat ut daret: pantomīmī chorum, nōn   107
patris familiae trīclīnium crēderēs.   108

---

101   puerīs . . . īnfundentibus aliīsque īnsequentibus . . . ac . . . tol-
      lentibus: ablatives absolute.
      puerīs Alexandrīnīs: prized slave boys from Egypt, a country
      proverbial among Romans for license and lax morals.
      īnsequentibus ad pedēs: i.e., approaching our feet.
      aquam . . . nivātam: Romans used snow and ice to cool water
      and wine for drinking; Nero is said to have initiated the prac-
      tice of first boiling water and then cooling it in a glass sur-
      rounded by snow (Pliny, *Natural History* 31.40). Moralists re-
      garded these practices as extravagant (Pliny, *Natural History*
      19.55–56, and Seneca, *Epistulae morales* 78.23), but Trimalchio
      goes further by chilling even the water used by his slaves to
      wash the hands of his guests.
      in manūs: *over/onto our hands.*
105   an . . . cantāret: indirect question with imperfect subjunctive in
      secondary sequence. For singing at Roman meals, see Seneca,
      On the Happy Life 11.4.
106   nōn minus . . . acidō canticō: *with no less shrill a song.*
      et quisquis aliquid rogātus erat ut daret: supply simul cantā-
      bat, lit., *and whoever* (i.e., *whatever slave/if any slave*) *was asked for
      something that he should give* (it), *he sang at the same time.* All the
      slaves sang whenever they performed any services.
107   ut daret: indirect command with imperfect subjunctive in sec-
      ondary sequence.
      pantomīmī chorum: pantomime was extremely popular under
      the early Empire (see *The Oxford Classical Dictionary*, "Panto-
      mimus," pp. 776–777) but was suppressed by some emperors
      as subversive of moral order. Pliny describes the pantomime
      as an effeminate art unworthy of the reign of Trajan (*Panegyric*
      46.4).
108   crēderēs: potential subjunctive, *you would have thought.*

109 *afferō [ad- + ferō], afferre, attulī, allātus, irreg. + dat., *to bring (to)*.

**tamen, adv., *yet, nevertheless.*

gustātiō, gustātiōnis, f. [gustō, -āre, -āvī, -ātus, *to taste*], *first course, antipasto, hors d'oeuvres.*

validē, adv., *strongly, mightily, very.*

valdē, syncopated variant (see p. 241).

*lautus, -a, -um, *neat, elegant, luxurious, sumptuous.*

*discumbō, discumbere, discubuī, discubitūrus, *to recline at table.*

110 *praeter, prep. + acc., *except for.*

mōs, mōris, m., *manner, custom, way.*

111 *prīmus, -a, -um, *first.*

servō, -āre, -āvī, -ātus, *to save.*

***cēterum, adv., *for the rest, moreover.*

prōmulsidāre, prōmulsidāris, prōmulsidārium, n. [rare word, see p. 246], *tray* (on which the prōmulsis was served).

prōmulsis, prōmulsidis, f. [prō-, *before* + mulsum, -ī, n., *honey and wine*], *hors d'oeuvre.*

asellus, -ī, m. [dim. of asinus, -ī, m., *ass, donkey*], *little ass/donkey.*

112 Corinthius, -a, -um, *Corinthian; made of Corinthian bronze.*

bisaccium, -ī, n. [word found only here, see p. 245)], *pair of saddle bags* [saccus, -ī, m.].

olīva, -ae, f., *olive.*

***alter, altera, alterum, *the one, the other* (of two).

113 albus, -a, -um, *white.*

niger, nigra, nigrum, *black.*

*tegō, tegere, tēxī, tēctus, *to cover.*

*asellus, -ī, m. [dim. of asinus, -ī, m., *ass, donkey*], *little ass/ donkey.*

*lānx, lancis, f., *plate, dish.*

114 margō, marginis, f., *edge, border, margin.*

nōmen, nōminis, n., *name.*

īnscrībō, īnscrībere, īnscrīpsī, īnscrīptus, *to write on, inscribe.*

argentum, -ī, n., *silver.*

115 pondus, ponderis, n., *weight.*

An extravagantly elegant hors d'oeuvre is served.

Allāta est tamen gustātiō valdē lauta; nam iam omnēs dis- 109
cubuerant praeter ūnum Trimalchiōnem, cui locus novō mōre 110
prīmus servābātur.   Cēterum   in   prōmulsidārī asellus erat 111
Corinthius cum bisacciō positus, quī habēbat olīvās in alterā 112
parte albās, in alterā nigrās. Tegēbant asellum duae lancēs, in 113
quārum marginibus nōmen Trimalchiōnis īnscrīptum erat et ar- 114
gentī pondus. 115

(paragraph continued on page 55)

110   **ūnum:** *only.*
      locus . . . prīmus: usually the host reclined at the place called
      summus in īmō; Trimalchio, however, reclines at what is here
      loosely called the **locus prīmus,** *the first/top place,* and is techni-
      cally called **summus in summō:** see the diagram below.
112   **Corinthius:** Corinthian bronze was highly valued in Rome;
      Seneca mocks the mania of those who collected Corinthian
      bronze vessels and spent their days fussing over them (*On the
      Shortness of Life* 12.2); see also Pliny, *Natural History* 34.6–8.
      positus: *placed* (on the table).
      olīvās . . . albās: i.e., light green as opposed to the black ripe
      olives.

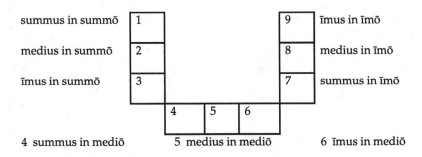

summus in summō   1   9   īmus in īmō

medius in summō   2   8   medius in īmō

īmus in summō   3   7   summus in īmō

4   5   6

4 summus in mediō   5 medius in mediō   6 īmus in mediō

116   **ponticulus, -ī,** m. [dim. of **pōns, pontis,** m., *bridge*], *little bridge.*

     ferrūminātus, -a, -um, *cemented, soldered.*

     sustineō [sub- + teneō], sustinēre, sustinuī, sustentus, *to hold up, support.*

     glīs, glīris, glīrium, m., *dormouse.*

     mel, mellis, n., *honey.*

     papāver, papāveris, n., *poppy seed.*

117   **spargō, spargere, sparsī, sparsus,** *to sprinkle.*

     tomāculum, -ī, n., *sausage.*

     ferveō, fervēre, ferbuī, *to boil, be hot.*

     ***suprā,** prep. + acc., *above.*

     crātīcula, -ae, f. [dim. of **crātis, crātis, crātium,** f., *wicker-work*], *gridiron.*

     *****argenteus, -a, -um,** *of silver.*

118   **īnfrā,** adv., *below, underneath.*

     Syriacus, -a, -um, *Syrian;* here = **Damascēnus, -a, -um,** *from Damascus, Damson.*

     prūnum, -ī, n., *plum.*

     grānum, -ī, n., *seed.*

     Pūnicus, -a, -um, *Punic, Carthaginian.*

     mālum, -ī, n., *apple.*

     Pūnicum mālum, *pomegranate.*

Ponticulī etiam ferrūminātī sustinēbant glīrēs melle ac papāvere 116
sparsōs. Fuērunt et tomācula ferventia suprā crātīculam argen- 117
team posita, et īnfrā Syriaca prūna cum grānīs Pūnicī mālī. 118

---

116 **Ponticulī . . . ferrūminātī**: bridge-like structures soldered to the
plates.
    glīrēs: a popular delicacy among the Romans; sometimes the ob-
ject of sumptuary legislation such as that passed during the
consulship of Marcus Scaurus in 115 B.C., which forbade eating
of dormice, shellfish, and imported birds at banquets (Pliny,
Natural History 8.223). Varro (*On Agriculture* 3.15) describes
how dormice were bred and raised outdoors in spaces sur-
rounded by walls to prevent their escape and in specially made
pottery jars kept inside the house.

118 **Syriaca prūna cum grānīs Pūnicī mālī**: the dark damson plums
and red pomegranate seeds represent coals and fire under the
gridiron (**crātīculam**).

For a variety of texts from ancient sources relating to Roman meals
and Roman dinner parties, see Jo-Ann Shelton, *As the Romans Did*,
"Meals," pp. 81–88, and "Dinner Parties," pp. 315–319.

119 *lautitia, -ae, f., *extravagance, elegance, splendor.*

ad, prep. + acc., *to;* here, *to the accompaniment of.*

symphōnia, -ae, f. [Greek loan word], *music.*

120 **afferō [ad- + ferō], afferre, attulī, allātus, irreg. + dat., *to bring (to).*

cervīcal, cervīcālis, cervīcālium, n., *pillow.*

minūtus, -a, -um, *little, small, minute.*

exprimō [ex- + premō, *to press*], exprimere, expressī, expressus, *to squeeze/force out.*

imprūdēns, imprūdentis, *unaware, unwary; ignorant; imprudent.*

121 *rīsus, -ūs, m., *laughter.*

***enim, particle,*for.*

coccineus, -a, -um [Greek root], *scarlet.*

adrāsus, -a, -um, *shaved.*

exclūdō [ex- + claudo, *to shut*], exclūdere, exclūsī, exclūsus, *to shut out; to leave uncovered* (by) + abl.

122 circā, prep. + acc., *around, about.*

onerō, -āre, -āvī, -ātus, *to burden, load.*

***vestis, vestis, vestium, f., *garment.*

cervīx, cervīcis, f., *neck.*

lāticlāvius, -a, -um, *having a broad purple stripe* [lātus clāvus, -ī, m.].

immittō [in- + mittō], immittere, immīsī, immissus, *to send, let loose; to throw; to put on/around.*

mappa, -ae, f., *napkin.*

123 fimbriae, -ārum, f. pl.,*fringe, tassels.*

hinc atque illinc,*from this side and that.*

**pendeō, pendēre, pependī, *to hang.*

124 minimus, -a, -um [superl. of parvus, -a, -um, *small*], *smallest, very little.*

sinister, sinistra, sinistrum,*left.*

ānulus, -ī, m., *ring.*

**grandis, -is, -e,*great, large.*

subaurātus, -a, -um,*gold-plated.*

125 *extrēmus, -a, -um, *outermost, farthest, last.*

*vērō, adv., *but, however.*

articulus, -ī, m., *joint, knuckle.*

sequēns, sequentis,*following, next.*

Trimalchio arrives with fanfare.

In hīs erāmus lautitiīs, cum ipse Trimalchiō ad symphōniam   119
allātus est positusque inter cervīcālia minūtissima expressit im-   120
prūdentibus rīsum. Palliō enim coccineō adrāsum exclūserat ca-   121
put circāque onerātās veste cervīcēs lāticlāviam immīserat map-   122
pam fimbriīs hinc atque illinc pendentibus. Habēbat etiam in   123
minimō digitō sinistrae manūs ānulum grandem subaurātum,   124
extrēmō vērō articulō digitī sequentis minōrem,   125

(paragraph continued on page 59)

120   **minūtissima**: another reading is **mūnītissima**, *very well forti-
       fied/protected/defended; well-padded.*
       expressit imprūdentibus rīsum: i.e., drew laughter from those
       of us who weren't expecting such a sight and were inconsid-
       erate enough to laugh at it.
121   **Palliō . . . coccineō adrāsum exclūserat caput**: *he had left his
       shaven head uncovered by. . . .* Compare Seneca's description of
       the eccentric way Maecenas dressed on public occasions—his
       head wrapped in his cloak with only his ears uncovered, re-
       sembling runaway slaves in a mime (*Epistulae morales* 114.6).
       coccineō: Martial tells of someone who regarded scarlet clothing
       as a sign of effeminacy (1.96.6).
       adrāsum . . . caput: slaves, when they received their freedom, of-
       ten shaved their heads, and many continued to do so.
122   **lāticlāviam . . . mappam**: the broad purple stripe on the napkin
       is a pretentious imitation of the broad purple stripe on the
       tunic worn by senators. Martial (4.46) describes gifts sent on
       the Saturnalia to a certain Sabellus, which included a napkin
       with the senatorial purple stripe, to which Sabellus was no
       more entitled than is Trimalchio.
123   **fimbriīs . . . pendentibus**: ablative absolute.
124   **subaurātum**: Trimalchio could have worn a gold ring during his
       term as **sēvir**, but normally only men of equestrian rank wore
       gold rings (see Pliny, *Natural History* 33.29); Trimalchio avoids
       transgressing this custom by wearing a gilt ring and by wear-
       ing his other ring studded with iron stars (lines 126–127).
       Martial (11.59) mocks a certain Charinus for wearing six rings
       on each of his fingers and not taking them off while either
       bathing or sleeping. Trimalchio appears moderate in contrast.
125   **minōrem**: supply **ānulum**.

126 ***aureus, -a, -um, *of gold.*
     ferreus, -a, -um, *of iron.*
     velutī, adv., *as if, like.*
     *stella, -ae, f., *star.*
127 *ferrūminātus, -a, -um, *cemented, soldered; encrusted.*
     *tantum, adv., *only.*
     ostendō, ostendere, ostendī, ostentus or ostēnsus, *to show, display.*
     dīvitiae, -ārum, f. pl., *riches, wealth.*
     ***dexter, dextra, dextrum, *right.*
128 nūdō, -āre, -āvī, -ātus, *to lay bare, expose.*
     lacertus, -ī, m., *upper arm.*
     armilla, -ae, f., *bracelet.*
     cultus, -a, -um, *adorned.*
     eboreus, -a, -um, *of ivory.*
     **circulus, -ī, m., *circle.*
     lāmina, -ae, f., *thin piece of metal plate, band.*
129 splendeō, -ēre, *to shine, gleam.*
     cōnectō [con- + nectō, *to tie*], cōnectere, cōnexuī, cōnexus, *to tie, bind, fasten.*

ut mihi vidēbātur, tōtum aureum, sed plānē ferreīs velutī stellīs   126
ferrūminātum. Et nē hās tantum ostenderet dīvitiās, dextrum   127
nūdāvit lacertum armillā aureā cultum et eboreō circulō lāminā   128
splendente cōnexō.   129

---

126   **ferreīs velutī stellīs**: *as if with.* . . . The stars are a charm against
     the evil eye.

127   **nē** . . . **ostenderet**: negative purpose clause with imperfect sub-
     junctive in secondary sequence. Note the virtual double nega-
     tive = *so as to display even greater.* . . .

128   **armillā aureā** . . . **et eboreō circulō**: ablative of means with **cul-
     tum**, *adorned.* Note the chiastic arrangement of the nouns and
     adjectives.

129   **cōnexō**: modifying both **armillā aureā** and **eboreō circulō**. The
     golden bracelet and the circle of ivory are joined by a gleaming
     band of metal.

130   *deinde, adv., *afterward, then, next.*
      pinna, -ae, f., *feather, quill* (here used as a toothpick).
      perfodiō, perfodere, perfōdī, perfossus, *to dig, pick.*
131   nōndum, adv., *not yet.*
      suāvis, -is, -e, *pleasant, agreeable.*
      diūtius, compar. adv., *longer.*
      absentīvus, -a, -um [vulgar, found only here, see p. 245; variant
      of absēns, absentis, *absent*], *absent.*
132   mora, -ae, f., *delay.*
      *voluptās, voluptātis, f., *pleasure.*
      *negō, -āre, -āvī, -ātus, *to say not, deny.*
133   permittō, permittere, permīsī, permissus, *to permit.*
      ***tamen, adv., *yet, nevertheless.*
      *fīniō, -īre, -īvī, -ītus, *to finish, end.*
      *lūsus, -ūs, m., *game.*
      **sequor, sequī, secūtus sum, *to follow.*
      *tabula, -ae, f., *waxed writing-tablet, board.*
134   terebinthinus, -a, -um, *of terebinth wood* (a dark black wood that
      takes a high polish).
      crystallīnus, -a, -um [Greek loan word], *made of crystal/glass.*
      tessera, -ae, f., *square piece of stone; die.*
135   dēlicātus, -a, -um, *charming; luxurious, extravagant.*
      ***prō, prep. + abl., *for, on behalf of; instead of.*
      calculus, -ī, m., *small stone; counter.*
      *albus, -a, -um, *white.*
      *niger, nigra, nigrum, *black.*
136   dēnārius, -ī, m., *denarius* (a silver coin originally worth ten assēs,
      later sixteen; the as, gen. assis, m., was the basic unit of Roman
      coinage; the golden denarius was worth twenty-five silver
      denarii).

Trimalchio picks his teeth and explains his tardiness.

    Ut deinde pinnā argenteā dentēs perfōdit, "Amīcī," inquit,   130
"nōndum mihi suāve erat in trīclīnium venīre, sed nē diūtius ab-   131
sentīvus morae vōbīs essem, omnem voluptātem mihi negāvī.   132
Permittitis tamen fīnīrī lūsum." Sequēbātur puer cum tabulā   133
terebinthinā et crystallīnīs tesserīs, notāvīque rem omnium   134
dēlicātissimam. Prō calculīs enim albīs ac nigrīs aureōs argen-   135
teōsque habēbat dēnāriōs.   136

---

130   **Ut . . . perfōdit**: **ut** with indicative = *when*; translate the perfect as
    a pluperfect, as is usually best with temporal clauses in Latin.

131   **nōndum mihi suāve erat**: *it was not yet my pleasure*, a pretentious
    phrase.

    nē . . . essem: negative purpose clause with imperfect subjunc-
    tive in secondary sequence.

132   **morae vōbīs essem**: double dative, *I be for a delay to you = I delay
    you.*

133   **Permittitis**: present indicative used colloquially instead of the
    future (see p. 248) or as a substitute for the imperative.

    lūsum: Trimalchio is probably playing **duodecim scrīpta** (*twelve
    lines*). For this he needs a board (**tabula**) having twelve verti-
    cal lines divided by one horizontal, fifteen markers (**calculī**) for
    each player, and three dice (**tesserae**). The players move their
    markers according to the throw of the dice. See Paoli, *Rome: Its
    People, Life and Customs*, p. 236, and R. G. Austin, "Roman
    Board Games," *Greece & Rome* 4 (1934–1935): 24–34 and 76–82.

137   ***interim, adv., *in the meantime, meanwhile.*
     textor, textōris, m., *weaver.*
     dictum, -ī, n., *saying, word;* pl., *sayings, words.*
     **lūsus, -ūs, m., *game.*
     cōnsūmō, cōnsūmere, cōnsūmpsī, cōnsūmptus, *to eat, devour.*
138   gustō, -āre, -āvī, -ātus, *to taste; to eat the gustātiō* (first course).
     **adhūc, adv., *until now, still, yet.*
     repositōrium, -ī, n., *portable stand for serving courses at meals.*
     ***afferō [ad- + ferō], afferre, attulī, allātus, irreg. + dat., *to bring (to).*
139   corbis, corbis, corbium, m. or f., *basket.*
     gallīna, -ae, f., *hen.*
     ligneus, -a, -um, *of wood.*
     pateō, patēre, patuī, *to lie open, stretch out, spread out.*
     orbis, orbis, orbium, m., *circle.*
     āla, -ae, f., *wing.*
     quālis, -is, -e, *such as.*
140   **soleō, solēre, solitus sum + infin., *to be accustomed* (to).
     incubō, -āre, -āvī, -ātus, *to lie upon, incubate.*
     ōvum, -ī, n., *egg.*
     continuō, adv., *immediately, without delay.*
141   *symphōnia, -ae, f. [Greek loan word], *music.*
     strepō, strepere, strepuī, *to make a noise; to sound.*
     scrūtor, -ārī, -ātus sum, *to examine thoroughly.*
     palea, -ae, f., *chaff, straw.*
     ēruō, ēruere, ēruī, ērutus, *to dig out.*
142   *subinde, adv., *thereupon, promptly; repeatedly, one after the other.*
     pāvōnīnus, -a, -um, *belonging to a peacock* [pāvō, pāvōnis, m.].
     *ōvum, -ī, n., *egg.*
     dīvidō, dīvidere, dīvīsī, dīvīsus, *to divide.*
     convīva, -ae, m., *guest.*

A second course of hors d'oeuvres is brought in.

Interim dum ille omnium textōrum dicta inter lūsum cōn- 137
sūmit, gustantibus adhūc nōbīs repositōrium allātum est cum 138
corbe, in quō gallīna erat lignea patentibus in orbem ālīs, quālēs 139
esse solent quae incubant ōva. Accessēre continuō duo servī et 140
symphōniā strepente scrūtārī paleam coepērunt ērutaque 141
subinde pāvōnīna ōva dīvīsēre convīvīs. 142

---

137 **omnium textōrum dicta**: perhaps = **omnia dicta textōrum**: *all the sayings of the weavers*, perhaps = *commonplace chatter*. The text, however, is probably corrupt here; perhaps **tesserāriōrum**, *of the dice-players*, should be read instead of **textōrum**.

138 **gustantibus . . . nōbīs**: dative with **allātum est**, *to us while we were still eating the gustātiō*.
repositōrium allātum est: a second round of hors d'oeuvres is brought on; serving a second round of hors d'oeuvres was unusual and reveals Trimalchio's extravagance, but it also provides the eggs that were traditionally served as part of the first course (thus the saying **ab ōvō usque ad māla**, Horace, *Satires* 1.3.6–7, *from the egg clear to the apples* = from A to Z, from beginning to end).

139 **patentibus in orbem ālīs**: ablative absolute. **in orbem**: *all around*.

140 **quae**: the implied antecedent is **gallīnae**.
Accessēre: = **Accessērunt**.

141 **symphōniā strepente**: ablative absolute.

142 **dīvīsēre**: = **dīvīsērunt**.

143   **convertō, convertere, convertī, conversus,** *to turn.*
      scaena, -ae, f., *stage, performance, scene.*
      *vultus, -ūs, m., *face.*
144   ****aiō,** defective verb used mainly in present and imperfect in-
      dicative, *to say.*
      pāvō, pāvōnis, m., *peacock.*
      **ōvum, -ī, n., *egg.*
      *gallīna, -ae, f., *hen.*
      suppōnō [sub- + pōnō], **suppōnere, supposuī, suppositus,** *to*
      put under.
      meherculēs, interj., *by Hercules!*
145   **concipiō** [con- + capiō], **concipere, concēpī, conceptus,** *to take*
      hold of; to conceive; to be fertilized.
      *temptō, -āre, -āvī, -ātus, *to handle, feel, test.*
      ***adhūc, adv., *until now, still, yet.*
      sorbilis, -is, -e, *able to be sucked.*
146   ****accipiō** [ad- + capiō], **accipere, accēpī, acceptus,** *to receive.*
      cochlear, cochleāris, cochleārium, n., *small spoon* (with a round
      bowl and a long, pointed handle, for eating eggs or snails [**co-**
      chlea, -ae, f., *snail*]).
      *minus, compar. adv., *less.*
      sēlībra, -ae, f., *half of a lībra* [**lībra, -ae,** f., a measure of weight
      equivalent to three-quarters of a pound]; roughly, *half a pound.*
      pendō, pendere, pependī, pēnsus, *to weigh.*
      ***ōvum, -ī, n., *egg.*
147   **farīna, -ae,** f., *flour.*
      pinguis, -is, -e, *fat, rich.*
      figūrō, -āre, -āvī, -ātus, *to form, fashion, shape.*
      pertundō, pertundere, pertūdī, pertūsus, *to make a hole through.*
148   **prōiciō** [prō- + iaciō, *to throw*], **prōicere, prōiēcī, prōiectus,** *to*
      throw away.
      pullus, -ī, m., *chick.*
      coeō, coīre, coiī, coitus, irreg., *to come together, unite.*
149   ****deinde,** adv., *afterward, then, next.*
      vetus, veteris, *old; experienced.*
      *convīva, -ae, m., *guest.*
      hīc, adv., *here.*
      nesciō quid, *I don't know what, something;* here + partitive gen.
        nesciō quid bonī, *something of good = something good/nice.*
      dēbeō, -ēre, -uī, -itus, *to owe; ought.*
150   ***persequor, persequī, persecūtus sum,** *to follow;* here, *to go over,*
      examine, explore.
      putāmen, putāminis, n., *shell.*
      *pinguis, -is, -e, *fat.*
      fīcēdula, -ae, f., *small bird, fig-pecker* [**fīcus, -ūs,** f., *fig*].

Trimalchio teases his guests with peacock eggs that aren't what they seem to be.

Convertit ad hanc scaenam Trimalchiō vultum et, "Amīcī," 143
ait, "pāvōnis ōva gallīnae iussī suppōnī. Et meherculēs timeō nē 144
iam conceptī sint; temptēmus tamen, sī adhūc sorbilia sunt." 145
Accipimus nōs cochleāria nōn minus sēlībrās pendentia ōvaque 146
ex farīnā linguī figūrāta pertundimus. Ego quidem paene 147
prōiēcī partem meam, nam vidēbātur mihi iam in pullum coīsse. 148
Deinde ut audīvī veterem convīvam: "Hīc nesciō quid bonī dē- 149
bet esse," persecūtus putāmen manū pinguissimam fīcēdulam 150
invēnī piperātō vitellō circumdatam. 151

---

151 *inveniō, invenīre, invēnī, inventus, *to find.*
    piperātus, -a, -um, *peppered.*
    vitellus, -ī, m., *yolk.*
    circumdō, circumdare, circumdedī, circumdatus, *to surround.*

---

143 Amīcī: vocative case.
144 gallīnae . . . suppōnī: gallīnae is dative with the compound
    verb.
    nē iam conceptī sint: supply pullī, *chicks*; nē is used with the
    subjunctive in positive clauses of fear, *that* (chicks) *have already*
    been conceived.
145 temptēmus: hortatory subjunctive, *let us test* (them).
    sorbilia: referring again to the eggs; eggs were eaten raw by
    piercing the shell and sucking.
146 nōn minus sēlībrās pendentia: *weighing no less* (than) *half a*
    pound; the ablative of comparison need not be used after mi-
    nus.
147 farīnā linguī: i.e., rich pastry.
    figūrāta: modifying ōva.
148 in pullum coīsse: *to have turned into a chick.*
149 ut audīvī: ut with indicative = *as, when.*
    dēbet esse: *ought to be* = *is sure to be, should be.*

1 **ferculum, -ī, n.**, *that on which something is carried* [**ferō, ferre**]; *dish*
   (on which food is served); *dish/course* (at a meal).
   lasanum, -ī, n. [Greek loan word], *chamber-pot.*
   surgō, surgere, surrēxī, surrēctūrus, *to rise, get up.*
2 **lībertās, lībertātis, f.,** *freedom.*
   tyrannus, -ī, m. [Greek loan word], *tyrant.*
   nancīscor, nancīscī, nactus sum, *to obtain, receive, get.*
   invītō, -āre, -āvī, -ātus, *to invite.*
   **convīva, -ae, m., *guest.*
3 **sermō, sermōnis, m.,** *talk, conversation.*
   Dāma, -ae, m., *Dama* (a typical slave-name in Horace and Martial;
   an unsavory freedman in Persius; here also a freedman).
   **prīmus, -a, -um, *first.*
   pataracina, -ōrum, n. pl. [vulgar, found only here, see p. 246],
   form and meaning uncertain, perhaps *large drinking cups.*
   **poscō, poscere, poposcī, *to ask for.*
4 **versō, -āre, -āvī, -ātus,** *to turn.*
   nox, noctis, noctium, f., *night.*
5 **cubiculum, -ī, n.,** *bedroom.*
   rēctus, -a, -um, *upright, straight.*
   rēctā (viā), adv., *straight, directly.*
   mundus, -a, -um, *clean, elegant, fine;* slang, *nice, tidy.*
   frīgus, frīgoris, n., *cold, frost.*
6 ***vix, adv.,** *scarcely.*
   ***balineum, -ī, n., *bath; baths* (i.e., a public bathing establishment
   or a set of rooms for bathing in a private home).
   balneus, syncopated variant; vulgar m. for n. (see pp. 241,
   242).
   *calefaciō, calefacere, calefēcī, calefactus, *to make warm/hot.*
   calfēcit: syncopated colloquial variant of **calefēcit** (see p. 241).
   calidus, -a, -um, *warm, hot.*
   calda, syncopated colloquial variant of **calida** (see p. 241).
   *pōtiō, pōtiōnis, f., *drink.*
7 **vestiārius, -ī, m.** [see p. 244; **vestis, vestis, vestium, f.,** *garment*],
   clothes-dealer.
   stāminātus, -a, -um [vulgar, found only here, see p. 246], meaning
   uncertain, perhaps *consisting of threads* [**stāmen, stāminis, n.,**
   thread; the vertical threads in a loom, the warp]; *threadbare;* of drink,
   neat, not tempered with water; or perhaps from Greek *stamnos,*
   "wine-jar," *as large as a wine-jar.*
   dūxī, *I have drunk/quaffed.*
   matus, -a, -um [word found only here, see p. 246; perhaps a
   vulgar equivalent of **madidus, -a, -um,** *wet, drunk*], *drunk.*
   *vīnum, -ī, n., *wine.*
   vīnus, vulgar m. for n. (see p. 242).

II.

TRIMALCHIO'S DINNER

2. Table Talk

Triamalchio leaves the table to go to the toilet, and in his absence the freedmen guests relax and enjoy the pleasure of each other's conversation. They philosophize on a wide range of subjects from the swift passage of time to the education of their children.

[41–46] Ab hōc ferculō Trimalchiō ad lasanum surrēxit. Nōs 1
lībertātem sine tyrannō nactī coepimus invītāre convīvārum 2
sermōnēs. Dāma itaque prīmus cum pataracina poposcisset, 3
"Diēs," inquit, "nihil est. Dum versās tē, nox fit. Itaque nihil est 4
melius quam dē cubiculō rēctā in trīclīnium īre. Et mundum frī- 5
gus habuimus. Vix mē balneus calfēcit. Tamen calda pōtiō 6
vestiārius est. Stāminātās dūxī, et plānē matus sum. Vīnus mihi 7
in cerebrum abiit." 8

---

8 **cerebrum, -ī,** n., *brain.*
*abeō, abīre, abiī, abitūrus, irreg., *to go away, depart.*

---

1 **Ab hōc ferulō:** *After this course.*
2 **lībertātem . . . nactī:** *having gotten. . . .* Past participles of deponent verbs are passive in form and active in meaning.
3 **cum . . . poposcisset:** pluperfect subjunctive in circumstantial clause, *after he had asked. . . .*
6 **calda pōtiō vestiārius est:** an original and strong metaphor, *a hot drink really dresses you up.*
7 **Stāminātās:** supply **pōtiōnēs,** *drinks: I have drunk/quaffed* (**dūxī,** lit., *I have led) threadbare drinks* = (perhaps) *I drank the wine straight* (without the usual mixture of water) or the drink was only slightly threaded with wine and therefore threadbare, yet nonetheless I got drunk. Or, **stāminātās** may be derived from the Greek word for a wine-jar (*stamnos*) and describe large drinks. Another original and strong metaphor, although of somewhat uncertain meaning to us.

9 **excipiō [ex- + capiō], excipere, excēpī, exceptus, *to take up.*
Seleucus, -ī, m. [Greek name], *Seleucus* (this freedman bears the name of the kings of the Seleucid Empire that extended from Asia Minor and Syria eastwards in the wake of the conquests of Alexander the Great).
fābula, -ae, f., *story; conversation.*

10 quōtīdiē, adv., *daily.*
cōtīdiē, colloquial variant (see p. 241).
*lavō, lavāre, lāvī, lavātus or lautus or lōtus, *to wash;* pass. in reflexive sense, *to bathe oneself.*
baliscus, -ī, m. [vulgar, found only here, see p. 245], *bath.*
fullō, fullōnis, m., *fuller* (a person who works with cloth to increase its bulk by shrinking, beating, and compressing it); *launderer.*
cor, cordis, n., heart.

11 *quōtīdiē, adv., *daily.*
cōtīdiē, colloquial variant (see p. 241).
liquēscō, liquēscere, *to melt, waste away.*
mulsum, -ī, n., *wine mixed with honey.*
pultārius, -ī, m. (see p. 244), *cooking-pot* (originally for cereal, puls, pultis, f.); here, *large drinking vessel.*
obdūcō, obdūcere, obdūxī, obductus, *to lead against;* here, *to drink down.*
*frīgus, frīgoris, n., *cold.*

12 laecasīn [vulgar, see p. 247], transliteration of a Greek infinitive, *laikazein,* "to fornicate."
laecasīn dīcere + dat., *to tell* (someone or something) *to go hang.*
sānē, adv., *soundly; truly, really.*
**lavō, lavāre, lāvī, lavātus or lautus or lōtus, *to wash;* pass. in reflexive sense, *to bathe oneself;* active here instead of the usual passive with reflexive sense.

13 fūnus, fūneris, n., *funeral.*
bellus, -a, -um, *beautiful; fine.*
**tam, adv., *as, so, such.*
Chrysanthus, -ī, m. [Greek name meaning "Gold-Flower"], *Chrysanthus.*
anima, -ae, f., *breath, spirit.*
ēbulliō, ēbullīre, ēbulliī or ēbullīvī, *to boil up, bubble forth.*
animam ēbullīre, *to give up the ghost, expire.*

14 modo, adv., here repeated for emphasis (see p. 251), *only recently, just now.*
appellō, -āre, -āvī, -ātus, *to call to, address, speak to.*
*loquor, loquī, locūtus sum, *to speak.*
heu or ēheu, interj., *oh! ah! alas!*

Seleucus sentimentalizes on the death of a friend named Chrysanthus (Greek for Gold-Flower), and reveals his cynical and hard-hearted attitude toward people in general and women in particular.

Excēpit Seleucus fābulae partem et, "Ego," inquit, "nōn   9
cōtīdiē lavor; baliscus enim fullō est, aqua dentēs habet, et cor   10
nostrum cōtīdiē liquēscit. Sed cum mulsī pultārium obdūxī, frī-   11
gorī laecasīn dīcō. Nec sānē lavāre potuī; fuī enim hodiē in   12
fūnus. Homō bellus, tam bonus Chrysanthus animam ēbulliit.   13
Modo modo mē appellāvit. Videor mihi cum illō loquī. Heu,   14
ēheu! Ūtrēs īnflātī ambulāmus. Minōris quam muscae sumus,   15
muscae tamen aliquam virtūtem habent, nōs nōn plūris sumus   16
quam bullae. Et quid sī nōn abstināx fuisset! Quīnque diēs   17
aquam in ōs suum nōn coniēcit, nōn mīcam pānis.   18

(paragraph continued on page 71)

15   **ūter, ūtris, ūtrium**, m., *leather bag* (used for holding liquids).
    īnflātus, -a, -um, *blown up.*
    musca, -ae, f., *fly.*
16   ***aliquī, aliqua, aliquod**, indef. adj., *some, any.*
    virtūs, virtūtis, f., *excellence; bravery; manliness.*
    plūs, plūris, n., *more.*
17   ***bulla, -ae**, f., *bubble.*
    abstināx, abstinācis [vulgar, found only here, see pp. 244, 245;
    variant of **abstinēns, abstinentis**, *self-restrained*], *abstemious.*
18   **ōs, ōris**, n., *mouth.*
    coniciō [**con-** + **iaciō**, *to throw*], **conicere, coniēcī, coniectus**, *to throw, hurl, cast, put.*
    mīca, -ae, f., *little bit, morsel, crumb.*
    pānis, pānis, pānium, m., *bread.*

10   **fullō est**: *is* (as bad as) *a fuller.*
    cor . . . liquēscit: excessive bathing was thought to be bad for one's
    health.
12   **fuī . . . in fūnus**: vulgar confusion of place in which (abl.) and
    place to which (acc.) (for other examples, see pp. 247–248) or use
    of the verb *to be* with **ad** or **in** instead of a verb of motion;
    translate *I was at. . . .* or *I went to. . . .*
15   **Ūtrēs īnflātī . . . muscae . . . bullae**: all proverbial comparisons
    expressing the transience and insignificance of human life.
    Minōris . . . plūris: genitive of value, *of smaller worth . . . of more*
    worth.   *(notes continued on next page)*

17   quid sī nōn . . . fuisset: pluperfect subjunctive in an unfulfillable
     wish, *if only he hadn't been.* . . .
     quīnque diēs: accusative of extent of time.

19   **abeō, abīre, abiī, abitūrus, irreg., *to go away, depart.*
     plūrēs, plūrum [compar. of multī], m./f., *more;* here, *the majority*
        (i.e., *the dead*).
     medicus, -ī, m., *doctor.*
     **perdō, perdere, perdidī, perditus, *to destroy; to lose; to kill.*
     *immō, particle, *nay, on the contrary, rather.*
     *magis, compar. adv., *more; rather.*
20   fātum, -ī, n., *fate; luck.*
        fātus, vulgar m. for n. (see p. 242).
     *medicus, -ī, m., *doctor.*
     animus, -ī, m., *mind.*
     cōnsōlātiō, cōnsōlātiōnis, f., *consolation, comfort.*
21   efferō [ex- + ferō], efferre, extulī, ēlātus, irreg., *to carry out* (for
        burial).
     vītālis, -is, -e, *of/belonging to life* [vīta, -ae, f.].
     lectus, -ī, m., *bed; couch; bier.*
        vītālis lectus, *bier* (funeral couch on which one is carried out
           when dead; vītālis is a euphemism).
     strāgula, -ae, f., *pall* (covering for a corpse).
     plangō, plangere, plānxī, plānctus, *to strike the breast; to bewail,*
        mourn.
22   optimē, superl. adv., *very well, excellently.*
     manū mittō, mittere, mīsī, missus, *to send by/from the hand,*
        emancipate, set free (of slaves).
     aliquot, indecl. adj., *several, some.*
        aliquot, supply servōs.
     etiam sī, *even if, although.*
     malignē, adv., *scantily, grudgingly.*
     plōrō, -āre, -āvī, -ātus, *to cry aloud; to lament.*
23   uxor, uxōris, f., *wife.*
     *optimē, superl. adv., *very well, excellently.*
     ***accipiō [ad- + capiō], accipere, accēpī, acceptus, *to receive; to*
        deal with, treat.
24   mīlvīnus, -a, -um, *kite-like* (a kite, mīlvus, -ī, m., is a rapacious
        bird of prey).
     **genus, generis, n., *birth; way; race, sort, species.*
     nēmō, nēminis, m., *no one.*
     oportet, -ēre, -uit, impersonal, *it is proper/right; ought.*
     aequē . . . ac, *the same as.*

"Tamen abiit ad plūrēs. Medicī illum perdidērunt, immō magis 19
malus fātus; medicus enim nihil aliud est quam animī cōnsōlātiō. 20
Tamen bene ēlātus est, vītālī lectō, strāgulīs bonīs. Plānctus est 21
optimē—manū mīsit aliquot—etiam sī malignē illum plōrāvit 22
uxor. Quid sī nōn illam optimē accēpisset! Sed mulier quae 23
mulier mīlvīnum genus. Nēminem nihil bonī facere oportet; ae- 24
quē est enim ac sī in puteum coniciās. Sed antīquus amor cancer 25
est." 26

---

25   **puteum, -ī,** n., *well.*
     ***coniciō, conicere, coniēcī, coniectus,** to throw, hurl.*
     antīquus, -a, -um, *old, former.*
     amor, amōris, m., *love.*
     cancer, cancrī, m., *crab; cancerous growth.*

---

19   **abiit ad plūrēs:** euphemism for *he died.*
20   **fātus:** vulgar m. for n., but the masculine form personifies the idea.
21   **bene ēlātus est:** for Roman funerals, see Paoli, *Rome: Its People, Life and Customs,* pp. 128–132.
     vītālī lectō, strāgulīs bonīs: ablatives of attendant circumstances: *on . . . , with. . . .*
22   **manū mīsit aliquot:** i.e., in his will.
23   **Quid sī nōn . . . accēpisset:** pluperfect subjunctive in an unfulfillable wish (cf. line 17), *If only he hadn't. . . .*
     mulier quae mulier: supply **est,** *a woman who is a* (true) *woman.*
24   **Nēminem nihil bonī facere oportet:** accusative and infinitive as grammatical subject of **oportet. Nēminem nihil:** vulgar pleonastic double negative in which the second negative takes the place of a positive (see p. 250). **nihil bonī:** partitive genitive, *nothing of good, no favors;* here, *any favors.* Translate: (For) *nobody to do* (them = women) *any favors is right = It's not right for anyone to do them any favors = Nobody ought to do them any favors.*
     aequē est enim ac sī: *for it's just the same as if.*
25   **ac sī in puteum coniciās:** *as if you should throw* (your favors); present subjunctive in a future less vivid protasis.
     in puteum coniciās: proverbial expression. **coniciās:** as direct object supply **beneficium,** (your) *kindness* (to a woman).
     cancer est: an old love is like a crab because it clings and like a cancerous growth because it is painful. The metaphor plays on the two meanings of **cancer.**

27   *molestus, -a, -um, *troublesome, annoying, boring;* as substantive, *a bore.*

Philerōs, Philerōtis, m. [Greek name = "Friend of Love," "Amorous"], *Phileros* (a freedman).

*prōclāmō, -āre, -āvī, -ātus, *to cry out, shout.*

vīvus, -a, -um, *alive, living.*

*meminī, meminisse [perfect forms with present sense] + gen., *to remember, be mindful of.*

28   *dēbeō, -ēre, -uī, -itus, *to owe;* pass., *to be due.*

honestē, adv., *honorably.*

vīvō, vīvere, vīxī, vīctūrus, *to live.*

29   obeō, obīre, obiī, obitus, irreg., *to meet with;* + **mortem** or **diem**, stated or implied, *to meet one's death, end one's days, die.*

*queror, querī, questus sum, *to complain of, bewail.*

as, assis, m., *as* (small copper coin).

crēscō, crēscere, crēvī, crētūrus, *to increase, grow.*

**parātus, -a, -um, *prepared, ready.*

30   quadrāns, quadrantis, m., *quadrans* (coin worth a quarter of an as, see above); as a token of minimal value, *farthing.*

stercus, stercoris, n., *excrement, dung, manure.*

mordicus, adv., *by biting, with the teeth.*

*tollō, tollere, sustulī, sublātus, *to lift; to pick up.*

*crēscō, crēscere, crēvī, crētūrus, *to increase, grow.*

*quisquis, quisquis, quidquid/quicquid, indef. pron., *whoever, whatever.*

31   tangō, tangere, tetigī, tāctus, *to touch.*

***tamquam, conj., *just as (if).*

favus, -ī, m., *honeycomb.*

*meherculēs, interj., *by Hercules!*

relinquō, relinquere, relīquī, relictus, *to leave (behind).*

32   solidus, -a, -um, *firm, solid.*

*nummus, -ī, m., *piece of money, coin; cash.*

33   vērum, -ī, n., *the truth.*

lingua, -ae, f., *tongue.*

canīnus, -a, -um, *of a dog* [canis, canis, m./f.].

comedō [con- + edō; see p. 246], comesse, comēdī, comēsus, *to consume, eat up.*

dūrus, -a, -um, *hard, harsh, rough.*

bucca, -ae, f., *cheek; mouth.*

34   linguōsus, -a, -um [vulgar, found only here and at II.4.56, see pp. 245, 246], *with an idle/malicious/garrulous tongue* [lingua, -ae, f.].

discordia, -ae, f., *dissension, discord.*

*Phileros becomes annoyed at this overly emotional description of Chrysanthus,
and so paints a more realistic portrait of him.*

Molestus fuit, Philerōsque prōclāmāvit: "Vīvōrum meminer- 27
imus. Ille habet, quod sibi dēbēbātur: honestē vīxit, honestē 28
obiit. Quid habet quod querātur? Ab asse crēvit et parātus fuit 29
quadrantem dē stercore mordicus tollere. Itaque crēvit, quic- 30
quid tetigit, tamquam favus. Putō meherculēs illum relīquisse 31
solida centum, et omnia in nummīs habuit. Dē rē tamen ego 32
vērum dīcam, quī linguam canīnam comēdī: dūrae buccae fuit, 33
linguōsus, discordia, nōn homō. 34

(paragraph continued on page 75)

27 **Vīvōrum meminerimus**: a proverbial phrase; **meminī** is perfect
tense used as present (= *I remember*), and accordingly the perfect
subjunctive (**meminerimus**) is equivalent to a present
subjunctive. The subjunctive is hortatory, *Let us be mindful of. . . .*
—a mild rebuke to Seleucus for dwelling on the dead.
28 **Ille**: Chrysanthus. Phileros continues to talk about the dead.
sibi: = **eī**, incorrect (vulgar) use of the reflexive pronoun instead of
a form of **is, ea, id**.
honestē . . . honestē: anaphora (see p. 251).
29 **quod querātur**: present subjunctive in a relative clause of characteristic, *what does he have to complain about?*
30 **quadrantem dē stercore**: exaggerated proverbial language.
32 **centum**: supply **mīlia sēstertium**, *hundred thousands of sesterces = a
hundred thousand sesterces.*
in nummīs: i.e., in cash and investments.
33 **linguam canīnam comēdī**: to eat a dog's tongue would make one
as truthful and outspoken as the cynic (= Greek *kynikos*,
"doglike") philosophers, who were proverbial for their outspoken criticism, such as their "barking" at liars and hypocrites.
comēdī: colloquial use of the compound instead of the simple
verb (see p. 246).
dūrae buccae: genitive of description, (a man) *of rough mouth*, i.e.,
with a sharp tongue.
34 **discordia**: (the very essence of) *discord*.

35 **fortis, -is, -e,** *brave, strong.*
****plēnus, -a, -um,** *full; generous.*
ūnctus, -a, -um, *annointed; luxurious, lavish.*
mēnsa, -ae, f., *table.*
36 **initium, -ī,** n., *beginning.*
malus, -a, -um, *bad; here, unlucky.*
parra, -ae, f., *barn owl, bird of ill-omen.*
pilō, -āre, -āvī, -ātus, *to deprive of hair/feathers, pluck.*
  malam parram pilāre, *to have bad luck.*
recorrigō [re- + con- + regō, *to direct;* see p. 247], **recorrigere,**
  recorrēxī, recorrēctus, *to mend, set right again.*
costa, -ae, f., *rib.*
37 *****prīmus, -a, -um,** *first.*
vindēmia, -ae, f., *vintage* (harvest of grapes).
***vēndō, vēndere, vēndidī, vēnditus,** *to sell.*
****vīnum, -ī,** n., *wine.*
quantī, gen. of price, *for as much as.*
  quantum, vulgar acc. instead of gen. (see p. 247), *for as much as.*
38 **quod,** *that which, what.*
***mentum, -ī,** n., *chin.*
***sufferō [sub- + ferō], sufferre, sustulī, sublātus,** irreg., *to lift up.*
hērēditās, hērēditātis, f., *inheritance.*
plūs . . . quam, *more . . . than.*
involō, -āre, -āvī, -ātus, *to fly at, rush upon* (to steal), *seize upon.*
39 ***relinquō, relinquere, relīquī, relictus,** *to leave (behind).*
stīpes, stīpitis, m., *trunk, stump* (of a tree); *branch, stick;* as a term
  of abuse, *blockhead, dolt.*
  stīps, variant of **stīpes.**
īrāscor, īrāscī, īrātus sum + dat., *to become angry, be angry* (at).
40 **nesciō quī,** *I don't know what, some.*
patrimōnium, -ī, n., *inheritance.*
ēlēgō [ex- + lēgō, -āre, *to bequeath***], -āre, -āvī, -ātus** [word found
  only here, see p. 246] *to will away* (one's property).
****longē,** adv., *far.*
fugiō, fugere, fūgī, *to flee.*
41 ****quisquis, quisquis, quidquid/quicquid,** indef. pron., *whoever,*
  whatever.
suōs, *his own* (family, kin).
ōrāculārius, -a, -um [vulgar, found only here, see pp. 244, 246],
  dealing in oracles [**ōrāculum, -ī,** n.] (and hence often deceptive).
42 **pessum,** adv., *to the bottom.*
  pessum dare, *to give/send to the bottom, to ruin.*

"Frāter eius fortis fuit, amīcus amīcō, manū plēnā, ūnctā mēnsā. 35
Et inter initia malam parram pilāvit, sed recorrēxit costās illīus 36
prīma vindēmia: vēndidit enim vīnum, quantum ipse voluit. Et 37
quod illīus mentum sustulit, hērēditātem accēpit, ex quā plūs in- 38
volāvit quam illī relictum est. Et ille stīps, dum frātrī suō īrāsci- 39
tur, nesciō cui terrae fīliō patrimōnium ēlēgāvit. Longē fugit, 40
quisquis suōs fugit. Habuit autem ōrāculāriōs servōs, quī illum 41
pessum dedērunt. 42

(paragraph continued on page 77)

35 **amīcus amīcō**: proverbial; note the jingle produced by the repetition of words (see p. 251).
manū plēnā, ūnctā mēnsā: ablative of description, *a man of. . . .*:
i.e., generous with gifts and invitations to dinner. Note the chi-
astic order of the words.

36 **inter initia**: *to begin with.* Chrysanthus is again the subject after the
brief parenthesis on his brother. The pronouns **illīus** (36), **illīus**
(38), **illī** (39), and the adjective **ille** (39) all refer to Chrysanthus.
malam parram pilāvit: proverbial, "plucked an unlucky jay,"
"caught a tartar," i.e., tangled with a formidable opponent, had
bad luck.
recorrēxit costās: i.e., he got back on his feet again. **recorrēxit**:
note the double prefix, a feature of colloquial Latin (see page
247).

37 **prīma vindēmia**: subject of **recorrēxit**.

38 **mentum sustulit**: cf. **levātum mentō** (II.1.57).

40 **nesciō cui terrae fīliō**: *to some son of the earth = to a stranger/nobody.*
Longē fugit. . . .: proverbial.

41 **ōrāculāriōs servōs . . . pessum dedērunt**: the sense is apparently
that Chrysanthus took the advice of his slaves as if they were oracles, but he was deceived by it and was ruined.

43   *numquam, adv. *never.*
     rēctē, adv., *rightly.*
     citō, adv., *quickly, too quickly.*
     crēdō, crēdere, crēdidī, crēditus, to lend (money); to trust.
     utīque, adv., *in any case, certainly, especially.*
44   negōtior, -ārī, -ātus sum, *to do business.*
     homō negōtiāns, *business man.*
     vērus, -a, -um, *true.*
     *quod, *the fact that.*
     fruor, fruī, frūctus sum + abl., *to enjoy.*
       frūnīscor, frūnīscī, frūnītus sum [archaic and vulgar variant of
       fruor] + acc. or abl., here with neither, *to enjoy oneself.*
     quam diū, *as long as.*
     vīvō, vīvere, vīxī, vīctūrus, to live.
45   *dēstinō, -āre, -āvī, -ātus, to fix, resolve, intend.*
46   plumbum, -ī, n., *lead.*
     aurum, -ī, n., *gold.*
     facilis, -is, -e, *easy.*
47   *quadrātus, -a, -um, *squared* , *square-cut* (of stone); *fitting, suitable.*
     currō, currere, cucurrī, cursūrus, *to run.*
     quot, indecl. interrog. adj., *how many?*
     sēcum, = cum sē.
48   septuāgintā, indecl. adj., *seventy.*
     suprā, adv., *above, more.*
     corneolus, -a, -um, *hard as horn* [cornū, -ūs, n.].
     aetās, aetātis, f., *age.*
49   **niger, nigra, nigrum, *black.*
     corvus, -ī, m., *crow.*
     nōscō, nōscere, nōvī, nōtus, to become acquainted with; pf., *to
     know;* plpf., *knew.*
     ōlim, adv., *once, formerly.*
     ōliōrum, facetious gen. pl. of ōlim.
       ōlim ōliōrum, *once upon a time, long ago.*
50   salāx, salācis, *fond of leaping* [saliō, salīre]; *lecherous.*
     **meherculēs, interj., *by Hercules!*
     domus, -ūs, f., *house, home.*
     domō, abl.
51   **relinquō, relinquere, relīquī, relictus, *to leave (alone).*
     **immō, particle, *nay, on the contrary, rather.*
     pullārius, -ī, m., *chicken-keeper* [pullus, -ī, m., *chick*]; *pederast.*
     minerva, -ae, f. [Minerva, -ae, f., *Minerva*, goddess of handicrafts
     and skills], *natural capacity, skill, art.*
52   improbō [in- + probō, *to approve of*], -āre, -āvī, -ātus, *to blame.*
     *sēcum, = cum sē.

"Numquam autem rēctē faciet, quī citō crēdit, utīque homō 43
negōtiāns. Tamen vērum quod frūnītus est, quam diū vīxit. Cui 44
datum est, nōn cui dēstinātum. Plānē Fortūnae fīlius, in manū 45
illīus plumbum aurum fīēbat. Facile est autem, ubi omnia 46
quadrāta currunt. Et quot putās illum annōs sēcum tulisse? 47
Septuāgintā et suprā. Sed corneolus fuit, aetātem bene ferēbat, 48
niger tamquam corvus. "Nōveram hominem ōlim ōliōrum, et 49
adhūc salāx erat. Nōn meherculēs illum putō in domō canem 50
relīquisse. Immō etiam pullārius erat, omnis minervae homō. 51
Nec improbō, hoc sōlum enim sēcum tulit." 52

---

43 **quī citō crēdit**: (the one) *who*. . . . ; subject of **faciet**; trusting too
quickly was proverbially dangerous.
homō negotiāns: these words activate a play on the other possible
meaning of **quī . . . crēdit**, (the one) *who lends* (money).
44 **Tamen vērum . . . dēstinātum**: text uncertain. Perhaps:
Nevertheless it's true that he enjoyed himself as long as he lived. (He)
to whom it (i.e., the inheritance mentioned in lines 38–39) *was
given, not* (the one) *for whom it was intended.*
45 **Fortūnae fīlius**: proverbial expression.
46 **plumbum aurum fīēbat**: allusion to King Midas of the golden
touch.
omnia quadrāta currunt: *everything runs smoothly* (i.e., square to, in
accord with, one's desires).
47 **sēcum tulisse**: a common formula in Roman gravestone inscriptions, "He/she took X number of years with him/her when
he/she died."
48 **corneolus**: perhaps suggesting dryness and therefore good health.
49 **niger**: of youthful dark hair rather than the white hair of old age.
ōlim ōliōrum: note the jingle produced by the repetition of words
and the nonce form **ōliōrum** (see p. 251).
50 **in domō**: for the more usual **domī** (locative).
canem relīquisse: **canem** is feminine here; supply **intāctam**: i.e.,
he didn't even leave the dog alone.
51 **omnis minervae**: genitive of description, *a man of.* . . . = a versatile
person (here in an obscene sense).
52 **hoc sōlum . . . sēcum tulit**: i.e., the pleasure he had in life was all
he took with him to the grave. The language again recalls
gravestone inscriptions; the epitaph of Sardanapalus, king of
Syria, was famous, in which he boasted that he had taken with
him to the grave all the sensual pleasures that he had enjoyed
while alive (**sē omnēs sēcum abstulisse libīdinum voluptātēs**,
Cicero, *De finibus* 2.106).

53 **Ganymēdēs, Ganymēdis,** m., *Ganymede* (Zeus'/Jupiter's cup-bearer; here the name of a freedman).

    nārrō, -āre, -āvī, -ātus, *to tell, report.*

54 **caelum, -ī,** n., *sky.*

    pertineō [per- + teneō], -ēre, -uī, *to reach to, concern, pertain to.*

    ***nēmō, nēminis,** m., *no one.*

    cūrō, -āre, -āvī, -ātus, *to care.*

    quid, here = **quantum,** *to what extent, how much.*

55 **annōna, -ae,** f., *supply of grain; price of grain.*

    mordeō, mordēre, momordī, morsus, *to bite, sting.*

    *****meherculēs,** interj., *by Hercules!*

    ***bucca, -ae,** f., *cheek;* colloquial, *mouthful.*

    ***pānis, pānis, pānium,** m., *bread.*

    ****inveniō, invenīre, invēnī, inventus,** *to find.*

56 **quōmodo,** adv., *how.*

    siccitās, siccitātis, f., *dryness, drought.*

    persevērō, -āre, -āvī, -ātūrus, *to continue, persist.*

    ēsurītiō, ēsurītiōnis, f., *hunger, famine.*

57 **aedīlis, aedīlis, aedīlium,** m., *aedile* (an official who superin-tended public works and markets and was responsible for maintaining a sufficient supply of grain at a reasonable price).

    ēveniō, ēvenīre, ēvēnī, ēventūrus, *to happen, come about; to turn out.*

    pīstor, pīstōris, m., *miller, baker.*

    collūdō [con- + lūdō, *to play*]**, collūdere, collūsī, collūsūrus,** *to play with; to have a secret understanding with, connive with.*

    ***servō, -āre, -āvī, -ātus,** *to serve; to save.*

58 **populus, -ī,** m., *people.*

    ***minūtus, -a, -um,** *little; poor, common* (when used of people).

    labōrō, -āre, -āvī, -ātus, *to work; to suffer.*

59 **maxilla, -ae,** f., *jaw.*

    semper, adv., *always.*

    Sāturnālia, Sāturnālium, n. pl., *Saturnalia* (the festival of Saturn, celebrated in December with presents and festivities, in which even slaves participated).

Ganymedes speaks and reveals his pessimism about the current state of politics, economics, and religion.

Haec Philerōs dixit, illa Ganymēdēs: "Nārrātis quod nec ad   53
caelum nec ad terram pertinet, cum interim nēmō cūrat, quid   54
annōna mordet. Nōn meherculēs hodiē buccam pānis invenīre   55
potuī. Et quōmodo siccitās persevērat! Iam annum ēsurītiō fuit.   56
Aedīlēs male ēveniat, quī cum pīstōribus collūdunt. 'Servā mē,   57
servābō tē.' Itaque populus minūtus labōrat; nam istī maiōrēs   58
maxillae semper Sāturnālia agunt.   59

(paragraph continued on page 81)

---

53 **nec ad caelum nec ad terram pertinet**: proverbial.
54 **cūrat, quid annōna mordet**: normally the **quid** clause would be subordinated as an indirect question with the subjunctive (**mordeat**). Here it remains in the direct form with the indicative and is simply positioned alongside the main clause (**nēmō cūrat**). Such parataxis is typical of vulgar Latin (see p. 249).
56 **annum**: accusative of duration of time.
57 **Aedīlēs male ēveniat**: normally **ēveniat** would take the dative (**Aedīlibus male ēveniat**), *May it turn out badly for . . . !* = *Curses on . . . !).* Here **aedīlēs** may be taken as a replacement of the dative with the accusative, found in vulgar Latin (see p. 247), or there may be a break in the grammatical structure of the sentence (anacoluthon), *The aediles—curse them!* **ēveniat**: jussive subjunctive.
    quī cum pīstōribus collūdunt: electoral graffiti found in Pompeii provide evidence of collusion between bakers and elected officials, e.g., **Trebium aedīlem ōrō vōs faciātis. Clībanāri rogant.** *I ask you to elect Trebius as aedile. The bakers support him (CIL VI.677).*
    Servā mē, servābō tē: proverbial; parataxis instead of subordination of the first clause as a condition (see p. 249).
58 **istī maiōrēs maxillae**: note that **istī** (masc.) does not agree with **maxillae** (fem.), but with the gender of the people referred to as *big jaws*; this lack of grammatical agreement is called "construction according to sense" or synesis; it is found in the Latin of educated writers as well as in vulgar Latin (see page 250).
59 **semper Sāturnālia agunt**: i.e., they are always having a holiday; a proverbial phrase that carries the implication that those who act as if they are always on holiday will have to pay for it later.

60 leō, leōnis, m., *lion.*
*hīc, adv., *here.*
***inveniō, invenīre, invēnī, inventus, *to find.*
prīmum, adv., *first.*

61 Asia, -ae, f., *Asia* (the Roman province in the western part of what is now Turkey).
**vīvō, vīvere, vīxī, vīctūrus, *to live.*
simila, -ae, f., *wheat flour* (of the finest kind.)
Sicilia, -ae, f., *Sicily.*
īnferior, īnferior, īnferius, īnferiōris [compar. of īnferus], *lower; of inferior quality.*

62 larva, -ae, f., *evil spirit, demon;* here, *rascal.*
iste, ista, istud, *that* (often contemptuous).
percolopō, -āre, -āvī, -ātus [vulgar form of unattested perco-laphō, with loss of aspiration, see p. 241; hybrid compound found only here, see p. 247; per- + colaphus, a Greek loan word meaning *a blow with the fist*], *to strike with the fist; to cuff.*
Iuppiter, Iovis, m., *Jupiter* (Roman god equated with the Greek Zeus, king of the gods).
īrātus, -a, -um, *angry.*

63 **meminī, meminisse [perfect forms with present sense] + acc. of persons one remembers as acquaintances (cf. II.2.27), *to remember.*
Safinius, -ī, m. [Oscan-Samnite name], *Safinius.*
habitō, -āre, -āvī, -ātus, *to live.*
arcus, -ūs, m., *arch.*
*vetus, veteris, *old, ancient.*

64 piper, piperis, n., *pepper* (here of a sharp, hot-tempered person).
quācumque, adv., *wherever.*
adūrō, adūrere, adussī, adustus, *to set fire to, scorch, singe.*
*rēctus, -a, -um, *upright, straight.*

65 certus, -a, -um, *fixed, determined; reliable.*
audācter, adv., *courageously, boldly, confidently.*
tenebrae, -ārum, f. pl., *darkness.*

66 micō, micāre, micuī, *to move quickly to and fro; to flash; to play morra* (the Italian name for an ancient game in which two players flash or raise a number of fingers on their right hands and simultaneously call out how many fingers altogether they guess have been shown).

"Ō sī habērēmus illōs leōnēs, quōs ego hīc invēnī, cum prīmum 60
ex Asiā vēnī. Illud erat vīvere. Sī simila Siciliae īnferior erat, 61
larvās sīc istōs percolopābant, ut illīs Iuppiter īrātus esset. 62
Meminī Safinium: tunc habitābat ad arcum veterem, mē puerō, 63
piper, nōn homō. Is quācumque ībat, terram adūrēbat. Sed rēc- 64
tus, sed certus, amīcus amīcō, cum quō audācter possēs in tene- 65
brīs micāre. 66

(paragraph continued on page 83)

60 **sī habērēmus**: imperfect subjunctive expressing an unfulfilled
wish in present time, *if only we had.* . . .
illōs leōnēs: slang metaphor for courageous folk who spoke out
when the aediles made illegal deals or did not keep the price of
grain down.

61 **vīvere**: infinitive used as a noun, *that was life!*
Sī simila Siciliae īnferior erat: i.e., if the flour of Sicily was not as
good as it should have been.

62 **larvās . . . istōs**: i.e., corrupt aediles. See note on line 58 for the lack
of agreement (construction according to sense, see page 250).
percolopābant: the subject is the people referred to above as **illōs
leōnēs**.
ut illīs Iuppiter īrātus esset: result clause with imperfect subjunctive in secondary sequence. The sense of this whole sentence is
something like the following: if there was trouble with the grain
supply, the "lions" beat up those rascals, the aediles, so badly
that you would think that Jupiter himself was angry at them.

63 **Safinium**: one of the "lions."
mē puerō: ablative absolute, *when.* . . .

64 **piper, nōn homō**: cf. line 34.
Sed rēctus, sed certus: anaphora (see p. 251).

65 **amīcus amīcō**: see line 35.
in tenebrīs micāre: to play *morra* in the dark requires complete
confidence in the honesty of your partner. The phrase was
proverbial.

67   cūria, -ae, f., *senate house.*
*quōmodo, adv., *how.*
*singulī, -ae, -a, *single, separate, individual.*
*pilō, -āre, -āvī, -ātus, *to deprive of hair/feathers, pluck; to dress down, trounce.*
schēma, schēmatis, n. [Greek loan word], *rhetorical figure of speech* (Greek technical term).
     schēmās, vulgar f. for n. and change of declension from third to first (see p. 243).
**loquor, loquī, locūtus sum, *to speak.*
68   dīrēctus [dērēctus], -a, -um, *straight, straightforward, direct.*
dērēctum, adverbial.
agō, agere, ēgī, āctus, *to do, drive; to plead* (a case in court).
agere in forō, *to address* (the people at a meeting) *in the forum.*
porrō, adv., *furthermore.*
vōx, vōcis, f., *voice.*
69   **crēscō, crēscere, crēvī, crētus, *to increase, grow.*
tuba, -ae, f., *trumpet.*
sūdō, -āre, -āvī, -ātūrus, *to sweat, perspire.*
umquam, adv., *ever.*
expuō, expuere, expuī, expūtus, *to spit.*
70   *nesciō quid, *I don't know what, something;* here + partitive gen.
assum, -ī, n., *dryness.*
     nesciō quid assī, *some dryness.*
ā dīs, *from the gods.*
quam, exclam. adv., *how!*
benignus, -a, -um, *kind, friendly.*
resalūtō, -āre, -āvī, -ātus, *to greet in return.*
71   *nōmen, nōminis, n., *name.*
72   *annōna, -ae, f., *grain.*
***prō, prep. + abl., *for, on behalf of;* here, *in a degree corresponding to, in proportion to.*
lutum, -ī, n., *mud.*
     prō lutō, *dirt cheap.*
*as, assis, m., *as* (small copper coin).
**pānis, pānis, pānium, m., *bread.*
73   *emō, emere, ēmī, ēmptus, *to buy.*
dēvorō, -āre, -āvī, -ātus, *to swallow, gobble up, devour.*
**oculus, -ī, m., *eye.*
74   būbulus, -a, -um, *belonging to an ox/bull* [bōs, bovis, m./f.].
     būblum, vulgar for būbulum by syncope (see p. 241).
*heu, interj., *oh! ah! alas!*
**quōtīdiē, adv., *daily.*

"In cūriā autem quōmodo singulōs pilābat, nec schēmās lo- 67
quēbātur sed dērēctum. Cum ageret porrō in forō, sīc illīus vōx 68
crēscēbat tamquam tuba. Nec sūdāvit umquam nec expuit, putō 69
eum nesciō quid assī ā dīs habuisse. Et quam benignus re- 70
salūtāre, nōmina omnium reddere, tamquam ūnus dē nōbīs. 71
Itaque illō tempore annōna prō lutō erat. Asse pānem quem 72
ēmissēs, nōn potuissēs cum alterō dēvorāre. Nunc oculum 73
būblum vīdī maiōrem. Heu heu, quōtīdiē peius! 74

(paragraph continued on page XX)

67 **singulōs pilābat:** i.e., he put down or exposed each and every corrupt official.

68 **Cum ageret . . . in forō:** circumstantial clause with imperfect subjunctive in secondary sequence.

69 **expuit:** Quintilian in his book on the training of an orator (11.3.56)
criticizes orators who frequently cough and spit while orating,
sometimes even sprinkling their audience with saliva.

70 **benignus:** supply **erat,** *how friendly he was in. . . .* Safinius knew
everyone's name and did not need a **nōmenclātor,** a slave who
would accompany a candidate for office to remind him of the
names of his clients and of other potential supporters when the
candidate met them on the streets.

72 **Asse pānem quem ēmissēs:** word order, **pānem quem asse
ēmissēs.**
pānem quem ēmissēs: = **quandōcumque ēmissēs,** pluperfect
subjunctive in past general temporal clause (a regular usage at
the time of Petronius; Ciceronian Latin used the pluperfect indicative in this kind of clause), *whenever you bought.*

73 **nōn potuissēs:** past potential, *you could not have. . . .*
Nunc oculum būblum vīdī maiōrem: i.e., a bull's eye is bigger
than the loaf you can buy now-a-days for an **as.**

74 **quōtīdiē:** see II.2.10, II.2.11, and II.2.157 for use of the colloquial
variant **cōtīdiē** (see p. 241); here Ganymedes uses the more formal word.

75 colōnia, -ae, f., *colony.*
retrōversus, adv., *backwards.*
***crēscō, crēscere, crēvī, crētūrus, *to increase, grow.*
cauda, -ae, f., *tail.*
cōda, vulgar for cauda (see p. 240).
vitulus, -ī, m., *calf.*
76 quārē, interrog. adv., *why?*
*aedīlis, aedīlis, aedīlium, m., *aedile* (an official who superin-
tended public works and markets and was responsible for
maintaining a sufficient supply of grain at a reasonable price).
trium, gen. of trēs.
cauneae, -ārum, f. pl., *dried figs* (from Caunus in Caria, Asia
Minor).
cauniārum, vulgar for cauneārum (see p. 241).
māvult, from mālō.
77 **as, assis, m., *as* (small copper coin).
*domus, -ūs, f., *house, home.*
domī, locative, *at home.*
gaudeō, gaudēre, gāvīsus sum, *to rejoice, be glad.*
*plūs . . . quam, *more . . . than.*
78 **nummus, -ī, m., *piece of money, coin.*
alter, here used colloquially (see p. 245) for alius, *another, any one
else.*
*patrimōnium, -ī, n., *inheritance.*
79 unde, adv., *from where; from whom.*
*dēnārius, -ī, m., *denarius* (a silver coin originally worth ten assēs,
later sixteen; the as, gen. assis, m., was the basic unit of Roman
coinage).
dēnārius aureus, *golden denarius* (a coin worth twenty-five
silver dēnāriī).
cōleī, -ōrum, m. pl., *testicles; manliness.*
80 **tantum, adv., *only, so much.*
*populus, -ī, m., *people.*
**domus, -ūs, f., *house, home.*
*domī, locative, *at home.*
*leō, leōnis, m., *lion.*
81 **forās, adv., *out of doors* (implying motion); vulgar use here of the
accusative form forās in the sense of the locative forīs, *out of
doors, abroad* (place where) (see p. 247).
vulpēs [vulpis], vulpis, vulpium, m., *fox.*
attineō [ad- + teneō], attinēre, attinuī, attentus, *to hold to; to concern; to pertain.*
pannus, -ī, m., *clothes, rags.*
*comedō [con- + edō; see p. 246], comesse, comēdī, comēsus, *to
consume, eat up.*

"Haec colōnia retrōversus crēscit tamquam cōda vitulī. Sed 75
quārē? Habēmus aedīlem nōn trium cauniārum, quī sibi māvult 76
assem quam vītam nostram. Itaque domī gaudet, plūs in diē 77
nummōrum accipit, quam alter patrimōnium habet. Iam sciō 78
unde accēperit dēnāriōs mīlle aureōs. Sed sī nōs cōleōs habērē- 79
mus, nōn tantum sibi placēret. Nunc populus est domī leōnēs, 80
forās vulpēs. Quod ad mē attinet, iam pannōs meōs comēdī, et sī 81
persevērat haec annōna, casulās meās vēndam. 82

(paragraph continued on page 87)

---

82 ***persevērō, -āre, -āvī, -ātūrus,** *to continue, persist.*
**annōna, -ae, f., *grain; price of grain.*
casula, -ae, f. [dim., see p. 245, of **casa, -ae,** f., *cottage*], *little/ humble cottage.*
**vēndō, vēndere, vēndidī, vēnditus, *to sell.*

---

76 **nōn trium cauniārum:** genitive of value, *not worth.* . . .
77 **plūs in diē nummōrum accipit:** from bribes and collusion with the bakers (as above).
79 **unde accēperit:** perfect subjunctive in indirect question in primary sequence.
dēnāriōs mīlle aureōs: 100,000 sesterces (the silver denarius was worth four sesterces, the gold, a hundred); apparently mentioned here as the amount of wealth one had to have to quality for the aedileship.
sī nōs cōleōs habērēmus . . . placēret: present contrary to fact condition with imperfect subjunctives: *if we only had the nerve* (to do something about him), *he wouldn't be so pleasing to himself* (i.e., so conceited, stuck up, selfish). Cf. above (line 60): **Ō sī habērēmus illōs leōnēs.** . . . , *If only we had.* . . .
80 **domī leōnēs, forās vulpēs:** proverbial; asyndeton (see p. 251). The people roar against the aediles in private (just as Ganymedes is doing now), but are cunning and crafty like the fox in public and look out only for their own selfish interests.
81 **Quod ad mē attinet:** (That) *which pertains to me.*
pānnōs meōs comēdī: i.e., he has sold his rags to be able to buy food to eat.
82 **casulās:** probably plural for singular.

83   **deus, -ī,** m., *god.*

     diī, nom. pl.

     ***colōnia, -ae,** f., *colony.*

84   **misereor, -ērī, -itus sum** + gen., *to feel sorry for, pity.*

     meōs, *my (family/kin/friends).*

     ***fruor, fruī, frūctus sum** + abl., *to enjoy.*

       ***frūnīscor, frūnīscī, frūnītus sum** [archaic and vulgar variant of **fruor**; see p. 247] + acc. or abl., *to enjoy.*

     ***deus, -ī,** m., *god.*

     diibus, third declension instead of second declension (**dīs/deīs**) to distinguish male gods from female (**deābus**), a distinction not allowed with the second declension forms (**diibus** is found in the everyday Latin of inscriptions).

85   ****nēmō, nēminis,** m., *no one.*

     ***caelum, -ī,** n., *sky; heaven* (as the abode of the gods).

     iēiūnium, -ī, n., *fast; fast day* (here in honor of Ceres, goddess of grain).

     ****servō, -āre, -āvī, -ātus,** *to serve; to save; to keep.*

86   *****nēmō, nēminis,** m., *no one.*

     pilus, -ī, m., *hair.*

     pilī facere, *to regard* (someone/something) *as worth a hair.*

     ***operiō, operīre, operuī, opertus,** *to cover; to shut, close.*

     *****oculus, -ī,** m., *eye.*

     bona, -ōrum, n. pl., *goods, possessions.*

     computō [con- + **putō,** *to add up and balance accounts*], **-āre, -āvī, -ātus,** *to count/reckon up.*

"Quid enim futūrum est, sī nec diī nec hominēs huius colōniae   83
miserentur? Ita meōs frūnsīcar, ut ego putō omnia illa ā diibus   84
fierī. Nēmō enim caelum caelum putat, nēmō iēiūnium servat,   85
nēmō Iovem pilī facit, sed omnēs opertīs oculīs bona sua com-   86
putant.   87

(paragraph continued on page 89)

83 **futūrum est**: colloquial circumlocution for **erit**, *will be* (see p. 248).
84 **Ita meōs frūnīscar, ut ego putō . . .** : **frūnīscar** is subjunctive of
    wish, *So may I enjoy. . . .* **ut ego putō . . . fierī**, *as I think that. . . .*
    The wish adds force of conviction to the main statement (see p.
    252). We might phrase the idea in the negative and say, "May I
    not enjoy . . . , if I don't think. . . ."
85 **Nēmō . . . nēmō . . . nēmō**: anaphora (see p. 251).
    caelum caelum: repetition with a play on the two meanings of the
    word (see p. 251).
    iēiūnium: such as the **iēiūnium Cereris**, the fast in honor of Ceres,
    the goddess of grain.
86 **Iovem**: as god of the sky, Jupiter was also the god of rain.
    pilī facit: genitive of value.
    opertīs oculīs: the usual practice was to pray to the gods with cov-
    ered head (**capite vēlātō**); now people count up their assets *with
    covered/closed eyes*. This could mean that they shade their eyes the
    better to concentrate on counting their money, that they count
    their money with their eyes closed to all other concerns, or that
    they pretend to pray with eyes covered but are mentally count-
    ing up their money.

88   **anteā**, adv., *previously, in the past.*
      stolātus, -a, -um, *wearing a* **stola** (dress worn by matrons).
        stolāta, -ae, f., *matron.*
      nūdus, -a, -um, *bare.*
      clīvus, -ī, m., *slope, hill.*
      pandō, pandere, _____, passus, *to spread out.*
      capillus, -ī, m., *hair.*
89   **mēns, mentis, mentium**, f., *mind.*
      pūrus, -a, -um, *clean, pure.*
      exōrō, -āre, -āvī, -ātus, *to ask* (someone) *for* (something).
      **statim, adv., *immediately.*
      urceātim, adv. [word found only here, see p. 246], *in pitcherfuls*
        [**urceus, -ī**, m., *pitcher*].
90   **pluit, pluere, pluit**, impersonal, *it rains.*
        plovēbat, vulgar for **pluēbat** (see p. 240).
      **numquam, adv., *never.*
      *redeō, redīre, rediī, reditūrus, irreg., *to come back, return.*
      ūdus, -a, -um, *wet.*
91   **mūs, mūris**, m./f., *mouse; rat.*
      **deus, -ī, m., *god.*
        *diī, nom. pl.
      lānātus, -a, -um, *wooly; covered with wool* [**lāna, -ae**, f.].
      religiōsus, -a, -um, *religious.*
92   **ager, agrī**, m., *field.*
      iaceō, iacēre, iacuī, iacitūrus, *to lie;* here perhaps, *to be unproduc-*
      tive.

"Anteā stolātae ībant nūdīs pedibus in clīvum, passīs capillīs,   88
mentibus pūrīs, et Iovem aquam exōrābant. Itaque statim urceā-   89
tim plovēbat: aut tunc aut numquam: et omnēs redībant ūdī   90
tamquam mūrēs. Itaque diī pedēs lānātōs habent, quia nōs re-   91
ligiōsī nōn sumus. Agrī iacent—"   92

---

89 **nūdīs pedibus**: ablative of manner; bare feet and loosening of
clothing and hair (**passīs capillīs**) were normal in ancient rituals.
Leather was taboo because it represented dead animals, and bare
feet would put the worshiper in direct contact with the powers of
the earth. The hair is loosened because nothing should be bound
or knotted in ritual acts. Horace describes a witch, Canidia, performing magic rituals **pedibus nūdīs passōque capillō** (*Satires*
1.8.24).
   in clīvum: up the hill on which temples of the gods were situated.
   passīs capillīs, mentibus pūrīs: ablatives of manner.
92 **tamquam mūrēs**: *like (drowned)*. . . .
   diī pedēs lānātōs habent: proverbial but of uncertain meaning;
the sense seems to be that the gods do not answer our prayers
and that they neglect us (cf. above, lines 83–84, **nec diī nec hominēs huius colōniae miserentur**). Saturn's feet were said to be
wrapped in wool except at the Saturnalia, perhaps because his
reign was over. The image of the feet wrapped in wool may owe
something to the practice of wrapping the feet of persons with
gout (who could therefore not walk) in bands of wool. Perhaps
the idea is that the gods enjoy life with their feet warmly clad in
wool and so neglect us—all because **nōs religiōsī nōn sumus**.

93   **ōrō, -āre, -āvī, -ātus,** *to ask, beg.*

     Echīōn, Echīonis, m. [Greek name], *Echion* (one of the mythical men born in Thebes from dragon's teeth sown by Cadmus; he was the father of Pentheus; here the name of a freedman.)

     centōnārius, -ī, m. [vulgar formation, see p. 244; rare word, see p. 246; **centō, centōnis, m.,** *quilt, blanket, mat made of old clothes stitched together*], *fireman* (who used mats made of rags to fight fires).

     melius, compar. adv., *better.*

     **loquor, loquī, locūtus sum, *to speak.*

        loquere, imperative.

     *modo . . . modo, *at one time . . . at another time, now . . . now.*

94   ***varius, -a, -um,** *many-colored, mottled, spotted.*

     porcus, -ī, m., *pig.*

     ***perdō, perdere, perdidī, perditus, *to destroy; to kill; to lose.*

95   **trūdō, trūdere, trūsī, trūsus,** *to thrust, shove forward, drive on.*

     patria, -ae, f., *fatherland, home-town.*

96   ***labōrō, -āre, -āvī, -ātus,** *to work; to suffer.*

97   ****dēbeō, -ēre, -uī, -itus,** *to owe; ought.*

     *dēlicātus, -a, -um, *charming; luxurious, extravagant; fastidious, spoiled, sentimental.*

     ubīque, adv., *everywhere.*

     medius, -a, -um, *middle, middle of.*

     **caelum, -ī, n., *sky.*

        caelus, vulgar m. for n. (see p. 242).

98   **aliubī,** adv., *elsewhere.*

     **hīc, adv., *here.*

     *porcus, -ī, m., *pig.*

     coctus, -a, -um, *cooked, roasted.*

     ecce, interj., *behold!*

99   ***mūnus, mūneris, n.,** *duty; gift; gladiatorial show.*

     excellēns, excellentis, *excellent.*

        excellente, vulgar for **excellēns,** neuter acc. sing., as if it were an adjective of three terminations such as **ācer, ācris, ācre** and formed from the stem found in the genitive (see p. 243).

     trīduum, -ī, n., *period of three days.*

     fēstus, -a, -um, *of/belonging to a festival/holiday.*

     familia, -ae, f., *family; company of gladiators.*

100   **lanisticius, -a, -um** [vulgar, found only here, see pp. 245, 246], *of/belonging to a lanista* (a professional trainer of gladiators).

     plūrimī, -ae, -a [superl. of **multī**], *most, the majority.*

     lībertus, -ī, m., *freedman.*

Echion wishes to talk about more optimistic things—such as the holiday the town is about to have and the real value of an education.

"Ōrō tē," inquit Echīōn centōnārius, "melius loquere. 'Modo   93
sīc, modo sīc,' inquit rūsticus; varium porcum perdiderat. Quod   94
hodiē nōn est, crās erit: sīc vīta trūditur. Nōn meherculēs patria   95
melior dīcī potest, sī hominēs habēret. Sed labōrat hōc tempore,   96
nec haec sōla. Nōn dēbēmus dēlicātī esse, ubīque medius caelus   97
est. Tū sī aliubī fueris, dīcēs hīc porcōs coctōs ambulāre. Et ecce   98
habitūrī sumus mūnus excellente in trīduō diē fēstā; familia nōn   99
lanisticia, sed plūrimī lībertī.   100

(paragraph continued on page 93)

---

93 **centōnārius:** Echion may have belonged to a guild (**collēgium**) of
centōnāriī.
Ōrō tē . . . melius loquere (imperative): vulgar parataxis of a direct command instead of subordination as an indirect command with **ut** and the subjunctive (**ōrō tē ut melius loquāris**) (see p. 249). **melius loquere:** i.e., don't speak words of ill omen.
Modo sīc, modo sīc: *Now this way, now that,* i.e., things have their ups and downs, said with a shrug of resignation (for the repetition of words, see p. 251).

94 **inquit rūsticus; varium porcum perdiderat:** *said the farmer* (when) *he. . . . :* parataxis again instead of subordination (see p. 249). The tone of resignation in **Modo sīc, modo sīc** is trivialized by the circumstances in which the peasant uttered the words.
Quod hodiē . . . crās erit: proverbial.

95 **patria melior dīcī potest, sī hominēs habēret:** the indicative (usually imperfect or pluperfect) of **posse** may be used in the apodosis of a contrary-to-fact condition, *no country can/could be said to be better* (than this one) *if* (only) *it had. . . .*

96 **hōc tempore:** ablative absolute, *times being thus.*

97 **ubīque medius caelus est:** proverbial, i.e., everything is the same no matter where you go.

98 **sī . . . fueris, dīcēs:** future more vivid condition, *if you are* (lit., *will have been*) *. . . , you will say. . . .* The future perfect is used colloquially in the protasis where the sense requires a simple future (see p. 248).
hīc (*here*) **porcōs coctōs ambulāre:** i.e., that our town is a utopian dream world with cooked food on the hoof, ready to eat.

99 **habitūrī sumus:** colloquial circumlocution for **habēbimus** (see p. 248).
in trīduō diē fēstā: *within three days* or *on the day after tomorrow*

(Romans counted the present day as the first day) *on the day of the festival*. **diē**: feminine when referring to a set day such as this. **nōn lanisticia, sed plūrimī lībertī**: i.e., not slaves training in a gladiatorial school but freedmen who have earned manumission and discharge from the gladiatorial school as a reward for their skill and success and choose to continue fighting at a higher fee.

101 **Titus, -ī, m.**, *Titus* (the magistrate who will sponsor the games).
*animus, -ī, m., *mind; soul; spirit.*
   magnum animum habet, = **magnanimus est.**
   magnanimus, -a, -um, *great-souled, magnanimous.*
   caldicerebrius, -a, -um [vulgar, found only here and one other place in Petronius, see p. 245] *hot-brained* [**calidus, -a, -um** + **cerebrum, -ī, n.**], *hot-headed.*
102 **quid**, = **aliquid**, *something.*
   *utīque, adv., *in any case, certainly, especially.*
   domesticus, -a, -um + dat., *familiar with.*
103 **mixcix** [vulgar, found only here, see p. 246], see note below text.
   ferrum, -ī, n., *iron; sword;* here, *gladiatorial fight.*
   *fuga, -ae, f., *flight, escape.*
   carnārium, -ī, n., *frame with hooks* (for hanging meat [**carō, carnis, f.**, *meat*] for smoking or drying); *butcher's shop; carnage.*
104 ***medium, -ī, n.**, *middle part, center.*
   amphitheātrum, -ī, n. [Greek loan word], *amphtheater.*
   amphitheāter, vulgar m. for n. (see p. 242).
   *unde, adv., *from where.*
   ***relinquō, relinquere, relīquī, relictus, *to leave.*
105 ***sēstertius, -ī, m.**, *sesterce* (small silver coin).
   sēstertium, gen. pl.
   trecentiēs, adv., *three hundred times.*
   sēstertium trecentiēs, short for **sēstertium trecentiēs centēna mīlia**, *30,000,000 sesterces.*
   dēcēdō, dēcēdere, dēcessī, dēcessūrus, *to go away; to die.*
   ut, conj. + subjn., *although.*
   quadringentī, -ae, -a, *four hundred.*
   quadringenta, short for **quadringenta mīlia sēstertium**, *400,000 sesterces.*
106 **impendō** [in- + **pendō, pendere**, *to place in the scales, weigh*], **impendere, impendī, impēnsus**, *to weigh out; to pay out; to expend, spend.*
   sentiō, sentīre, sēnsī, sēnsus, *to feel, perceive.*
   **patrimōnium, -ī, n., *inheritance.*
   sempiternō, adv., *forever.*
107 **nōminō, -āre, -āvī, -ātus**, *to name;* pass., *to be celebrated.*

"Et Titus noster magnum animum habet et est caldicerebrius: 101
aut hoc aut illud, erit quid utīque. Nam illī domesticus sum, nōn 102
est mixcix. Ferrum optimum datūrus est, sine fugā, carnārium 103
in mediō, ut amphitheāter videat. Et habet unde: relictum est illī 104
sēstertium trecentiēs, dēcessit illīus pater. Male! Ut quadrin- 105
genta impendat, nōn sentiet patrimōnium illīus, et sempiternō 106
nōminābitur. 107

(paragraph continued on page 95)

101 **Titus**: use of the praenomen implies familiarity, confirmed by
     noster = almost, *my good friend.*
102 **aut hoc aut illud, erit quid utīque**: i.e., I don't know what it'll
     be, but it'll be something good in any case.
103 **mixcix**: vulgar nonce word savored for its onomatopoetic effect
     (cf. English "shilly-shally"); meaning unknown, but the sug-
     gestion is that Titus is not a man not to do or to do badly what-
     ever he promises—that he is not given to half measures.
     datūrus est: colloquial circumlocution for **dabit** (see p. 248).
     sine fugā: i.e., to the death.
104 **ut amphitheāter videat**: purpose clause with present subjunc-
     tive. The gladiators will be put to death in the middle of the
     arena so that all the spectators can see, rather than being
     dragged into the pits and dispatched out of sight. Seneca,
     Epistulae morales 7.3–5, gives a vivid picture of the kind of
     butchery in the arena that Echion is looking forward to with
     relish.
     Et habet unde: supply **solvat** [**solvō, solvere**, *to pay*], *And he has
     the wherewithal* (to pay for this expensive gladiatorial show).
     relictum est: i.e., by his father.
105 **Male!**: *What a pity!*
     Ut . . . impendat: concessive, *Although he may spend . . .* (on the
     gladiatorial show).
106 **patrimōnium**: subject of **sentiet**.

108 **nannus, -ī**, m., *dwarf.*

*aliquot, indecl. adj., *several, some.*

essedārius, -a, -um, *fighting from a war-chariot* [**essēdum, -ī**, n., *war-chariot*, used by Gauls and Britons].

109 **Glycō, Glycōnis**, m. [Greek word, "sweet-one"], *Glyco.*

dēprehendō, dēprehendere, dēprehendī, dēprehēnsus, *to catch, apprehend.*

domina, -ae, f., *mistress.*

110 **dēlectō, -āre, -āvī, -ātus**, *to please, charm, delight.*

dēlectārētur, vulgar, affected conjugation as deponent instead of active (see p. 244).

**populus, -ī, m., *people.*

rixa, -ae, f., *quarrel, dispute, brawl.*

zēlotypus, -ī, m. [Greek loan word], *jealous man.*

amāsiunculus, -ī, m. [word found only here; dim., see p. 245, of **amāsius, -ī**, m., *lover*], *fond lover; adulterer.*

111 **sēstertiārius, -a, -um** [vulgar, found only here and at II.2.123 with this meaning, see pp. 244, 246], *worth but a sesterce.*

112 **bēstia, -ae**, f., *beast; wild beast* (used in shows in the arena).

ad bēstiās dare, *to condemn to fight with wild beasts in the arena.*

*trādūcō [**trāns-** + **dūcō**], **trādūcere, trādūxī, trāductus**, *to lead across; to exhibit as a spectacle; to expose to public ridicule/disgrace.*

peccō, -āre, -āvī, -ātūrus, *to commit a fault, offend, sin.*

113 **cōgō, cōgere, coēgī, coāctus**, *to force, compel.*

**magis, compar. adv., *more; rather.*

**matella, -ae, f., *chamber-pot.*

*dignus, -a, -um, *worthy.*

taurus, -ī, m., *bull.*

114 **iactō, -āre, -āvī, -ātus**, *to throw.*

quī, = **is quī**, *he who.*

asinus, -ī, m., *ass, donkey.*

strātum, -ī, n., *something spread out* [**sternō, sternere, strāvī, strātus**]; *horse-blanket, saddle-cloth.*

caedō, caedere, cecīdī, caesus, *to cut; to strike, beat.*

"Iam nannōs aliquot habet et mulierem essedāriam et dispēn- 108
sātōrem Glycōnis, quī dēprehēnsus est, cum dominam suam 109
dēlectārētur. Vidēbis populī rixam inter zēlotypōs et amāsiun- 110
culōs. Glycō autem, sēstertiārius homō, dispēnsātōrem ad 111
bēstiās dedit. Hoc est sē ipsum trādūcere. Quid servus peccāvit, 112
quī coāctus est facere? Magis illa matella digna fuit quam taurus 113
iactāret. Sed quī asinum nōn potest, strātum caedit. 114

(paragraph continued on page 97)

---

109 **mulierem essedāriam**: for women even of good family as gladiators, see Tacitus, *Annals* 15.32. One type of gladiatorial show
involved combatants fighting from British war chariorts; the
combatants were called **essēdāriī** (see Suetonius, *Claudius*
21.5).

110 **populī rixam**: there will be a brawl in the amphitheater between
those who side with Glyco, the jealous husband who has condemned his wife's lover to the arena, and those who side with
the lover; the former are the **zēlotypī**, the latter the **amāsiun-
culī**. Tacitus (*Annals* 14.17) describes a famous and bloody
brawl between Nucerini and Pompeiani in the amphitheater at
Pompeii in A.D. 59.

112 **Quid servus peccāvit . . . ?**: i.e., Glyco's **dispēnsātor** was not to
blame, because Glyco's wife forced him to make love with her.
Thus, in punishing the **dispēnsātor**, Glyco is merely exposing
himself as a cuckolded husband (**sē ipsum trādūcere**).

113 **illa matella**: i.e., Glyco's wife.
digna . . . quam . . . iactāret: **dignus** is regularly followed by a
relative clause in the subjunctive; we would say, *she was worthy
of being*. . . . There may be an allusion to the myth of Dirce,
who was punished by Amphion and Zethus for abusing their
mother Antiope. Amphion and Zethus tied Dirce to a bull,
which dragged her to her death.

114 **quī asinum nōn potest**: supply **caedere**; proverbial: if you can't
beat the donkey, beat the saddle. Glyco did not dare punish
his wife, presumably because she had a large dowry or influential parents, so he punished the **dispēnsātor**.

115 **Hermogenēs, Hermogenis,** m. [Greek name, "Born from Hermes"], *Hermogenes* (father of Glyco's wife).
filix, filicis, f., *fern;* figuratively, *worthless person.*
***umquam,** adv., *ever.*

116 **exitus, -ūs,** m., *outcome, end.*
mīlvus, -ī, m., *kite* (rapacious bird of prey).
volō, -āre, -āvī, -ātūrus, *to fly.*
unguis, unguis, unguium, m., *fingernail; hoof; claw; talon.*

117 **resecō, -āre, -āvī, -ātus,** *to cut off.*
colubra, -ae, f., *snake.*
restis, restis, restium, f., *rope, cord.*
pariō, parere, peperī, partus, *to bring forth, bear.*

118 ***quamdiū [quam diū],** adv., *as long as.*
*****vīvō, vīvere, vīxī, vīctūrus,** *to live.*
stigma, stigmatis, n. [Greek loan word], *mark* (burned onto the skin of runaway slaves, criminals, etc.).
    stigmam, vulgar f. for n. and first declension instead of third (see p. 243).
****nisi,** conj., *unless, except.*
Orcus, -ī, m., *Orcus* (god of the underworld); *the underworld; death.*

119 **dēleō, dēlēre, dēlēvī, dēlētus,** *to destroy, blot out, efface.*
***quisque, quaeque, quidque/quicque,** indef. pron., *each one, every one.*
***peccō, -āre, -āvī, -ātūrus,** *to commit a fault, offend, sin.*
subolfaciō, subolfacere [compound verb found only here and used with the same meaning as the simple verb **olfaciō,** see pp. 246, 247], *to smell out, perceive by the scent; to get wind of, hear about.*
quia, conj., *that* (here introducing indirect statement).

120 **epulum, -ī,** n., *banquet, feast.*
Mammea, -ae, m., *Mammea* (a candidate for some political position).
bīnī, -ae, -a, *two each.*
****dēnārius, -ī,** m., *denarius* (a silver coin originally worth ten **assēs,** later sixteen; the **as,** gen. **assis,** m., was the basic unit of Roman coinage).

121 **quod sī,** *but if, and if.*
***ēripiō [ex- + rapiō], ēripere, ēripuī, ēreptus,** *to snatch away, take away.*
Norbānus, -ī, m., *Norbanus* (a rival candidate).
favor, favōris, m., *favor, popularity.*

122 ***oportet, -ēre, -uit,** impersonal + subjn. without **ut,** *it is proper/ right; ought.*
*****plēnus, -a, -um,** *full.*

"Quid autem Glycō putābat Hermogenis filicem umquam 115
bonum exitum factūram? Ille mīlvō volantī poterat unguēs 116
resecāre; colubra restem nōn parit. Glycō, Glycō dedit suās; 117
itaque quamdiū vīxerit, habēbit stigmam, nec illam nisi Orcus 118
dēlēbit. Sed sibi quisque peccat. Sed subolfaciō quia nōbīs 119
epulum datūrus est Mammea, bīnōs dēnāriōs mihi et meīs. 120
Quod sī hoc fēcerit, ēripiet Norbānō tōtum favōrem. Sciās 121
oportet plēnīs vēlīs hunc vincitūrum. 122

(paragraph continued on page 99)

---

vēlum, -ī, n., *sail.*
*vincō, vincere, vīcī, victus, *to conquer; to be victorious, win.*
vincitūrus, vulgar future participle for victūrus (see p. 244).

---

115 **Hermogenis filicem**: *the fern of Hermogenes* = Hermogenes'
daughter, now Glyco's wife. **filicem**: disparaging and contemptuous, with a pun on **fīliam.**
116 **Ille**: Hermogenes.
milvō volantī . . . unguēs resecāre: proverbial for a real sharp-
ster. **milvō volantī**: dative of separation.
117 **colubra restem nōn parit**: proverbial, "Like breeds like." Hermogenes' daughter is as sharp and unprincipled as her father.
Glycō, Glycō: note the effect produced by the repetition of the
name (see p. 251).
dedit suās: supply **poenās;** he has paid his penalty, gotten his
punishment (for marrying a woman like Hermogenes' daughter).
118 **quamdiū vīxerit, habēbit**: future more vivid, *as long as he lives*
(lit., *will have lived*), *he will.* . . . The future perfect is used colloquially in the temporal clause where the sense requires a simple future (see p. 248).
119 **sibi quisque peccat**: dative of disadvantage, *each person sins to
his own loss* (because he will pay for it sooner or later). Having
concluded that a man's misdeeds are his own concern, Echion
now changes the subject.
subolfaciō quia . . . datūrus est: vulgar use of **quia,** *that,* and
indicative instead of the normal accusative and infinitive in indirect statement (see p. 250).
120 **datūrus est**: colloquial circumlocution for **dabit** (see p. 248).
Mammea: a candidate currying favor with the electorate by giving a free banquet.
bīnōs dēnāriōs: in apposition to **epulum,** *worth two denarii per*

person.
mihi et meīs: *to me and my* (associates—perhaps his fellow guild members; see note on line 93 above).
121 fēcerit, ēripiet: future more vivid condition.
Sciās oportet: *It is right* (that) *you may think* = *You can be sure that.* . . .
122 plēnīs vēlīs: ablative of manner, *with.* . . . = *easily.*
hunc: i.e., Mammea.
vincitūrum: intransitive here, *will win.*

123 rēvērā [rē vērā], adv., *in fact, in truth, in reality.*
gladiātor, gladiātōris [gladius, -ī, m., *sword*], m., *gladiator*
*sēstertiārius, -a, -um [vulgar, found only here and at II.2.111 with this meaning, see pp. 244, 246], *worth but a sesterce.*
124 dēcrepitus, -a, -um, *worn out* (with age), *decrepit.*
sufflō [sub- + flō, *to blow*], -āre, -āvī, -ātus, *to blow at.*
sufflāssēs, = sufflāvissēs.
cadō, cadere, cecidī, cāsūrus, *to fall, fall down.*
125 bēstiārius, -ī, m., *beast-fighter* (sometimes common criminals condemned to fight with wild beasts in the arena).
occīdō [ob- + caedō, *to cut*], occīdere, occīdī, occīsus, *to cut down; to kill, slay.*
*lucerna, -ae, f., *oil-lamp.*
*eques, equitis, m., *horseman.*
126 gallus, -ī, m., *cock.*
gallīnāceus, -a, -um, *of/belonging to the domestic breed of poultry.*
gallus gallīnāceus, *poultry-cock.*
alter . . . alter, *the one . . . the other.*
burdubasta, -ae, f. [vulgar, found only here, see p. 245], meaning uncertain, perhaps from burdō, burdōnis, m., *mule* + Greek *bastazō,* "to carry" = perhaps, *packhorse*; or the second element may mean *stave,* and **bourdubasta** may mean *stick to drive a mule,* and the gladiator is being described as "thin as a rail."
lōripēs, lōripedis [see p. 246], *strap-footed* [lōrum, -ī, n. + pēs, pedis, m.], *crook-footed, bandy-legged.*
tertiārius, -a, -um, *containing a third part*; as substantive, *gladiator* (who replaced the victim or challenged the winner in the first duel).
mortuus, -a, -um, *dead.*
127 ***prō, prep. + abl., *for, on behalf of; instead of, in place of.*
nervus, -ī, m., *sinew, tendon, nerve.*
nervia, vulgar, affected n. for m. and third declension instead of second (see p. 242).
praecīdō [prae- + caedō, *to cut*], praecīdere, praecīdī, praecīsus, *to cut through; to hamstring.*

"Et rēvērā, quid ille nōbīs bonī fēcit? Dedit gladiātōrēs sēster- 123
tiāriōs iam dēcrepitōs, quōs sī sufflāssēs cecidissent; iam 124
meliōrēs bēstiāriōs vīdī. Occīdit dē lucernā equitēs, putārēs eōs 125
gallōs gallīnāceōs; alter burdubasta, alter lōripēs, tertiārius mor- 126
tuus prō mortuō, quī habēbat nervia praecīsa. 127

(paragraph continued on page 101)

123 **ille:** i.e., Norbanus.
124 **sī sufflāssēs cecidissent:** pluperfect subjunctives in past contrary-to-fact condition, *if you had . . . , they would have. . . . .*
125 **bēstiāriōs:** inferior to gladiators because they were often mere
criminals thrown to the beasts with little bodily protection and
sometimes with no weapons with which to defend themselves.
Occīdit: i.e., he sent them into the arena to be killed.
dē lucernā equitēs: perhaps horsemen or mounted gladiators so
small that they resembled small figures in relief on oil lamps.
126 **mortuus prō mortuō:** the **tertiārius** was no better than the dead
man he replaced; note the jingle produced by the repetition of
words (see p. 251).

128 **aliquī, aliqua, aliquod**, indef. adj., *some, any.*
flātūra, -ae, f., *blowing; the casting of metals* (using a bellows); here, figuratively from the coining of metals, *stamp, quality* (of a person), *spirit, courage.*
Thraex, Thraecis, *Thracian* (a class of gladiators who fought with small square shields and short swords).
ad, prep. + acc., *to;* here, *according to.*
dictāta, -ōrum, n. pl., *things dictated by a teacher, lessons, rules.*
129 **pugnō, -āre, -āvī, -ātūrus**, *to fight.*
ad summam, *in short, to be brief.*
posteā, adv., *afterward.*
secō, secāre, secuī, sectus, *to cut; to cut up; to cut* (with a whip or lash); *to whip.*
adeō, adv., *so true is it that, to such an extent* (introducing an explanation of the preceding statement).
130 *turba, -ae*, f., *crowd, mob.*
adhibeō [ad- + habeō], adhibēre, adhibuī, adhibitus, *to hold out; to bring; to apply.*
****fuga, -ae**, f., *flight; rout* (running away in battle).
merus, -a, -um, *pure, simple.*
****mūnus, mūneris**, n., *duty; gift; gladiatorial show.*
131 **plaudō, plaudere, plausī, plausus**, *to applaud.*
plōdō, vulgar for **plaudō** (see p. 240).
computō [con- + putō, to add up and balance accounts], -āre, -āvī, -ātus, to count/reckon up.
****plūs . . . quam**, *more . . . than.*
132 ***lavō, lavāre, lāvī, lavātus** or **lautus** or **lōtus**, *to wash.*

"Ūnus alicuius flātūrae fuit Thraex, quī et ipse ad dictāta 128
pugnāvit. Ad summam, omnēs posteā sectī sunt; adeō dē 129
magnā turbā 'Adhibēte!' accēperant, plānē fugae merae. 'Mūnus 130
tamen,' inquit, 'tibi dedī': et ego tibi plōdō. Computā, et tibi plūs 131
dō quam accēpī. Manus manum lavat. 132

(paragraph continued on page 103)

---

128 alicuius flātūrae: genitive of description, *with some* (consider-
able)....
ad dictāta: i.e., merely in accordance with the rules laid down by
his trainer, not with any real gusto.

129 sectī sunt: either they had to be whipped into combat or they
were whipped for fighting poorly.

130 'Adhibēte!' accēperant: the bad gladiators received or heard the
spectators shouting "Adhibēte!" Supply **virgās ferrumque**,
rods (used for corporal punishment) *and the sword*, as direct
objects of **Adhibēte**, = *Punish them!* Compare Seneca, *Epistulae
morales* 7.5, who records the spectators at a gladiatorial combat
shouting "**Occīde, verberā, ūre!**" *Kill him, whip him, burn him!*
fugae merae: plural for singular, *a pure rout;* or possibly *pure
runaways, cowards.*

131 inquit: the subject is Norbanus; the sense is: in spite of the fact
that you don't appreciate it, at least I gave you a show!
Computā.... : i.e., you gave a rotten show; I applauded. Figure
it up; you're the gainer.

132 **Manus manum lavat:** proverbial for returning like for like;
Echion means "You get what you deserve."

For passages from ancient sources dealing with gladiatorial combats in
the arena, see Jo-Ann Shelton, *As the Romans Did*, "Amphitheater
Events," pp. 342–350.

133 *iste, ista, istud, *that* (often contemptuous).
argūtor, -ārī, -ātus sum, *to chatter, prattle, babble.*
argūtat, vulgar active for deponent (argūtātur) (see p. 243).
**molestus, -a, -um, *troublesome, annoying;* as substantive, *a bore.*
134 ***loquor, loquī, locūtus sum , *to speak.*
loquere, vulgar active for deponent (loquī) (see p. 243).
loquis, vulgar active for deponent (loqueris) (see p. 243).
fascia, -ae, f., *ribbon, band* (of material); *fascia* (architectural term);
here, idiom, nōn es nostrae fasciae, *you're not one of us.*
135 ideō, adv., *for that/this reason, therefore.*
pauper, pauperis, m./f., *poor person.*
pauperōrum, vulgar second declension gen. pl. instead of
third (pauperum) (see p. 243).
*verbum, -ī, n., *word.*
dērīdeō, dērīdēre, dērīsī, dērīsus, *to laugh at, mock.*
prae, prep. here + acc. (vulgar, see p. 247) instead of abl., *in view
of, on account of.*
litterae, -ārum, f. pl., *letter* (i.e., an epistle); *literature; learning; liberal education.*
fatuus, -a, -um, *silly, foolish.*
136 ***aliquī, aliqua, aliquod, indef. adj., *some, any.*
persuādeō, persuādēre, persuāsī, persuāsus + dat., but here +
acc. (vulgar, see p. 247), *to persuade, prevail upon* (someone to do
something, ut + subjn.).
vīlla, -ae, f., *country estate.*
137 *casula, -ae, f. [dim. of casa, -ae, f., *cottage*], *little/humble cottage.*
mandūcō, mandūcere, mandūxī, manductus, *to chew, eat.*
138 *pullus, -ī, m., *chick; chicken.*
bellē, adv., *in an agreeable manner, nicely.*
bellē esse, *to have a nice time;* impersonal, bellē est, *a nice time
is had.*
*etiam sī, *even if, although.*
tempestās, tempestātis, f., *weather* (good or bad).
139 disparpallō, -āre, -āvī, -ātus [the word is an editorial conjecture,
if right, a vulgar coinage, see p. 246], meaning uncertain, perhaps *to scatter.*
**unde, adv., *from where;* here, *with which.*
*satur, satura, saturum + abl., here implied in unde, *full* (of),
satisfied (with), *filled* (with).
140 discipulus, -ī, m., *pupil.*
cicarō, cicarōnis, m. [vulgar word-formation with ending in -ō,
see p. 244; found only here and at II.5.33, see p. 246], meaning
uncertain, perhaps *small boy.*

"Vidēris mihi, Agamemnōn, dīcere: 'Quid iste argūtat molestus?' 133
Quia tū, quī potes loquere, nōn loquis. Nōn es nostrae fasciae, et 134
ideō pauperōrum verba dērīdēs. Scīmus tē prae litterās fatuum 135
esse. Quid ergō est? Aliquā diē tē persuādeam ut ad vīllam 136
veniās et videās casulās nostrās? Inveniēmus quod mandūcē- 137
mus, pullum, ōva: bellē erit, etiam sī omnia hōc annō tempestās 138
disparpallāvit: inveniēmus ergō unde saturī fīāmus. Et iam tibi 139
discipulus crēscit cicarō meus. 140

(paragraph continued on page 105)

133 **Agamemnōn:** the well-educated teacher of rhetoric (see II.1.4).
134 **nostrae fasciae:** genitive of description, *you're not of.* . . .
135 **fatuum:** perhaps with a play on the word as if it could describe
one *who is able to speak* (**fārī**), cf. **tū, quī potes loquere**, line 134.
136 **Aliquā diē:** feminine when a specific day is referred to.
persuādeam: potential subjunctive, *could I persuade* . . . ? or present subjunctive used colloquially instead of a future indicative.
ut . . . veniās . . . videās: indirect commands with subjunctive
dependent on **persuādeam**.
137 **casulās nostrās:** perhaps plural for singular.
quod mandūcēmus: relative clause of characteristic with present
subjunctive.
138 **hōc annō:** ablative of time within which or perhaps ablative instead of accusative of duration of time.
139 **unde saturī fīāmus:** relative clause of characteristic with present
subjunctive.
tibi discipulus: predicate, (to be) *your pupil* (in rhetoric).

141 **latus, lateris,** n., *side, flank.*
servulus, -ī, m. [dim. of **servus, -ī,** m., *slave*], *little slave.*

142 *****quisquis, quisquis, quidquid/quicquid,** indef. pron., *whoever, whatever.*
vacō, -āre, -āvī, -ātūrus, *to be empty;* impersonal, *there is time/leisure.*
****tabula, -ae,** f., *waxed writing-tablet.*
****tollō, tollere, sustulī, sublātus,** *to lift; to take away, remove.*
ingeniōsus, -a, -um, *intellectual, gifted, clever.*

143 **fīlum, -ī,** n., *thread; style* (of a speech); *character* (of a person).
****etiam sī,** *even if, although.*
avis, avis, avium, f., *bird.*
morbōsus, -a, -um, *sickly, ailing; morbidly lustful; wild about, crazy about.*

144 **carduēlis, carduēlis, carduēlium,** f., *goldfinch.*
cardēlēs, vulgar for **carduēlēs** (see p. 241).
***occīdō** [**ob-** + **caedō,** *to cut*], **occīdere, occīdī, occīsus,** *to cut down; to kill, slay.*
***quia,** conj., *that* (here introducing indirect statement).
mustella, -ae, f., *weasel* (sometimes kept as household pets by the Romans).
****comedō** [**con-** + **edō;** see p. 246], **comesse, comēdī, comēsus,** *to consume, eat up.*

145 **nēnia, -ae,** f., *funeral song, dirge; jingle;* pl., *trifles; hobby.*
***libentissimē,** superl. adv., *very willingly; most gladly, with the greatest pleasure.*
*****pingō, pingere, pīnxī, pictus,** *to paint.*
Graeculus, -a, -um [dim. of **Graecus, -a, -um,** *Greek*], *Greek.*
Graeculīs, supply **litterīs,** *letters, literature.*
calx, calcis, calcium, f., *heel.*

146 ***impingō** [**in-** + **pangō,** *to fix*], **impingere, impēgī, impactus,** *to fasten, fix on; to push, thrust at/upon; to strike/drive into.*
Latīnus, -a, -um, *Latin.*
Latīnās, supply **litterās,** *letters, literature.*
appetō [**ad-** + **petō,** *to seek*], **appetere, appetīvī, appetītus,** *to grasp after, seek, pursue.*
*****etiam sī,** *even if, although.*
***magister, magistrī,** m., *teacher.*

147 **placēns, placentis,** *pleasing.*
cōnsistō, cōnsistere, cōnstitī, *to stop, stand still; to pause.*

148 ***litterae, -ārum,** f. pl., *letters* (of the alphabet); *letter* (i.e., an epistle); *literature; learning; liberal education.*
****labōrō, -āre, -āvī, -ātus,** *to work.*

"Iam quattuor partēs dīcit; sī vīxerit, habēbis ad latus servulum. 141
Nam quicquid illī vacat, caput dē tabulā nōn tollit. Ingeniōsus 142
est et bonō fīlō, etiam sī in avēs morbōsus est. Ego illī iam trēs 143
cardēlēs occīdī, et dīxī quia mustella comēdit. Invēnit tamen ali- 144
ās nēniās, et libentissimē pingit. Cēterum iam Graeculīs calcem 145
impingit et Latīnās coepit nōn male appetere, etiam sī magister 146
eius sibi placēns sit nec ūnō locō cōnsistit, sed venit. . . . scit qui- 147
dem litterās, sed nōn vult labōrāre. 148

(paragraph continued on page 107)

141 quattuor partēs: his table of division by fours.
     sī vīxerit, habēbis: future more vivid condition; the future per-
     fect is used colloquially in the protasis where the sense re-
     quires a simple future (see p. 248).
142 quicquid illī vacat: *whatever spart time he has.*
     dē: here used where ā would be expected.
143 bonō fīlō: ablative of description, *of.* . . .
     in avēs morbōsus: M. Cornelius Fronto (ca. A.D. 100–166) de-
     scribes his son as fond of little birds, especially chickens, pi-
     geons, and sparrows; Fronto admits that he himself was at-
     tracted to birds from his earliest infancy (Fronto, Loeb, Vol. 2,
     pp. 172–173).
     illī: colloquial for *eī.*
144 dīxī quia . . . comēdit: vulgar use of quia, *that,* and indicative in-
     stead of the normal accusative and infinitive in indirect state-
     ment; see II.2.119–120 (see p. 250).
145 Graeculīs (litterīs) calcem impingit: Echion seems to mean
     simply that his son has now put aside his Greek and advanced
     to Latin studies (the normal sequence), but the language he
     uses is stronger than is necessary to convey this idea and sug-
     gests rebellion against Greek studies. The diminutive Grae-
     culīs seems contemptuous.
147 sibi placēns: *self-satisfied, conceited.*
     sit: subjunctive used as a vulgar affectation where the indicative
     would be correct, see p. 250; some editors, however, read fit, *is
     becoming.*
     nec ūnō locō cōnsistit: perhaps = he does not stick to his job.
     sed venit: some words appear to have been lost from the sen-
     tence here; perhaps the teacher comes to Echion to demand
     higher pay or looking for some further employment.
     scit . . . labōrāre: the subject is now probably Echion's son,
     whom Echion thinks is now literate enough but lazy.

149   doctus, -a, -um [doceō, docēre, docuī, doctus, *to teach*], *learned,*
      scholarly.
      **cūriōsus, -a, -um, *careful, thoughtful, diligent.*
      ***plūs . . . quam, *more than.*
      doceō, docēre, docuī, doctus, *to teach.*
150   fēriātus, -a, -um, *keeping holiday; idle.*
      fēriātus diēs, *holiday.*
      ***soleō, solēre, solitus sum + infin., *to be accustomed* (to).
      ***domus, -ūs, f., *house, home.*
      domum, *to home, home.*
151   contentus, -a, -um, *content.*
      **emō, emere, ēmī, ēmptus, *to buy.*
      **aliquot, indecl. adj., *several, some.*
      liber, librī, m., *book.*
      libra, vulgar, affected n. for m. (see p. 242).
152   rubricātus, -a, -um, *colored red, having rubrics* (headings) *in red.*
      libra rubricāta, *law books with titles of laws in red.*
      domūsiō, domūsiōnis, f. [rare vulgar compound, see p. 246],
      home-use [domus, -ūs, f., *home* + ūsiō, ūsiōnis, f., *use*], *use at*
      home.
      ***aliquis, aliquis, aliquid, indef. pron., *someone, anything, some-*
      thing, anything.
      **iūs, iūris, n., *law.*
153   *gustō, -āre, -āvī, -ātus, *to taste; to have superficial knowledge of.*
      ***pānis, pānis, pānium, m., *bread.*
      **litterae, -ārum, f. pl., *letters* (of the alphabet); *letter* (i.e., an epis-
      tle); *literature; learning; liberal education.*
      satis, adv., *enough, sufficiently.*
      inquinō, -āre, -āvī, -ātus, *to befoul, pollute, stain.*
154   *quod sī, *but if, and if.*
      resiliō [re- + saliō, *to jump*], resilīre, resiliī, *to spring back from,*
      to shrink from.
      **dēstinō, -āre, -āvī, -ātus, *to fix, resolve, intend.*
      artificium, -ī, n., *profession, trade.*
      *doceō, docēre, docuī, doctus, *to teach.*
155   tōnstrīnum, -ī, n. [tōnsor, tōnsōris, m., *barber*], *barber's trade.*
      praecō, praecōnis, m., *crier, herald, auctioneer.*
      certē, adv., *certainly.*
      causidicus, -ī, m., *pleader of causes, advocate* [causa, -ae, f., *cause;*
      case + dīcō, dīcere, *to say; to plead*].
156   *auferō [ab- + ferō], auferre, abstulī, ablātus, irreg., *to carry off,*
      take away.
      ***nisi, conj., *unless, except.*

"Est et alter nōn quidem doctus, sed cūriōsus, quī plūs docet 149
quam scit. Itaque fēriātīs diēbus solet domum venīre, et quic- 150
quid dederis, contentus est. Ēmī ergō nunc puerō aliquot libra 151
rubricāta, quia volō illum ad domūsiōnem aliquid dē iūre 152
gustāre. Habet haec rēs pānem. Nam litterīs satis inquinātus 153
est. Quod sī resilierit, dēstināvī illum artificium docēre, aut 154
tōnstrīnum aut praecōnem aut certē causidicum, quod illī 155
auferre nōn possit nisi Orcus. 156

(paragraph continued on page 109)

149 **Est et alter**: supply **magister**.
  doctus . . . docet: note the play on words.
150 **domum**: to Echion's house, not his own home. He comes on
  holidays expecting a handout from his pupil's father. It was
  customary to eke out the scanty pay of teachers with presents.
  quicquid dederis: = **sī quid dederis**, *if you give* (lit., *will have
  given*) (him) *anything*.
151 **est**: instead of **erit**, as being more vivid.
  nunc: not *now*, but *under these circumstances*.
152 **aliquid dē iūre**: informal use of prepositional phrase instead of
  partitive genitive (**aliquid iūris**) (see p. 248).
  aliquid dē iūre gustāre: the double meaning (see vocabulary
  list) of **gustāre** triggers a pun on **iūre** by calling to mind the
  homonym **iūs, iūris**, n., *broth, sauce*.
153 **Habet haec rēs** (i.e., law) **pānem**: proverbial, there's money in it.
  inquinātus: *befouled*, a vulgar expression for the more usual **im-
  būtus**, *tinged, imbued, initiated*.
154 **resilierit**: i.e., rebels (lit., will have rebelled) against the study of
  law.
155 **tōnstrīnum**: for the intellectual limitations of the barber's trade,
  see Martial 7.64, who comments that Cinnamus, the best barber
  in Rome, when he received a windfall, became a knight, and
  moved to Sicily, could do nothing interesting with his new-
  found leisure such as becoming a rhetorician, professor,
  teacher, or philosopher because of his lack of education but
  could only become a barber again.
  praecōnem: in another epigram (5.56) Martial, perhaps with
  tongue in cheek, recommends that a certain man named Lupus
  not entrust his son to teachers of grammar or rhetoric and not
  allow him to read Cicero or Vergil or to become a poet. If the
  son wishes to make money, he should become a harp- or flute-
  player, and if he is not very bright he should become an auc-
  tioneer (**praecō**) or an architect. *(notes continued on next page)*

causidicum: for a satirical picture of the life, activities, and earnings of advocates in Rome, see Juvenal 7.105–149.

quod . . . nōn possit: relative clause of characteristic, *which* (nothing) *except Orcus* (i.e., death) *could take from him* (illī, dative of separation).

157 *ideō, adv., *for that/this reason, therefore.*
***quōtīdiē, adv., *daily.*
    cōtīdiē, colloquial variant (see p. 241).
clāmō, -āre, -āvī, -ātus, *to shout.*
Prīmigenius, -ī, m. [see p. 246], *First-Born* (a common name given to the sons of slaves; the name of Echion's son).
    Prīmigenī, vocative.
**crēdō, crēdere, crēdidī, crēditus + dat., *to believe.*
*discō, discere, didicī, *to learn.*
158 *causidicus, -ī, m., *pleader of causes, advocate* [causa, -ae, f., *cause; case* + dīcō, dīcere, *to say; to plead*].
**discō, discere, didicī, *to learn.*
159 famēs, famis, f., *hunger.*
labrum, -ī, n., *lip, mouth.*
abigō [ab- + agō], abigere, abēgī, abāctus, *to drive away.*
**modo, adv., *only recently, just now.*
collum, -ī, n., *neck.*
circumferō, circumferre, circumtulī, circumlātus, irreg., *to carry around.*
160 onus, oneris, n., *burden.*
*vēnālis, -is, -e, *for sale.*
adversus, prep. + acc., *against.*
161 extendō, extendere, extendī, extentus, *to stretch out, extend.*
***litterae, -ārum, f. pl., *letter* (i.e., an epistle); *literature; learning; liberal education.*
***thēsaurus, -ī, m. [Greek loan word], *treasure.*
    thēsaurum, vulgar, affected n. for m. (see p. 242).
*artificium, -ī, n., *profession, trade.*
***numquam, adv., *never.*
162 morior, morī, mortuus sum, *to die.*

"Ideō illī cōtīdiē clāmō: 'Prīmigenī, crēde mihi, quicquid discis,   157
tibi discis. Vidēs Philerōnem causidicum: sī nōn didicisset,   158
hodiē famem ā labrīs nōn abigeret. Modo modo collō suō cir-   159
cumferēbat onera vēnālia, nunc etiam adversus Norbānum sē   160
extendit. Litterae thēsaurum est, et artificium numquam   161
moritur.'"   162

---

158   **tibi discis**: dative of advantage, *for your own good.*
Philerōnem: Echion declines the name incorrectly, as if the nominative were **Philerō** and the genitive **Philerōnis**; the correct
accusative form is **Philerōtem** (see the vocabulary entry at line
27) (see p. 243).
sī nōn didicisset: i.e., if he hadn't gone to school; pluperfect
subjunctive in past contrary-to-fact protasis with present contrary-to-fact apodosis (**abigeret**).

159   **Modo modo**: colloquial repetition of words (see p. 251).
collō suō: ablative of means.

160   **onera vēnālia**: perhaps firewood.
adversus Norbānum sē extendit: i.e., he is beginning to com-
pete for political popularity with Norbanus; see line 121.

161   **Litterae . . . moritur**: the two halves of Echion's sentence are
given equal grammatical weight, but clearly his view is that although learning is a treasure, still a trade is a good thing.
Litterae . . . est: the verb agrees with the predicate nominative,
thēsaurum.

For further background on freedmen in the Roman world, see Jo-Ann
Shelton, *As the Romans Did*, "Freedmen," pp. 190–205.

1   ***medius, -a, -um,** *middle, middle of.*

  ***aiō, defective verb used mainly in present and imperfect indicative, *to say.*

  *clīvus, -ī, m., *slope, hill.*

2   *****labōrō, -āre, -āvī, -ātus,** *to work; to labor, toil.*

  commundō [con- + mundō, *to make clean***], -āre, -āvī, -ātus,** *to clean thoroughly.*

  **symphōnia, -ae, f. [Greek loan word], *music.*

  *mēnsa, -ae, f., *table.*

  **albus, -a, -um, *white.*

3   **sūs, suis,** m./f., *pig.*

  *addūcō, addūcere, addūxī, adductus, *to bring (in)*

  capistrum, -ī, n., *halter, muzzle.*

  tintinnābulum, -ī, n., *bell.*

  *cultus, -a, -um, *adorned.*

4   **bīmus, -a, -um,** *two years old.*

  nōmenclātor, nōmenclātōris, m., *name-caller* (slave who tells his master the names of the people he meets and who announces the courses as they are served at a banquet; here he gives the ages of the pigs).

    nōmenculātor, variant spelling.

  trīmus, -a, -um, *three years old.*

5   ***tertius, -a, -um,** *third.*

  **vērō, adv., *but, however, indeed.*

  sexennis, -is, -e, *six years old.*

  petauristārius, -ī, m. [Greek base, *peteuron* = Latin **peteurum/ petaurum, -ī, n.,** *trapeze*], *tumbler, rope dancer, acrobat.*

6   **intrāsse, = intrāvisse.**

  **porcus, -ī, m., *pig.*

  sīcut, conj., *just as.*

  ***circulus, -ī, m., *circle, group of people* (here of circles of spectators watching acrobats or jugglers perform in the streets).

  *mōs, mōris, m., *manner, custom.*

  portentum, -ī, n., *omen; unnatural happening; marvelous trick.*

II.

TRIMALCHIO'S DINNER

3. A Joke on the Guests

During a pause in the incredible extravagance of a dinner that Trimalchio has prepared for his friends—a dinner full of vulgar surprises, buglers, tumblers, and luxury galore—Trimalchio plays an elaborate joke on his guests. To the surprise of Encolpius, the narrator, three live white pigs are brought into the dining room.

[47–49] Nec adhūc sciēbāmus nōs in mediō, quod aiunt, clīvō   1
labōrāre. Nam commundātīs ad symphōniam mēnsīs trēs albī   2
suēs in trīclīnium adductī sunt capitrīs et tintinnābulīs cultī, quō-   3
rum ūnum bīmum nōmenculātor esse dīcēbat, alterum trīmum,   4
tertium vērō iam sexennem. Ego putābam petauristāriōs intrās-   5
se et porcōs, sīcut in circulīs mōs est, portenta aliqua factūrōs.   6

(paragraph continued on page 113)

1 **quod aiunt:** *as they say,* underscoring the proverbial expression **in mediō . . . clīvō labōrāre.**
6 **factūrōs:** supply **esse,** *that the pigs would. . . .*

111

7   expectātiō, expectātiōnis, f., *waiting, expectation.*
    *discutiō [dis- + quatiō, *to shake; to strike*], discutere, discussī, discussus, *to strike apart, shatter; to dispel.*
8   ***statim, adv., *immediately.*
    *gallus, -ī, m., *cock.*
    *gallīnāceus, -a, -um, *of/belonging to the domestic breed of poultry.*
    *gallus gallīnāceus, *poultry-cock.*
    penthiacum, -ī, n. [vulgar, found only here, see p. 247; Greek base], *hash* (as if made from the fragments of Pentheus, king of Thebes, who was torn to pieces by frenzied women).
9   eiusmodī, *of that kind, such.*
    *nēnia, -ae, f., *funeral song, dirge; jingle;* pl., *trifles, nonsense.*
    coquus, -ī, m., *cook.*
    cocī, colloquial variant of coquī (see p. 241).
    *vitulus, -ī, m., *calf.*
10   aēnum, -ī, n., *bronze vessel/cauldron.*
    coquō, coquere, coxī, coctus, *to cook.*
    aēnō coctōs, *pot-roasted.*
    *continuō, adv., *immediately, without delay.*
    *coquus, -ī, m., *cook.*
    cocum, colloquial variant of coquum (see p. 241).
    vocō, -āre, -āvī, -ātus, *to call.*
11   expectō [ex- + spectō, *to look at*], -āre, -āvī, -ātus, *to await, wait for.*
    ēlectiō, ēlectiōnis, f., *choice, selection.*
    nātus, -ūs, m., *birth.*
    **occīdō [ob- + caedō, *to cut*], occīdere, occīdī, occīsus, *to cut down; to kill, slay.*

Sed Trimalchiō expectātiōne discussā, "Quem," inquit, "ex eīs   7
vultis in cēnam statim fierī? Gallum enim gallīnāceum, penthi-   8
acum et eiusmodī nēniās rūsticī faciunt: meī cocī etiam vitulōs   9
aēnō coctōs solent facere." Continuōque cocum vocārī iussit, et   10
nōn expectātā ēlectiōne nostrā maximum nātū iussit occīdī.   11

---

  7 **expectātiōne discussā**: ablative absolute, i.e., making us wait no
      longer.
      Quem . . . ex eīs: *which one of them. . . .*
  9 **vitulōs**: i.e., whole calves.
11 **nōn expectātā ēlectiōne nostrā**: ablative absolute, i.e., without
      waiting for us to choose.
      maximum nātū: *the biggest with respect to birth = the oldest.*

12　clārus, -a, -um, *clear, distinct.*
　　*vōx, vōcis, f., voice.
　　quotus, -a, -um, *which, what* (in number, order).
　　decuria, -ae, f., *group of ten; division; squad.*
13　quadrāgēsimus, -a, -um, *fortieth.*
　　respondeō, respondēre, respondī, respōnsūrus, *to answer, reply.*
　　ēmptīcius [emō, emere, ēmī, ēmptus, *to buy*], -a, -um, *bought,*
　　　purchased.
　　*an, particle, *whether; or.*
　　nāscor, nāscī, nātus sum, *to be born.*
14　neuter, neutra, neutrum, *neither (of two).*
　　**coquus, -ī, m., *cook.*
　　cocus, colloquial variant of coquus (see p. 241).
　　testāmentum, -ī, n., *will, testament.*
　　Pānsa, -ae, m., *Pansa.*
15　**dīligenter, adv., *carefully, diligently.*
　　pōnō, pōnere, posuī, positus, *to put, place;* here = appōnō [ad- +
　　　pōnō], *to set before one, serve.*
16　*decuria, -ae, f., *group of ten; division; squad.*
　　viātor, viātōris, m., *runner; messenger; official agent.*
　　**conicio, conicere, coniēcī, coniectus, *to throw, hurl, cast, put.*
　　***coquus, -ī, m., *cook.*
　　cocum, colloquial variant of coquum (see p. 241).
　　potentia, -ae, f., *force, power.*
17　admoneō, -ēre, -uī, -itus + gen., *to remind* (of).
　　culīna, -ae, f., *kitchen.*
　　obsōnium, -ī, n. [Greek loan word], *shopping items, food* (here the
　　　pig).

Trimalchio diverts the attention of the guests by taking the opportunity to pa-
rade his grand status. One of the pigs is led off to be cooked.

Et clārā vōce: "Ex quotā decuriā es?" Cum ille sē ex   12
quadrāgēsimā respondisset, "Ēmptīcius an," inquit, "domī nā-   13
tus?" "Neutrum," inquit cocus, "sed testāmentō Pānsae tibi re-   14
lictus sum." "Vidē ergō," ait, "ut dīligenter pōnās; sī nōn, tē   15
iubēbō in decuriam viātōrum conicī." Et cocum quidem poten-   16
tiae admonitum in culīnam obsōnium dūxit.   17

---

12 **decuriā**: Trimalchio's organization of his domestic slaves would be
    applauded by Columella, who in his book on agriculture (1.9.7–
    8) recommends that slaves working on large farms be organized
    into squads of ten men each so that they can be easily supervised
    and so that they will take an interest in their work and compete
    with one another.

13 **quadrāgēsima**: Trimalchio had at least 400 slaves.

16 **in decuriam viātōrum**: the terms **decuria viātōrum** and **collē-
    gium viātōrum** were titles of associations or guilds of agents
    employed by Roman magistrates on official errands. Trimalchio
    has such a **decuria** in his own household!
    conicī: present passive infinitive.
    potentiae: i.e., of Trimalchio.

17 **obsōnium dūxit**: i.e., the pig led the cook to the kitchen.

18   mītis, -is, -e, *ripe, mellow, gentle.*
     **vultus, -ūs, m., *face; expression.*
     respiciō [re- + speciō, *to see*], respicere, respexī, respectus, *to look at.*
     ***vīnum, -ī, n., *wine.*
19   mūtō, -āre, -āvī, -ātus, *to change, replace.*
     **oportet, -ēre, -uit, impersonal + subjn. without ut, *it is proper/right; ought.*
20   ***deus, -ī, m., *god.*
     **beneficium, -ī, n., *kindness, favor.*
     ***emō, emere, ēmī, ēmptus, *to buy.*
     salīva, -ae, f., *flavor, taste.*
21   suburbānum, -ī, n., *estate/farm near the city.*
     *nāscor, nāscī, nātus sum, *to be born, be produced.*
     **nōscō, nōscere, nōvī, nōtus, *to become acquainted with; pf., to know.*
22   cōnfīnis, -is, -e, *having common boundaries* [fīnis, fīnis, fīnium, m.], *bordering, adjoining.*
     Terraciniēnsis [Tarraciniēnsis], Terraciniēnsis, Terraciniēnsium, m., *citizen of Terracina/Tarracina* (city on the western coast of Italy about half way between Rome and Naples).
     Tarentīnus, -ī, m., *citizen of Tarentum* (a town in the heel of Italy).
     coniungō, coniungere, coniūnxī, coniūnctus, *to join, connect.*
23   agellus, -ī, m. [dim. of ager, agrī, m., *field*], *little field.*
     Āfrica, -ae, f., *Africa* (Roman province on the north coast of the continent of Africa).
     libet, libēre, libuit or libitum est, impersonal, *it pleases.*
     fīnis, fīnis, fīnium, m., *boundary;* pl., *territory, land, country.*
24   nāvigō, -āre, -āvī, -ātus, *to sail.*

Further diversion: Trimalchio the megalomanic.

Trimalchiō autem mītī ad nōs vultū respexit et, "Vīnum," in- 18
quit, "sī nōn placet, mūtābō: vōs illud oportet bonum faciātis. 19
Deōrum beneficiō nōn emō, sed nunc quicquid ad salīvam facit, 20
in suburbānō nāscitur eō, quod ego adhūc nōn nōvī. Dīcitur 21
cōnfīne esse Terraciniēnsibus et Tarentīnīs. Nunc coniungere 22
agellīs Siciliam volō, ut cum Āfricam libuerit īre, per meōs fīnēs 23
nāvigem." 24

---

18 **mītī . . . vultū:** ablative of manner.
19 **vōs** (nom., subject of **faciātis**) **illud oportet bonum faciātis:** i.e.,
   it's up to you to make it good by drinking it; cf. Martial (5.78.16),
   who invites a friend to a modest dinner and comments, **vīnum
   tū faciēs bonum bibendō;** in both Petronius and Martial the
   wine is not of the highest quality, and the guests' drinking it is its
   only recommendation.
20 **nōn emō:** = **nihil emō,** *I buy nothing* (because everything he needs
   grows on his own farms).
   quicquid ad salīvam facit: i.e., whatever makes your mouth water.
21 **eō, quod ego adhūc nōn nōvī:** i.e., on that farm that I have not
   even visited yet (as opposed to his numerous other farms that he
   does not mention here).
22 **cōnfīne esse Terraciniēnsibus et Tarentīnīs:** a huge farm if it ad-
   joins both Terracina and Tarentum, which are about 150 miles
   apart! Seneca (*Epistulae morales* 89.20) inveighs against those who
   would enlarge their farms to the size of whole provinces and
   nations and even surround whole seas with their estates.
23 **agellīs:** i.e., the farm just referred to; the diminutive is ironic, but it
   also expresses endearment. Trimalchio is fond of his dear little
   fields, even though he has not visited them yet.
   Āfricam: vulgar Latin often omits the preposition (**ad** or **in**) with
   names of countries (see p. 248).

25 *nārrō, -āre, -āvī, -ātus, *to tell, report, relate.*
   *contrōversia, -ae, f., *debate, controversy; matter* (for discussion);
   formal debate (in schools of rhetoric with pupils taking opposite
   sides); *subject* (of such a debate, usually involving a fictitious
   situation).
26 dēclāmō, -āre, -āvī, -ātus, *to declaim.*
   dēclāmāstī, = dēclāmāvistī.
   ***causa, -ae, f., *lawsuit, case.*
   *causās agere, *to plead cases.*
   *domūsiō, domūsiōnis, f. [rare vulgar compound, see p. 246,
   home-use [domus, -ūs, f., *home* + ūsus, -ūs, m., *use*], *use at home.*
27 ***discō, discere, didicī, *to learn.*
   studium, -ī, n., *eagerness; study.*
   fastīdiō, -īre, -īvī, -ītus, *to disdain.*
      fastīdītum (esse), perfect infinitive, vulgar, affected formation
      as if from a deponent verb (see p. 244).
   bybliothēca, -ae, f. [Greek loan word], *library.*
28 dīc, imperative of dīcō, dīcere.
29 peristasis, peristasis, f. [Greek loan word], *facts/circumstances* (of
   a case).
   dēclāmātiō, dēclāmātiōnis, f., *declamation, speech.*
30 *pauper, pauperis, m./f., *poor person.*
   dīves, dīvitis, *wealthy, rich;* as substantive, *rich man.*
   inimīcus, -a, -um, *hostile, unfriendly;* as substantive, *personal enemy.*
31 urbānus, -a, -um, *of the city* [urbs, urbis, urbium, f., *city*], *sophisti-
   cated, witty, clever.*
      urbānē (dictum), *cleverly stated.*
   *nesciō quam, *I don't know what, some.*
   **contrōversia, -ae, f., *debate, controversy; matter* (for discussion);
   formal debate (in schools of rhetoric with pupils taking opposite
   sides); *subject* (of such a debate, usually involving a fictitious
   situation).
32 expōnō, expōnere, exposuī, expositus, *to put forth, expound.*
33 ***contrōversia, -ae, f., *debate, controversy; matter* (for discussion);
   formal debate (in schools of rhetoric with pupils taking opposite
   sides); *subject* (of such a debate, usually involving a fictitious
   situation).

Yet further diversion: Trimalchio puts down the teacher of rhetoric

"Sed nārrā tū mihi, Agamemnōn, quam contrōversiam hodiē 25
dēclāmāstī? Ego etiam sī causās nōn agō, in domūsiōnem tamen 26
litterās didicī. Et nē mē putēs studia fastīdītum, III bybliothēcās 27
habeō, ūnam Graecam, alteram Latīnam. Dīc ergō, sī mē amās, 28
peristasim dēclāmātiōnis tuae." Cum dīxisset Agamemnōn: 29
"Pauper et dīves inimīcī erant," ait Trimalchiō, "Quid est pau- 30
per?" "Urbānē," inquit Agamemnōn et nesciō quam contrōver- 31
siam exposuit. Statim Trimalchiō, "Hoc," inquit, "sī factum est, 32
contrōversia nōn est; sī factum nōn est, nihil est." 33

---

25 **nārrā . . . quam contrōversiam . . . dēclāmāstī:** colloquial
parataxis of direct question instead of subordination with the
subjunctive (see p. 249).
Agamemnōn: the professor of rhetoric, see above, II.1.4.
27 **litterās didicī:** i.e., I learned to read and write.
nē . . . putēs: colloquial for **nōlī . . . putāre**, the usual expression of
a negative command.
III: changed to II by some editors. Defending **trēs**, Sedgwick remarks, "an absurd reading, and so probably right."
28 **sī mē amās:** = if you please.
29 **Cum dīxisset:** circumstantial clause with pluperfect subjunctive in
secondary sequence (**ait** = *he said*).
30 **Pauper et dīves inimīcī erant:** a commonplace theme for declamation.
Quid est pauper?: although Trimalchio rose from slavery to his
present fortune, he pretends not to know what a poor man is.
And in the manner of rhetorical debate, he interrupts and de-
mands a definition of terms. Agamemnon, who as a professor of
rhetoric is so poor that he has to sponge invitations to dinner
from the rich, pretends not to mind the boorish interruption of
his speech and actually flatters Trimalchio for his wit.
32 **Statim Trimalchiō:** Trimalchio interrupts again.
Hoc . . . sī factum est . . . : *if it was done, it's not a* **contrōversia** (in
the strict sense of a debate on a fictitious situation).

34 effūsus, -a, -um, *abundant, profuse.*
prōsequor, prōsequī, prōsecūtus sum, *to follow, attend, accompany.*
laudātiō, laudātiōnis, f., *praise; applause.*
35 ***rogō, -āre, -āvī, -ātus, *to ask.*
*cārus, -a, -um, *dear.*
numquid, interrog. particle = num, *surely not* (introducing a direct question expecting a negative answer).
36 duodecim, indecl. adj., *twelve.*
aerumna, -ae, f., *hardship, trouble, labor.*
Herculēs, Herculis, m., *Hercules* (Greek hero).
teneō, tenēre, tenuī, tentus, *to hold;* with or without memōriā, *to hold (in one's memory), remember.*
Ūlixēs, Ūlixis, m., *Ulysses* (= Odysseus, Greek hero).
*fābula, -ae, f., *story, tale.*
37 *quemadmodum, adv., *in what manner, how.*
Cyclōps, Cyclōpos, m., *Cyclops* (one-eyed monster of Greek mythology).
pollex, pollicis, m., *thumb.*
poricinō [vulgar, found only here, see p. 246], abl., meaning uncertain, perhaps *ring.*
extorqueō, extorquēre, extorsī, extortus, *to twist off, wrench away; to dislocate.*
38 **apud, prep. + acc., *at, in.*
Homērus, -ī, m., *Homer* (Greek epic poet).
legō, legere, lēgī, lēctus, *to read.*
Sibylla, -ae, f., *Sibyl* (the prophetess of Cumae in Campania near Naples, famed by Vergil as Aeneas' guide to the underworld).
39 Cūmae, -ārum, f. pl., *Cumae.*
Cūmīs, locative, *at Cumae.*
ampulla, -ae, f. [dim. of amphora, -ae, f., Greek loan word, *large, two-handled earthenware jar for holding wine*], *bottle, flask.*
***pendeō, pendēre, pependī, *to hang, hang down.*
illī, dat.
40 *respondeō, respondēre, respondī, respōnsus, *to answer, reply.*

Trimalchio shows up the scholar.

Haec aliaque cum effūsissimīs prōsequerēmur laudātiōnibus, 34
"Rogō," inquit, "Agamemnōn mihi cārissime, numquid 35
duodecim aerumnās Herculis tenēs, aut dē Ūlixe fābulam, 36
quemadmodum illī Cyclōps pollicem poricinō extorsit? Solēbam 37
haec ego puer apud Homērum legere. Nam Sibyllam quidem 38
Cūmīs ego ipse oculīs meīs vīdī in ampullā pendēre, et cum illī 39
puerī dīcerent: 'Σίβυλλα, τί θέλεις;' respondēbat illa: 'ἀποθανεῖν 40
θέλω.'" 41

---

34 **cum . . . prōsequerēmur**: circumstantial clause with imperfect subjunctive.
35 **Rogō . . . numquid . . . tenēs**: colloquial parataxis of direct question instead of subordination with the subjunctive (see p. 249). **Rogō** functions here merely as a bid for attention.
37 **illī**: dative of reference, *his.*
    pollicem poricinō extorsit: the uneducated Trimalchio displays his ignorance, as he garbles even the most familiar mythological tale. Compare Seneca's description of the pretentious and embarrassingly ignorant Calvisius Sabinus, a man "with the bank account and brains of a freedman," as Seneca describes him, who had great pretensions to learning but would forget the names of even the greatest Greek and Trojan heroes, Ulysses, Achilles, and Priam, and ended up buying slaves, each a specialist in one of the Greek poets. Calvisius made life miserable for his guests at banquets by asking the slaves to recite verses. He would try to repeat them but would break down in the middle of a word (*Epistulae morales* 27.5–6).
38 **Nam**: this should imply that Trimalchio also read about the Cumaean Sibyl in Homer.
39 **in ampullā pendēre**: the Sibyl, who had been granted immortality but not eternal youth, has grown so old and shrivelled that she lives in a bottle and longs to die. For her full story, see Ovid, *Metamorphoses* 14.130–153.
    cum . . . dīcerent: circumstantial clause with imperfect subjunctive in secondary sequence.
40 The Greek means: "Sibyl, what do you want? . . . I want to die." T. S. Eliot prefaced his "The Waste Land" with the sentence in lines 38–41 above.

42   *nōndum, adv., *not yet.*
efflō [ex- + flō, *to blow*], -āre, -āvī, -ātus, *to breathe out, blow out; to blether.*
*repositōrium, -ī, n., *portable stand for serving courses at meals.*
*sūs, suis, m./f., *pig.*
43   **mēnsa, -ae, f., *table.*
occupō, -āre, -āvī, -ātus, *to occupy, take up, fill.*
**mīror, -ārī, -ātus sum, *to wonder; to marvel at.*
celeritās, celeritātis, f., *speed, quickness, rapidity.*
44   iūrō, -āre, -āvī, -ātus, *to swear.*
**gallus, -ī, m., *cock.*
**gallīnāceus, -a, -um, *of/belonging to the domestic breed of poultry.*
**gallus gallīnāceus, *poultry-cock.*
***tam, adv., *so.*
*citō, adv., *quickly.*
percoquō, percoquere, percoxī, percoctus, *to cook through and through.*
45   tantō, *by so much.*
***magis, compar. adv., *more.*
***longē, adv., *far, by far.*
***porcus, -ī, m., *pig.*
46   paulō, adv., *by a little, a little.*
ante, adv., *before.*
**appāreō [ad- + pāreō, *to obey*], -ēre, -uī, -itūrus, *to appear.*
47   ***deinde, adv., *afterward, then, next.*
intueor, -ērī, -itus sum, *to consider, look at.*
48   exenterō [ex- + Greek *entera*, "guts, bowels"], -āre, -āvī, -ātus, *to gut* (clean out the inner organs, intestīna, -ōrum, n. pl.).
exinterātus, colloquial for exenterātus.
49   *vocō, -āre, -āvī, -ātus, *to call.*
**medium, -ī, n., *middle part, center.*
*cōnsistō, cōnsistere, cōnstitī, *to stand.*
***mēnsa, -ae, f., *table.*
50   trīstis, -is, -e, *sad.*
*oblīvīscor, oblīvīscī, oblītus sum, *to forget.*
*exenterō [ex- + Greek *entera*, "guts, bowels"], -āre, -āvī, -ātus, *to gut* (clean out the inner organs, intestīna, -ōrum, n. pl.).
exinterāre, colloquial for exenterāre.
51   *exclāmō, -āre, -āvī, -ātus, *to shout out.*
*piper, piperis, n., *pepper.*
cumīnum, -ī, n., *cumin* (a spice).
52   ***cōniciō [con- + iaciō, *to throw*], cōnicere, cōniēcī, cōniectus, *to throw together, put in, include.*
dēspoliō, -āre, -āvī, -ātus, *to rob, plunder; to undress.*
*mora, -ae, f., *delay.*

Re-enter the pig.

Nōndum efflāverat omnia, cum repositōrium cum sue in-   42
gentī mēnsam occupāvit. Mīrārī nōs celeritātem coepimus et   43
iūrāre, nē gallum quidem gallīnāceum tam citō percoquī po-   44
tuisse, tantō quidem magis, quod longē maior nōbīs porcus   45
vidēbātur esse quam paulō ante appāruerat.   46

---

42 **Nōndum efflāverat omnia:** a comic, satirical expression.
43 **mēnsam:** apparently a large table in the center (as opposed to the
    small tables that the individual guests have in front of them).
45 **tantō ... magis, quod:** *the more so because. . . .*

The forgetful cook about to be punished

Deinde magis magisque Trimalchiō intuēns eum, "Quid?   47
Quid?" inquit, "porcus hic nōn est exinterātus? Nōn meherculēs   48
est. Vocā, vocā cocum in mediō." Cum cōnstitisset ad mēnsam   49
cocus trīstis et dīceret sē oblītum esse exinterāre, "Quid? Oblī-   50
tus?" Trimalchiō exclāmat. "Putēs illum piper et cumīnum nōn   51
cōniēcisse. Dēspoliā." Nōn fit mora, dēspoliātur cocus atque in-   52
ter duōs tortōrēs maestus cōnsistit.   53

---

53 **tortor, tortōris,** m., *torturer.*
    ***maestus, -a, -um,** sad, dejected.*
    ****cōnsistō, cōnsistere, cōnstitī,** to stand.*

---

47 **magis magisque ... intuēns:** *looking at ... closer and closer.*
    Quid? Quid?: colloquial repetition of words (see p. 251); cf. **magis
    magisque** (47) and **Vocā, vocā** (49).
49 **in mediō:** instead of the correct **in medium**; confusion of place in
    which (abl.) and place to which (acc.) is common in vulgar Latin;
    cf. **fuī ... in fūnus** (II.2.12–13) (see pp. 247–248).
    Cum cōnstitisset ... dīceret: circumstantial clauses with pluper-
    fect and imperfect subjunctives.
50 **Oblītus?:** supply **es.**
51 **Putēs:** potential subjunctive, *you would think ...* (from the way he
    talks so lightly about not gutting it).
53 **tortōrēs:** for torturers in private homes, see Juvenal (6.474–485),
    who claims that some women hire torturers to punish their
    slaves.

54   *dēprecor, -ārī, -ātus sum, *to beg; to ask for pardon; to intercede.*
55   mittō, mittere, mīsī, missus, *to send; to dismiss, release.*
     *posteā, adv., *afterward.*
     *nostrum, gen. of nōs.
56   crūdēlis, -is, -e, *hard-hearted, cruel.*
     sevēritās, sevēritātis, f., *strictness, severity.*
     tenēre, = retinēre, *to hold* (myself) *back, restrain* (myself).
57   inclīnō, -āre, -āvī, -ātus, *to bend;* pass. in middle sense, *to bend oneself, lean.*
     *auris, auris, aurium, f., *ear.*
     inquam, I say.
58   ***dēbeō, -ēre, -uī, -itus, *to owe; ought, must.*
     *nēquissimus, -a, -um [superl. of nēquam, *wothless*], *most/very worthless.*
     **oblīvīscor, oblīvīscī, oblītus sum, *to forget.*
59   **exenterō [exinterō], -āre, -āvī, -ātus, *to gut, clean.*
     ignōscō, [in- + gnōscō, *to get to know*], ignōscere, ignōvī, ignō-tus + dat., *to forgive, pardon.*
     piscis, piscis, piscium, m., *fish.*
     praetereō, praeterīre, praeteriī, praeteritus, irreg., *to go past, ne-glect.*

61   at, conj., *but.*
     relaxō, -āre, -āvī, -ātus, *to loosen, ease, relax.*
     hilaritās, hilaritātis, f., *cheerfulness, gaiety, merriment.*
     ***vultus, -ūs, m., *face; expression.*
62   memoria, -ae, f., *memory.*
     palam, adv., *openly, publicly;* + abl., *in the presence of.*
     ***exenterō [exinterō], -āre, -āvī, -ātus, *to gut, clean.*
63   *recipiō [re- + capiō], recipere, recēpī, receptus, *to take/get back, regain.*
     culter, cultrī, m., *knife.*
     arripiō [ad- + rapiō, *to seize*], arripere, arripuī, arreptus, *to seize, snatch.*
     venter, ventris, m., *stomach, belly.*
64   *hinc atque illinc, *from this side and that.*
     timidus, -a, -um, *timid.*
     *secō, secāre, secuī, sectus, *to cut; to cut up.*
     **mora, -ae, f., *delay.*
     *plāga, -ae, f., *strike, blow; wound, cut, slit.*
     *pondus, ponderis, n., *weight.*
65   inclīnātiō, inclīnātiōnis, f., *leaning, bending, inclining.*
     *tomāculum, -ī, n., *sausage* (made from brain or liver).
     botulus, -ī, m., *black pudding, sausage,* German *Blutwurst.*

Reactions of the guests

Dēprecārī tamen omnēs coepērunt et dīcere: "Solet fierī;   54
rogāmus, mittās; posteā sī fēcerit, nēmō nostrum prō illō   55
rogābit." Ego, crūdēlissimae sevēritātis, nōn potuī mē tenēre,   56
sed inclīnātus ad aurem Agamemnonis, "Plānē," inquam, "hic   57
dēbet servus esse nēquissimus; aliquis oblīvīscerētur porcum   58
exinterāre? Nōn meherculēs illī ignōscerem, sī piscem praeterīs-   59
set."   60

---

55 **rogāmus, mittās:** = **rogāmus ut mittās,** indirect command with
    colloquial omission of **ut** (asyndeton; see p. 251).
    sī fēcerit . . . rogābit: future more vivid condition.
56 **crūdēlissimae sevēritātis:** genitive of description without the
    usual noun for it to depend on; translate *a man of. . . .*
58 **oblīvīscerētur:** deliberative subjunctive implying indignation,
    could anyone have . . . ?
59 **ignōscerem, sī . . . praeterīsset:** mixed contrary-to-fact condition
    with imperfect and pluperfect subjunctives, *I would not . . . if he
    had. . . .*

The climax of the joke: gutting the cooked pig

At nōn Trimalchiō, quī relaxātō in hilaritātem vultū, "Ergō,"   61
inquit, "quia tam malae memoriae es, palam nōbīs illum exin-   62
terā." Receptā cocus tunicā cultrum arripuit porcīque ventrem   63
hinc atque illinc timidā manū secuit. Nec mora, ex plāgīs pon-   64
deris inclīnātiōne crēscentibus tomācula cum botulīs effūsa sunt.   65

---

*effundō [ex- + fundō, to pour], effundere, effūdī, effūsus, to
pour out/forth; pass. with intransitive active sense, to flow forth.*

---

61 **At nōn Trimalchiō:** ellipsis, *But Trimalchio* (was) *not* (as severe as I
    would have been).
    relaxātō in hilaritātem vultū: ablative absolute.
62 **tam malae memoriae:** genitive of description.
63 **Receptā . . . tunicā:** ablative absolute.
64 **ponderis inclīnātiōne:** ablative of cause with **crēscentibus,** *because
    of the inclination/sagging of the weight* (of the sausages inside).
65 **crēscentibus:** modifying **plāgīs,** *the slits that were growing larger. . . .*

1 **Nīcerōs, Nīcerōtis,** m. [Greek word, "Lover of Victory"], *Niceros* (one of the freedmen).
   *respiciō [re- + speciō, *to see*], **respicere, respexī, respectus,** *to look at.*
2 **suāvius,** compar. adv., *more/rather pleasantly, agreeably, cheerfully.*
   suāvius esse, *to be rather/more cheerful.*
   convīctus, -ūs, m., *a living together, feast, banquet.*
   **nesciō quid, *I don't know what, something; I don't know why = for some reason.*
   *taceō, -ēre, -uī, *to be silent.*
   muttiō, -īre, -īvī, *to make the sound "mu"; to mutter, murmur.*
3 ***ōrō, -āre, -āvī, -ātus,** *to ask, beg.*
   fēlīx, fēlīcis, *fortunate, prosperous, happy.*
   **nārrō, -āre, -āvī, -ātus, *to tell, report, relate.*
   ūsus, -ūs, m., *use; habit; custom; occasion, opportunity.*
      ūsū venīre + dat., *to happen (to one) in the course of one's experience.*
4 ***dēlectō, -āre, -āvī, -ātus,** *to please, charm, delight.*
   affābilitās, affābilitātis, f., *courtesy, kindness.*
5 **lucrum, -ī,** n., *gain, profit; wealth, riches.*
   *trānseō, trānsīre, trānsiī, trānsitus, irreg., *to go over/across; to pass over/by.*
   dūdum, adv., *a short time ago, formerly.*
      iam dūdum, *some while ago now.*
   gaudimōnium -ī, n. [vulgar, found only here, see pp. 244, 246, = **gaudium, -ī,** n., *joy*], *joy, delight.*
   dissiliō [dis- + saliō, *to jump*], **dissilīre, dissiluī,** *to leap/burst asunder, fly apart.*
6 **tālis, -is, -e,** *such.*
   hilaris, -is, -e, *cheerful, merry, gay;* as neuter pl. substantive, *festivities.*
   *merus, -a, -um, *pure, unmixed, straight.*
   *etsī, conj. + indic., *even if, although.*
   **iste, ista, istud, *that* (often contemptuous).
   scholasticus, -ī, m. [Greek loan word], *teacher/student of rhetoric.*
7 *****nārrō, -āre, -āvī, -ātus,** *to tell, report, relate.*
8 ****auferō [ab- + ferō], auferre, abstulī, ablātus,** *to carry off, take/ carry away, remove.*
   satius, indecl. substantive, compar. adv., *better, preferable.*
   *dērīdeō, dērīdēre, dērīsī, dērīsus, *to laugh at, mock, deride, make a fool of.*
   *dictum, -ī, n., *saying, word.*
9 ***tālis, -is, -e,** *such.*
   **fābula, -ae, f., *story.*
   exordior, exordīrī, exorsus sum, *to begin.*

II.

TRIMALCHIO'S DINNER

4. Two Ghost Stories

Trimalchio invites Niceros to tell his story about what happened to him.

[61–64] Trimalchiō ad Nīcerōtem respexit et, "Solēbās," in-   1
quit, "suāvius esse in convīctū; nesciō quid nunc tacēs nec mut-   2
tīs. Ōrō tē, sīc fēlīcem mē videās, nārrā illud quod tibi ūsū   3
vēnit." Nīcerōs dēlectātus affābilitāte amīcī, "Omne mē," inquit,   4
"lucrum trānseat, nisi iam dūdum gaudimōniō dissiliō, quod tē   5
tālem videō. Itaque hilaria mera sint, etsī timeō istōs scholas-   6
ticōs, nē mē rīdeant. Vīderint: nārrābō tamen; quid enim mihi   7
aufert quī rīdet? Satius est rīdērī quam dērīdērī." Haec ubi dicta   8
dedit, tālem fābulam exorsus est.   9

---

3 **Ōrō tē . . . nārrā. . . . :** parataxis of direct command instead of subordination with **ut** and subjunctive (see p. 249).

sīc fēlīcem mē videās: subjunctive of wish, *so may you* (hope to) *see
me happy*, almost, *if you wish to see me happy.* The wish adds force
to the imperative **nārrā** (cf. II.2.84; see p. 252).

illud quod tibi ūsū vēnit: Niceros' story is his sole claim to fame,
and Trimalchio apparently asks him to tell it at every dinner he
attends.

5 **iam dūdum . . . dissiliō:** *I have been . . . for some while now* (and still
am. . . .).

tē tālem: i.e., **affābilem**, *courteous, kind.* Niceros has said nothing so
far at this dinner, and Trimalchio, knowing he has one good story
to tell, has courteously invited him to tell it.

6 **istōs** (contemptuous) **scholasticōs:** i.e., Agamemnon and Menelaus,
rhetoric teachers, and Eumolpus and Ascyltos, their companions.

7 **nē . . . rīdeant:** subjunctive dependent on a verb of fearing, introduced by **nē** for a positive fear, *I am afraid they may/will laugh at me.*

Vīderint: future perfect indicative with an admonitory or jussive
force, *Let them see to it,* i.e., I don't care: I'll tell my story anyway,
even if they laugh at me.

quid . . . mihi aufert: *what does it take away from me?* (dative of separation) = *what does it matter to me?*

8 **rīdērī quam dērīdērī:** *to be a source of laughter than of derision.*

Haec ubi dicta dedit: a formula found in several earlier authors, including Vergil, *Aeneid* 2.790, where it occurs in the context of a su-

pernatural occurrence. Aeneas, telling Dido about the fall of Troy and his escape from the city, quotes the words that the ghost of his wife Creusa spoke to him when he tried to find her in the burning city. After quoting her words, he says, "When thus she had spoken (**Haec ubi dicta dedit**), she left me weeping and wishing to say many things, and she withdrew into thin air." The freedman Niceros ironically echoes these words of Aeneas as he begins his own story of the supernatural.

---

10   **serviō, -īre, -īvī, -ītūrus**, *to be a slave.*
    ***habitō, -āre, -āvī, -ātus**, *to live.*
    vīcus, -ī, m., *row of houses, street.*
    angustus, -a, -um, *narrow.*
11   **Gāvilla, -ae**, f. [dim. of **Gāvia, -ae**, f., *Gavia*], *Gavilla.*
    ibi, adv., *there.*
    ****quōmodo**, adv., *how, as.*
12   ***uxor, uxōris**, f., *wife.*
    Terentius, -ī, m., *Terentius* (a Roman **nōmen**).
    caupō, caupōnis, m., *innkeeper.*
      cōpōnis, vulgar for **caupōnis** (see p. 240).
    *****nōscō, nōscere, nōvī, nōtus**, *to become acquainted with;* pf., *to know;* plpf., *knew.*
    Melissa, -ae, f. [Greek loan word meaning "bee"], *Melissa.*
    Tarentīnus, -a, -um, *of Tarentum* (a town in the heel of Italy).
13   **bacciballum, -ī**, n. [vulgar, found only here, see p. 245], onomatopoetic compound of uncertain derivation and meaning; perhaps from **bacca, -ae**, f., *berry;* the word probably refers to the woman's plumpness.
    corporāliter, adv., *bodily* [**corpus, corporis**, n.], *physically.*
14   ***propter**, prep. + acc., *because of, on account of.*
    venerius, -a, -um, *of/belonging to love* [**Venus, Veneris**, f. *Venus*, goddess of love], *sexual.*
    ***cūrō, -āre, -āvī, -ātus**, *to care (for).*
    benemōrius, -a, -um, an editorial conjecture [**bene**, adv., *well* + **mōrēs, mōrum**, m. pl., *character*] = **bonōrum mōrum**, *of good character.*
15   ***quis, qua/quae, quid**, indef. pron. [used after **sī, nisi, num**, and **nē**], *anyone, anything.*
    petō, petere, petiī, petītus, *to beg, ask; to seek.*
    ****negō, -āre, -āvī, -ātus**, *to say not, deny.*
    *****as, assis**, m., *as* (small copper coin).

Niceros begins his tale; his love for Melissa

"Cum adhūc servīrem, habitābāmus in vīcō angustō; nunc   10
Gāvillae domus est. Ibi, quōmodo diī volunt, amāre coepī   11
uxōrem Terentiī cōpōnis: nōverātis Melissam Tarentīnam, pul-   12
cherrimum bacciballum. Sed ego nōn meherculēs corporāliter   13
illam aut propter rēs veneriās cūrāvī, sed magis quod benemōria 14
fuit. Sī quid ab illā petiī, numquam mihi negātum; fēcit assem, 15
sēmissem habuī; quicquid habuī in illīus sinum dēmandāvī, nec 16
umquam fefellitus sum.   17

---

16 **sēmis, sēmissis, m.,** *half an* **as.**
   sinus, -ūs, m., *curve; fold of a garment over the breast; hanging fold of a*
   garment used as a purse.
   dēmandō, -āre, -āvī, -ātus, *to give, entrust, commit.*
17 ****umquam, adv.,** *ever.*
   fallō, fallere, fefellī, falsus, *to cheat, deceive.*
   fefellitus, vulgar reduplicated form based on the third principal
   part = **falsus** (see p. 244).

---

12 **uxōrem Terentiī cōpōnis . . . Melissam Tarentīnam:** Melissa is
   here described as the wife of an innkeeper with the **nōmen**
   Terentius, which indicates that he is not a slave. Apparently
   Melissa had previously been the mate (**contubernālis**) of an un-
   named slave, whose death is mentioned in line 18. The name
   Melissa suggests a courtesan. The details of her life are unclear,
   but they are not central to the story.
15 **negātum:** supply **est.**
   fēcit assem: = **sī assem fēcit,** colloquial parataxis instead of subordination as a condition (see p. 249).
16 **quidquid habuī:** i.e., whatever he earned as a slave, his **pecūlium.**

18   **contubernālis, contubernālis, contubernālium**, m./f., *tent-companion; mate* (of a slave, having the relationship but not the legal status of a husband or wife).

  ***vīlla, -ae**, f., *country estate*.

  suprēmus, -a, -um, superl. adj., *highest, last*.

  ***obeō, obīre, obiī, obitus**, irreg., *to meet with;* + **mortem** or **diem**, stated or implied, *to meet one's death, end one's days, die*.

19   **per**, prep. + acc., *through, by means of*.

  scūtum, -ī, n., *oblong shield*.

  ocrea, -ae, f., *greave* (usually pl., pieces of armor to cover a soldier's legs below the knees).

  aginō, -āre, -āvī [vulgar, found only here, see p. 245], meaning uncertain, perhaps, *to do one's best, hasten, scheme*.

  ****quemadmodum**, adv., *in what manner, how*.

20   ****perveniō, pervenīre, pervēnī, perventūrus**, *to come to, arrive*.

  angustiae, -ārum, f. pl., *narrowness, straightness; difficulty, distress*.

  *****appāreō** [ad- + **pāreō**, *to obey*], **-ēre, -uī**, *to appear, come in sight; to be revealed*.

21   ***forte**, adv., *by chance* [**fors, fortis**, f.].

  Capua, -ae, f., *Capua* (city just north of Naples).

  ****exeō, exīre, exiī, exitus**, irreg., *to go out, depart*.

  scrūta, -ōrum, n. pl., *odds and ends, junk*.

  scītus, -a, -um, *wise to, expert; nice, excellent*.

  expediō, -īre, -īvī, -ītus, *to free the feet* [**pēs, pedis**, m.], *set free, bring out; to prepare for use; to supply, provide;* here, *to dispose of by sale*.

  ***nancīscor, nancīscī, nactus sum**, *to obtain, receive, get*.

22   ***occāsiō, occāsiōnis**, f., *opportunity, occasion*.

  ***persuādeō, persuādēre, persuāsī, persuāsus** + dat., but here + acc. (vulgar, cf. II.2.136, see p. 247), *to persuade, prevail upon* (someone to do something, **ut** + subjn.).

  hospes, hospitis, m., *visitor; guest; friend*.

  mēcum, = **cum mē**.

23   **quīntus, -a, -um**, *fifth*.

  mīliārium, -ī, n., *mile-stone*.

When Melissa's mate dies, Niceros decides to go to her side; a soldier accompanies him as he sets out before sunrise.

"Huius contubernālis ad vīllam suprēmum diem obiit. 18
Itaque per scūtum per ocream ēgī agināvī, quemadmodum ad 19
illam pervenīrem: scītis autem, in angustiīs amīcī appārent. 20
Forte dominus Capuae exierat ad scrūta scīta expedienda. Nac- 21
tus ego occāsiōnem persuādeō hospitem nostrum ut mēcum ad 22
quīntum mīliārium veniat. 23

(paragraph continued on page 133)

18 **ad vīllam**: colloquial for **apud vīllam**.
19 **per scūtum per ocream**: colloquial asyndeton (see p. 251); the expression may come from soldiers' or gladiators' slang, cf. our "by hook or by crook."
   ēgī agināvī: asyndeton again; the sound of the words is more important than their sense, perhaps *I hustled and bustled.*
20 **in angustiīs amīcī appārent**: proverbial, cf. the Latin saying **Amīcus certus in rē incertā cernitur** and our "A friend in need is a friend indeed."
21 **Capuae**: vulgar use of locative instead of accusative of place to which, *to Capua* (see p. 248).
   ad scrūta scīta expedienda: ad + gerundive to express purpose; perhaps *to sell some fine odds and ends.* Niceros' master was a merchant, and Capua was an important trading center. With his master out of the way, Niceros is free to go to visit his Melissa.
22 **ad quīntum mīliārium**: *as far as. . . .*

24	**mīles, mīlitis,** m., *soldier.*
	***fortis, -is, -e,** brave, strong.*
	apocūlō, -āre [hybrid vulgar coinage, found only here and one other place in Petronius, see pp. 245, 247], meaning uncertain; see note below text.
	***circā,** prep. + acc., *around, about.*
25	**gallicinium, -ī,** n. [colloquial compound, see p. 246], *cock-crowing* [**gallus, -ī,** m., *cock* + **canō, canere,** *to sing, crow*]; *daybreak, dawn.*
	***lūna, -ae,** f., *moon.*
	lūceō, lūcēre, lūxī, *to shine.*
	merīdiēs, merīdiēī, m., *midday, noon.*
	merīdiē, *at noon.*
	monumentum [monimentum], -ī, n., *funerary monument, tomb.*
26	**stēla, -ae,** f. [Greek loan word], *tombstone.*
	sēcēdō, sēcēdere, sēcessī, sēcessūrus, *to withdraw.*
	cantābundus, -a, -um [rare word, see p. 246; **cantō, -āre,** *to sing*], *singing.*
27	****numerō, -āre, -āvī, -ātus,** *to count.*

Erat autem mīles, fortis tamquam Orcus. Apocūlāmus nōs circā   24
gallicinia, lūna lūcēbat tamquam merīdiē. Vēnimus inter moni-   25
menta: homō meus coepit ad stēlās facere, sēcēdō ego cantābun-   26
dus et stēlās numerō.   27

---

24 **Erat autem. . . . numerō** (27): the particle **autem** connects the first
    sentence here with the previous sentence, but note that none of
    the other clauses in this breathless narrative contains a connect-
    ing particle; each clause stands by itself without connectives
    (asyndeton, see p. 252).
    Apoculāmus nōs (nom.): *We take off*; the root of the word may be
    Latin **oculus, -ī**, m., *eye* (with Greek *apo-* "from, out of") = *we take
    ourselves out of sight.* Or more probably, the root may be Latin
    cūlus, *buttocks, ass,* and the word may be obscene slang, *We arse
    off.*
25 **Vēnimus inter monimenta:** the tombs that line the road just out-
    side the walls of the town.
26 **ad stēlās:** colloquial for **apud stēlās.**
    facere: slang, = *to relieve himself.*

28   **respiciō [re- + speciō, *to see*], respicere, respexī, respectus, *to look at.*
     *comes, comitis, m./f., *companion.*
     exuō, exuere, exuī, exūtus, *to pull off, strip off; to disrobe.*
     **vestīmentum, -ī, n., *clothing;* pl., *clothes.*
28   secundum, prep. + acc., *by, next to.*
     *anima, -ae, f., *breath, spirit; breath of life.*
     nāsus, -ī, m., *nose.*
30   *mortuus, -a, -um, *dead.*
     *at, conj., *but.*
     circummingō, circummingere, circummīnxī, *to urinate around* (something).
     ***vestīmentum, -ī, n., *clothing;* pl., *clothes.*
31   **subitō, adv., *suddenly.*
     lupus, -ī, m., *wolf.*
     *iocor, -ārī, -ātus sum, *to jest, joke.*
     mentior, -īrī, -ītus sum, *to lie.*
     **nūllus, -a, -um, *no;* as pronoun, *no one.*
     nūllīus, gen. sing.
32   ***patrimōnium, -ī, n., *inheritance.*
     tantus, -a, -um, *of such a size, so great.*
33   *lupus, -ī, m., *wolf.*
     ululō, -āre, -āvī, -ātus, *to howl.*
     silva, -ae, f., *woods.*
     *fugiō, fugere, fūgī, *to flee.*

Suddenly Niceros sees an astonishing sight.

"Deinde ut respexī ad comitem, ille exuit sē et omnia vestī-   28
menta secundum viam posuit. Mihi anima in nāsō esse, stābam   29
tamquam mortuus. At ille circummīnxit vestīmenta sua, et   30
subitō lupus factus est. Nōlīte mē iocārī putāre; ut mentiar, nūl-   31
līus patrimōnium tantī faciō. Sed, quod coeperam dīcere,   32
postquam lupus factus est, ululāre coepit et in silvās fūgit.   33

---

29   **anima . . . esse:** historical infinitive used in excited narrative instead of a finite verb, = **erat.**
anima in nāsō: the ancients believed that at death the vital spirit
left the body through the nose or mouth. Niceros means he almost died of fright.

30   **circummīnxit:** with the magical purpose of protecting his clothing
while he was changed into a wolf.

31   **Nōlīte . . . putāre:** the usual negative imperative, lit., *don't wish to
think = don't think. . . .*
ut mentiar: result clause dependent on **tantī faciō,** *I consider . . . of
such great value that. . . . = no one's inheritance could make me lie.*

34   prīmitus, adv. [colloquial for prīmum], *at first.*
     *nesciō, -īre, -īvī, -ītus, *not to know, to be ignorant.*
35   ***tollō, tollere, sustulī, sublātus, *to lift; to take away, remove.*
     lapideus, -a, -um, *of stone, stony.*
     *morior, morī, mortuus sum, *to die.*
36   timor, timōris, m., *fear.*
     gladius, -ī, m., *sword.*
     stringō, stringere, strīnxī, strictus, *to draw* (a sword).
     matauitatau [vulgar, found only here, see p. 246], apotropaic
      magical syllables (cf. abracadabra).
     umbra, -ae, f., *shadow, shade, ghost.*
37   *caedō, caedere, cecīdī, caesus, *to cut; to cut down; to slay.*
     dōnec, conj., *until.*
     **vīlla, -ae, f., *country estate.*
     ***perveniō, pervenīre, pervēnī, perventūrus, *to come to, arrive.*
     *larva, -ae, f., *evil spirit, demon; ghost.*
38   **anima, -ae, f., *breath, spirit; breath of life.*
     *ēbulliō, ēbullīre, ēbulliī or ēbullīvī, *to boil up, bubble forth.*
     *sūdor, sūdōris, m., *sweat.*
     bifurcum, -ī, n., *crotch.*
     *volō, -āre, -āvī, -ātūrus, *to fly, move swiftly.*
39   **mortuus, -a, -um, *dead.*
     **vix, adv., *scarcely, with difficulty.*
     ***umquam, adv., *ever.*
     reficiō [re- + faciō], reficere, refēcī, refectus, *to make again; to*
      make strong again, revive.

He hesitates, then acts.

"Ego prīmitus nesciēbam ubi essem, deinde accessī, ut 34
vestīmenta eius tollerem: illa autem lapidea facta sunt. Quī morī 35
timōre nisi ego? Gladium tamen strīnxī et—matauitatau!—um- 36
brās cecīdī, dōnec ad vīllam amīcae meae pervenīrem. In larvam 37
intrāvī, paene animam ēbullīvī, sūdor mihi per bifurcum volā- 38
bat, oculī mortuī, vix umquam refectus sum. 39

---

34 **ut ... tollerem**: purpose clause with imperfect subjunctive in secondary sequence.

35 **lapidea**: the magic worked; the clothes will be protected until the soldier (now a wolf) turns back into a man.
Quī morī ... : Quī = Quis, *Who ...?* **morī**: historical infinitive = **mortuus est.**

37 **dōnec ... pervenīrem**: the perfect indicative would be normal here for an actual fact in past time; the use of the subjunctive is a vulgar affectation (see p. 250).
In larvam: vulgar for **Velut larva**, *Like a ghost.*

39 **volābat**: a strong metaphor; or read **undābat**, *was swelling forth.*

40 ***mīror, -ārī, -ātus sum, *to wonder.*
    sērō, adv., *late.*
41 *ante, adv., *before.*
    saltem, adv., *at least.*
    adiūtō, -āre, -āvī, -ātus + dat. here instead of usual acc., *to help.*
    adiūtāssēs, = adiūtāvissēs.
    **lupus, -ī, m., *wolf.*
    ***vīlla, -ae, f., *country estate* (here referring to the enclosure within which the house stood).
42 pecus, pecoris, n., *cattle, sheep.*
    lanius, -ī, m., *butcher.*
    sanguis, sanguinis, m., *blood.*
43 **dērīdeō, dērīdēre, dērīsī, dērīsus, *to laugh at, mock, deride, make a fool of.*
    **fugiō, fugere, fūgī, *to flee.*
44 lancea, -ae, f., *lance, spear.*
    *collum, -ī, n., *neck.*
    trāiciō [trāns- + iaciō, *to throw*], trāicere, trāiēcī, trāiectus, *to pierce, stab.*
    **operiō, operīre, operuī, opertus, *to close.*
    *amplius, compar. adv., *more, longer, further, again.*
45 lūx, lūcis, f., *light.*
    *clārus, -a, -um, *clear; bright.*
    raptim, adv., *by snatching/hurrying away; in a hurry/rush.*
    ***fugiō, fugere, fūgī, *to flee.*
46 *caupō, caupōnis, m., *innkeeper.*
    cōpō, vulgar for caupō (see p. 240).
    compīlō, -āre, -āvī, -ātus, *to plunder, rob.*
    *lapideus, -a, -um, *of stone, stony.*
47 *sanguis, sanguinis, m., *blood.*

Melissa tells him something else that is strange.

"Melissa mea mīrārī coepit, quod tam sērō ambulārem, et, 'Sī 40
ante,' inquit, 'vēnissēs, saltem nōbīs adiūtāssēs; lupus enim vīl- 41
lam intrāvit et omnia pecora tamquam lanius sanguinem illīs 42
mīsit. Nec tamen dērīsit, etiam sī fūgit; servus enim noster 43
lanceā collum eius trāiēcit.' Haec ut audīvī, operīre oculōs am- 44
plius nōn potuī, sed lūce clārā raptim domum fūgī tamquam 45
cōpō compīlātus, et postquam vēnī in illum locum in quō lapi- 46
dea vestīmenta erant facta, nihil invēnī nisi sanguinem. 47

---

40 **mīrārī coepit:** = mīrāta est.
quod . . . ambulārem: quod generally takes the subjunctive when
the reason is given as that of someone other than the speaker.
Sī . . . vēnissēs . . . adiūtāssēs: past contrary-to-fact condition with
pluperfect subjunctive, *If you had . . . , you would have. . . .*
41 **nōbīs adiūtāssēs:** unusual use of dative instead of accusative.
42 **omnia pecora tamquam . . . :** anacoluthon (a change of construction in the same sentence, leaving the first part unfinished); she
was going to say **omnia pecora occīdit,** *killed all our sheep,* but
backs off from such an exaggeration and concludes, *it let blood
from them* (**sanguinem illīs mīsit**) *just like a butcher.*
44 **operīre oculōs:** i.e., in order to go to sleep.
45 **lūce clārā:** *at dawn.*
cōpō compīlātus: the reference may be to a fable of Aesop (196, ed.
Halm), which combines the theme of an innkeeper who is robbed
with the tale of a werewolf. It goes as follows. A thief, wishing
to rob an inn, takes lodging there. On a festival day, the
innkeeper dresses in his best clothes. The thief is seated with
him in front of the inn, and he opens his mouth and howls. The
innkeeper asks why he does this. Before explaining, he says that
he will need the innkeeper to guard his clothes. Then he explains
that he often turns into a wolf and eats men after he has howled
three times. He opens his mouth and howls a second time. The
innkeeper, terrified, wants to flee, but the thief takes hold of his
beautiful new clothes and says, "Stay here and keep my clothes
so that I don't lose them." As he opens his mouth to howl a third
time, the innkeeper flees inside, leaving (in his haste to get away)
his beautiful new clothes in the hands of the thief.

48 ***vērō, adv., *but, however, indeed.*
  *iaceō, iacēre, iacuī, iacitūrus, *to lie.*
  *mīles, mīlitis, m., *soldier.*
  *lectus, -ī, m., *bed.*
49 bōs, bovis, m./f., *ox, bull, cow.*
    bovis, vulgar nom. sing. formed from stem found in gen. sing
      (see p. 243).
  **collum, -ī, n., *neck.*
  **medicus, -ī, m., *doctor.*
  **cūrō, -āre, -āvī, -ātus, *to care (for), look after.*
  intellegō, intellegere, intellēxī, intellēctus, *to understand.*
  versipellis [versō, *to keep turning* + pellis, pellis, pellium, f.,
    skin], versipellis, versipellium, m./f., *werewolf.*
50 **posteā, adv., *afterward.*
  **gustō, -āre, -āvī, -ātus, *to taste.*
51 ***occīdō [ob- + caedō, *to cut*], occīdere, occīdī, occīsus, *to cut
    down; to kill, slay.*
  exopīnissō, -āre [vulgar, found only here, see p. 246; formed from
    opīnor, -ārī, -ātus sum, *to think, believe* + -issō by analogy with
    the Greek verbal suffix -izō], *to think, believe.*
52 *mentior, -īrī, -ītus sum, *to lie.*
  genius, -ī, m., *genius* (tutelar deity of a person, one's guardian
    spirit/angel).
  *īrātus, -a, -um, *angry.*

When he returns home, he finally understands all.

"Ut vērō domum vēnī, iacēbat mīles meus in lectō tamquam   48
bovis, et collum illīus medicus cūrābat. Intellēxī illum ver-   49
sipellem esse, nec posteā cum illō pānem gustāre potuī, nōn sī   50
mē occīdissēs. Vīderint aliī quid dē hōc exopīnissent; ego sī   51
mentior, geniōs vestrōs īrātōs habeam."   52

---

48   **ut . . . vēnī: ut** + indicative = *as, when.*
49   **versipellem:** see Pliny, *Natural History* 8.80–82, for other stories of
     men turned into wolves, stories in which Pliny expresses disbe-
     lief.
50   **sī . . . occīdissēs:** protasis of past contrary-to-fact condition, *if you
     had. . . .*
51   **Vīderint aliī:** see note to line 7 above; *Let others see/decide. . . .*
     exopīnissent: indirect question with present subjunctive.
52   **habeam:** subjunctive of wish, *may I have. . . .*

53   **attonitus, -a, -um,** *amazed, astonished.*
*admīrātiō, admīrātiōnis,** f., *admiration, wonder.*
ūniversī, ūniversōrum, m. pl., *everyone.*
salvus, -a, -um, *safe, well, sound.*
*sermō, sermōnis,** m., *talk, conversation, speech.*
54   *quī, qua, quod,** indef. adj. [used after **sī, nisi, num,** and **nē**], *any.*
***fidēs, fideī,** f., *faith; trust; credibility.*
ut, exclamatory adv., *how!*
*pilus, -ī,** m., *hair.*
inhorrēscō, inhorrēscere, inhorruī, *to bristle, stand on end.*
55   **nūgae, -ārum,** f. pl., *idle talk, nonsense.*
***immō,** particle, *nay, on the contrary, rather.*
*certus, -a, -um,** *fixed, determined; dependable, reliable.*
56   **minimē,** adv., *least of all, not at all.*
*linguōsus, -a, -um** [vulgar, found only here and at II.2.34, see pp. 245, 246], *with an idle/malicious/garrulous tongue* [**lingua, -ae,** f.], *loquacious.*
horribilis, -is, -e, *terrible, fearful, dreadful.*
57   *asinus, -ī,** m., *ass, donkey.*
tēgulae, -ārum, f. pl., *roof-tiles.*

Trimalchio also decides to tell a ghost story

Attonitīs admīrātiōne ūniversīs, "Salvō," inquit, "tuō ser-   53
mōne," Trimalchiō, "sī qua fidēs est, ut mihi pilī inhorruērunt,   54
quia sciō Nīcerōnem nihil nūgārum nārrāre: immō certus est et   55
minimē linguōsus. Nam et ipse vōbīs rem horribilem nārrābō: 56
asinus in tēgulīs.   57

---

53 **Attontīs admīrātiōne ūniversīs**: ablative absolute.
    Salvō . . . tuō sermōne: ablative absolute, *your tale being sound =
    with all respect to the truth of your tale*; this would usually be said
    by someone about to correct a statement made by the other per-
    son. Trimalchio is instead trying (rather inelegantly) to make a
    transition to his own ghost story.
54 **sī qua fidēs est**: supply **mihi**, possessive dative, *if I have any credi-
    bility*, i.e., if you'll believe me.
    ut mihi pilī inhorruērunt: i.e., as I listened to Niceros' story.
55 **Nīcerōnem**: Trimalchio declines the name incorrectly as if the
    nominative were **Nīcerō** and the genitive **Nīcerōnis**; the correct
    accusative form is **Nīcerōtem** (see lines 1 and 4 above and the
    note on **Philerōnem**, II.2.158) (see p. 243).
    nihil nūgārum: *nothing of idle talk = no idle talk*.
57 **asinus in tēgulīs**: proverbial for a marvel or a portent—like a don-
    key that succeeded in getting onto the roof! Livy (36.37) records
    a portent of two head of cattle climbing a stairway to the roof of a
    house (**bovēs duōs . . . per scalās pervēnisse in tēgulīs aedifi-
    ciī**).

58 **capillātus, -a, -um, *having long hair* [capillus, -ī, m.].
   Chīus, -a, -um, *of Chios* (a Greek island).
59 gerō, gerere, gessī, gestus, *to bear; to behave; to conduct, carry on.*
   ipsimus, -ī, m. [superlative of ipse, which may be used to mean
      master = the man himself], *master.*
   dēlicātus, -ī, m., *favorite slave, sexual pet.*
   *dēcēdō, dēcēdere, dēcessī, dēcessūrus, *to go away; to die.*
   margarīta, -ae, f., *pearl; treasure.*
      margarītum, vulgar, affected n. for f. (see p. 243).
60 catamītus, -ī, m. [from Etruscan *Catmite*, from Greek *Ganymedes*,
      Zeus's/Jupiter's cup-bearer and homosexual pet], *homosexual
      pet.*
   numerus, -ī, m., *number;* here, pl., *the parts that form a whole.*
      numerum, = numerōrum.
   misellus, -a, -um [dim. of miser, misera, miserum], *wretched.*
61 *plangō, plangere, plānxī, plānctus, *to strike the breast; to bewail,
      mourn.*
   **nostrum, gen. of nōs.
   *plūrēs, plūrum [compar. of multī], m./f., *more; the majority;* here,
      a number of us.
   trīstimōnium, -ī, n. [vulgar, see pp. 244, 246, = trīstitia, -ae, f.; cf.
      gaudimōnium, line 5], *sadness, sorrow.*
   ***subitō, adv., *suddenly.*
   strix, strigis, f., *screech-owl* (which, according to ancient belief,
      sucked the blood of young children); *vampire, witch.*
      strīgae, vulgar first declension variant of strigēs (see p. 243).
62 lepus, leporis, m., *hare.*
   **persequor, persequī, persecūtus sum, *to follow after, pursue.*

It happened when he was still a child.

"Cum adhūc capillātus essem, nam ā puerō vītam Chīam 58
gessī, ipsimī nostrī dēlicātus dēcessit, meherculēs margarītum, 59
catamītus et omnium numerum. Cum ergō illum māter misella 60
plangeret et nostrum plūrēs in trīstimōniō essēmus, subitō strī- 61
gae coepērunt: putārēs canem leporem persequī. 62

---

58 **Cum . . . essem**: circumstantial clause with imperfect subjunctive.
vītam Chīam: the Chians were proverbial for effeminacy and soft-living.

60 **omnium numerum**: genitive of description, (a lad) *of all the parts* =
a boy of every perfection, one in a thousand; cf. the phrase **omnibus numerīs perfectus**, *perfect in every detail*.
Cum . . . plangeret . . . essēmus: circumstantial clause with imperfect subjunctives.

61 **strīgae coepērunt**: supply **strīdere**, *to screech*.

62 **putārēs**: potential subjunctive, *you would have thought*.

63   **Cappadox, Cappadocis,** *Cappadocian* (proverbially husky people).
     *validē, adv., *strongly, mightily, very.*
     valdē, syncopated variant (see p. 241).

64   **audāculus, -a, -um** [rare dim., see p. 245, of **audāx, audācis,** *bold*],
     bold.
     quī, exclamatory adv., *how!*
     valeō, -ēre, -uī, *to be strong.*
     *bōs, bovis, m./f., *ox, bull, cow.*
     **īrātus, -a, -um, *angry.*

65   ***audācter,** adv., *courageously, boldly, confidently.*
     *stringō, stringere, strīnxī, strictus, *to draw* (a sword).
     *gladius, -ī, m., *sword.*
     extrā, prep. + acc., *out, outside of.*
     ōstium, -ī, n., *door.*
     prōcurrō, prōcurrere, prōcucurrī, prōcursūrus, *to run/rush forward.*
     *involvō, involvere, involvī, involūtus, *to roll up, wrap up, cover.*
     *sinister, sinistra, sinistrum, *left.*

66   **cūriōsē,** adv., *carefully; in a special way.*
     *salvus, -a, -um, *safe, well, sound.*

67   ***tangō, tangere, tetigī, tāctus,** *to touch.*
     **medius, -a, -um, *middle, middle of.*
     *trāiciō [trāns- + iaciō, *to throw*], **trāicere, trāiēcī, trāiectus,** *to pierce, stab.*
     gemitus, -ūs, m., *groan.*

68   ****mentior, -īrī, -ītus sum,** *to lie.*

A slave decides to act.

"Habēbāmus tunc hominem Cappadocem, longum, valdē 63
audāculum et quī valēbat: poterat bovem īrātum tollere. Hic 64
audācter strictō gladiō extrā ōstium prōcucurrit, involūtā sinistrā 65
manū cūriōsē, et mulierem tamquam hōc locō—salvum sit quod 66
tangō—mediam trāiēcit. Audīmus gemitum, et—plānē nōn 67
mentiar—ipsās nōn vīdimus. 68

---

63 **valdē audāculum**: the colloquial abuse of diminutives is illus-
trated here where the diminutive (which has lost any real force)
is modified by **valdē**, *very*.
64 **quī valēbat**: **quī** is here exclamatory, *how strong he was!*
bovem īrātum tollere: i.e., he could outdo the feat of the leg-
endary athlete Milo of Croton (6th century B.C.), who carried a
heifer down the race course.
66 **cūriōsē**: *carefully* or *in a special way*—in either case as a protection
against the witches.
hōc locō: Trimalchio touches his chest or stomach.
salvum sit quod tangō: a parenthetical wish to avert any magical
effect of his having touched the same place where the witch was
struck.
67 **nōn mentiar**: potential subjunctive, *I wouldn't lie.*

69 **bārō, bārōnis,** m. [vulgar word-formation with ending in **-ō**, see p. 244; probably from Etruscan], *blockhead, simpleton.*
intrōversus, adv., *towards the inside, back inside, within the house.*
*__*prōiciō__ [**prō-** + **iaciō,** *to throw*], **prōicere, prōiēcī, prōiectus,** *to throw (forth), hurl.*
****lectus, -ī,** m., *bed.*
corpus, corporis, n., *body.*
70 **līvidus, -a, -um,** *leaden-colored, black and blue.*
*__*quasi,__ conj., *as if.*
flagellum, -ī, n., *whip.*
****caedō, caedere, cecīdī, caesus,** *to cut; to strike, beat.*
claudō , claudere, clausī, clausus, *to shut.*
  clūsō, vulgar for **clausō** (see p. 240).
*__*ōstium, -ī,__ n., *door.*
71 ****redeō, redīre, rediī, reditūrus,** irreg., *to go/come back, return.*
iterum, adv., *again, a second time.*
*****officium, -ī,** n., *duty, task.*
amplexor, -ārī, -ātus sum, *to embrace.*
  amplexāret, vulgar active for deponent (see p. 243).
*__*corpus, corporis,__ n., *body.*
72 ****tangō, tangere, tetigī, tāctus,** *to touch.*
maniceolum, -ī, n. or **-us, -ī,** m. [unattested variant of **maniculus, -ī,** m., *handful, bundle,* from **manus, -ūs,** f., *hand*], *little handful, bundle.*
  manuciolum, vulgar variant with *u* instead of *i* and *i* instead of *e* (see pp. 240, 241, 246).
strāmentum, -ī, n., *straw.*
73 *__*cor, cordis,__ n., *heart.*
intestīna, -ōrum, n. pl., *guts, intestines.*
quisquam, quisquam, quidquam/quicquam, indef. pron., *somebody, anybody, something, anything.*
*__*scīlicet,__ particle, *of course, certainly, evidently.*
74 *__*strix, strigis,__ f., *screech-owl* (which, according to ancient belief, sucked the blood of young children); *vampire, witch.*
  strīgae, vulgar first declension variant of **strigēs** (see p. 243).
*__*involō, -āre, -āvī, -ātus,__ *to fly at, rush upon* (to steal), *seize upon.*
*__*suppōnō__ [**sub-** + **pōnō**], **suppōnere, supposuī, suppositus,** *to put under; to put in the place of, substitute.*
strāmentīcius, -a, -um, *made of straw* [**strāmentum, -ī,** n.].
vavatō, vavatōnis, m. [vulgar word-formation with ending in **-ō,** see p. 244, found only here, see p. 246; based on baby syllables **va, va**], *doll, puppet.*

But he fails.

"Bārō autem noster intrōversus sē prōiēcit in lectum, et cor- 69
pus tōtum līvidum habēbat quasi flagellīs caesus. Nōs clūsō ōs- 70
tiō redīmus iterum ad officium, sed dum māter amplexāret cor- 71
pus fīliī suī, tangit et videt manuciolum dē strāmentīs factum. 72
Nōn cor habēbat, nōn intestīna, nōn quicquam: scīlicet iam 73
puerum strīgae involāverant et supposuerant strāmentīcium va- 74
vatōnem. 75

---

70 **clūsō ōstiō**: i.e., as soon as the door was closed.
71 **ad officium**: i.e., to our task of lamenting the dead boy.
dum . . . amplexāret: vulgar use of active for deponent and affected use of the imperfect subjunctive instead of the usual present indicative (see pp. 243, 250).
73 **Nōn . . . nōn . . . nōn**: anaphora (see p. 251).

76 ***oportet, -ēre, -uit, impersonal + subjn. without ut, *it is proper/ right; ought.*

***crēdō, crēdere, crēdidī, crēditus, *to trust; to believe.*

plūsscius, -a, -um [vulgar, found only here, see p. 246; plūs, adv., *more* + sciō, scīre, *to know*], *who know more* (than we do), *overwise, uncanny*

77 Nocturna, -ae, f., *woman of the night* [nox, noctis, noctium, f.], *witch.*

sūrsum, adv., *up, upward.*

deorsum, adv., *down, downward.*

*bārō, bārōnis, m. [vulgar word-formation with ending in -ō, see p. 244; probably from Etruscan], *blockhead, simpleton.*

78 post, prep. + acc., *after.*

factum, -ī, n., *happening, event.*

color, colōris, m., *color.*

*post, prep. + acc., *after.*

79 paucī, -ae, -a, *few.*

phrenēticus, -a, -um [Greek loan word], *mad, delirious.*

pereō, perīre, periī, peritūrus, irreg., *to pass away, die.*

80 *pariter, adv., *equally; at the same time, together.*

ōsculor, -ārī, -ātus sum, *to kiss.*

81 *Nocturna, -ae, f., *woman of the night* [nox, noctis, noctium, f.], *witch.*

***redeō, redīre, rediī, reditūrus, irreg., *to go/come back, return.*

Witches do exist!

"Rogō vōs, oportet crēdātis, sunt mulierēs plūssciae, sunt 76
Nocturnae, et quod sūrsum est, deorsum faciunt. Cēterum bārō 77
ille longus post hoc factum numquam colōris suī fuit, immō post 78
paucōs diēs phrenēticus periit." 79
Mīrāmur nōs et pariter crēdimus, ōsculātīque mēnsam rogā- 80
mus Nocturnās ut suīs sē teneant, dum redīmus ā cēnā. 81

---

77 **sunt . . . sunt**: anaphora (see p. 251).
78 **quod sūrsum est, deorsum faciunt**: i.e., they turn things upside
down, topsy turvy.
79 **colōris suī**: genitive of description; he never got his color back
again.
81 **ut suīs sē teneant**: subjunctive in indirect command. **suīs**: that
they keep themselves *to their own* (and not bother us).

1   **diffūsus, -a, -um**, *spread out; loosened; cheered, gladdened.*
     contentiō, contentiōnis, f., *contest, dispute.*
2   **aequē**, adv., *equally.*
     lac, lactis, n., *milk.*
     lactem, vulgar m. for n. (see p. 242).
     bibō, bibere, bibī, *to drink.*
3   ***fātum, -ī**, n., *fate; luck.*
     fātus, vulgar m. for n. (see p. 242).
     opprimō [ob- + **premō**, *to press*], **opprimere, oppressī, oppres-**
     sus, *to press down, oppress.*
     ****salvus, -a, -um**, *safe, well, sound.*
     ****citō**, adv., *quickly; speedily; soon.*
4   **līber, lībera, līberum**, *free.*
     *****gustō, -āre, -āvī, -ātus**, *to taste.*
     ****ad summam**, *in short, to be brief.*
     ***testāmentum, -ī**, n., *will, testament.*
5   ***manū mittō, mittere, mīsī, missus**, *to send by/from the hand,*
     emancipate, set free (of slaves).
     Philargyrus, -ī, m. [Greek word meaning "fond of money, avari-
     cious"], *Philargyrus.*
     fundus, -ī, m., *farm, estate.*
     lēgō, -āre, -āvī, -ātus, *to leave, bequeath.*
     ***contubernālis, contubernālis, contubernālium**, m./f., *tent-com-
     panion; mate* (of a slave, having the relationship but not the legal
     status of a husband or wife).
6   **Cariō, Cariōnis**, m. [Greek name meaning "a little Carian"], *Cario*
     (a common Greek slave name).
     īnsula, -ae, f., *island; apartment house; single apartment.*
     vīcēsima, -ae, f., *the twentieth part* [**pars, partis, partium**, f.] *or five
     percent of the value of a slave* (paid as a tax when a slave was
     freed).
     *****lectus, -ī**, m., *bed.*
     sternō, sternere, strāvī, strātus, *to spread, prepare, arrange.*
7   **Fortūnāta, -ae**, f., *Fortunata* (Trimalchio's wife; the common Latin
     adjective means *fortunate, lucky, successful; wealthy; happy, blessed,*
     as of the gods).
     hērēs, hērēdis, m./f., *heir/heiress.*
     commendō [con- + **mandō**, *to consign*], **-āre, -āvī, -ātus**, *to en-
     trust, commend.*
8   ****ideō**, adv., *for that/this reason, therefore.*
     pūblicō, -āre, -āvī, -ātus, *to make known, publish, announce.*
9   *****mortuus, -a, -um**, *dead.*

II.

TRIMALCHIO'S DINNER

5. Trimalchio's Tomb and Funeral

Trimalchio's enlightened attitude toward his slaves; he decides to read his will.

[71–78] Diffūsus hāc contentiōne Trimalchiō, "Amīcī," inquit, 1
"et servī hominēs sunt et aequē ūnum lactem bibērunt, etiam sī 2
illōs malus fātus oppresserit. Tamen mē salvō citō aquam 3
līberam gustābunt. Ad summam, omnēs illōs in testāmentō meō 4
manū mittō. Philargyrō etiam fundum lēgō et contubernālem 5
suam, Cariōnī quoque īnsulam et vīcēsimam et lectum strātum. 6
Nam Fortūnātam meam hērēdem faciō, et commendō illam om- 7
nibus amīcīs meīs. Et haec ideō omnia pūblicō, ut familia mea 8
iam nunc sīc mē amet tamquam mortuum." 9

---

1 **hāc contentiōne**: the cook has just been challenging Trimalchio to a
wager over who would win the races at the circus.
Amīcī: vocative.
2 **et servī**: *even slaves.* Seneca the philosopher argues at length that
slaves are men, **hominēs**, and not just **servī** (*Epistulae morales*
47.1).
aequē: i.e., as much as we.
ūnum lactem: *the same* (mother's) *milk* (that we have drunk).
etiam sī . . . oppresserit: perfect subjunctive used as an affectation
where an indicative would be correct (see p. 250).
3 **mē salvō**: ablative absolute, *while I am alive*; a seemingly meaning-
less phrase in context, since presumably the slaves will taste the
proverbial water of freedom only after Trimalchio's death.
6 **vīcēsimam**: in his generosity, Trimalchio promises to bequeath
Cario the amount of this tax that will have to be paid when he is
freed.
lectum strātum: lectum sternere = *to make a bed;* **lectus strātus** = *a
bed made and ready for use.*
8 **ut familia . . . mē amet**: purpose clause with present subjunctive.

10 *grātiās agere + dat., *to give thanks* (to/for).
  indulgentia, -ae, f., *indulgence.*
11 ***oblīvīscor, oblīvīscī, oblītus sum + gen., *to forget.*
  *oblītus, -a, -um + gen., *forgetful* (of).
  *nūgae, -ārum, f. pl., *idle talk, nonsense.*
  exemplar, exemplāris, n., *copy.*
  **testāmentum, -ī, n., *will, testament.*
12 prīmum, -ī, n., *beginning.*
  ultimum, -ī, n., *end.*
  ingemēscō, ingemēscere, ingemuī, *to groan, sigh.*
  recitō, -āre, -āvī, -ātus, *to recite.*
  ***respiciō [re- + speciō, *to see*], respicere, respexī, respectus, *to look at.*
13 Habinnās, -ae, m., *Habinnas* (a stonemason, undertaker, and close friend of Trimalchio; he arrived late at dinner with his wife Scintilla).
  **cārus, -a, -um, *dear.*
  aedificō, -āre, -āvī, -ātus, *to build.*
14 *monumentum [monimentum], -ī, n., *funerary monument, tomb.*
  ***quemadmodum, adv., *in what manner, how, just as.*
  **validē, adv., *strongly, mightily, very.*
  valdē, syncopated variant (see p. 241).
15 *secundum, prep. + acc., *by, next to.*
  catella, -ae, f. [dim. of catulus, -ī, m., *young dog*], *little dog.*
  fingō, fingere, fīnxī, fictus, *to form, fashion, make.*
  corōna, -ae, f., *garland, wreath.*
16 *unguentum, -ī, n., *ointment, perfume.*
  Petraitēs, Petraitis, m., *Petraites* (gladiators with this name are known from the reigns of Caligula and Nero).
  pugna, -ae, f., *fight.*
  *contingō [con- + tangō, *to touch*], contingere, contigī, contāctus, *to touch*; + dat., *to happen* (to one), *befall.*
17 ***beneficium, -ī, n., *kindness, favor; benefit, service.*
  mors, mortis, mortium, f., *death.*
  *praetereā, adv., *besides, moreover.*
  *frōns, frontis, frontium, f., *forehead; front; frontage.*
18 *ager, agrī, m., *field; length, breadth, depth.*
  ducentī, -ae, -a, *two hundred.*

Instructions for building Trimalchio's tomb

Grātiās agere omnēs indulgentiae coeperant dominī, cum ille 10
oblītus nūgārum exemplar testāmentī iussit afferrī et tōtum ā 11
prīmō ad ultimum ingemēscente familiā recitāvit. Respiciēns 12
deinde Habinnam, "Quid dīcis," inquit, "amīce cārissime? Aedi- 13
ficās monumentum meum, quemadmodum tē iussī? Valdē tē 14
rogō ut secundum pedēs statuae meae catellam fingās et corōnās 15
et unguenta et Petraitis omnēs pugnās, ut mihi contingat tuō 16
beneficiō post mortem vīvere; praetereā ut sint in fronte pedēs 17
centum, in agrum pedēs ducentī. 18

(paragraph continued on page 157)

11 **oblītus nūgārum**: i.e., becoming serious.
12 **ingemēscente familiā**: ablative absolute.
13 **Aedificās**: either progressive present (*Are you building . . . ?*) or
present used colloquially for the future (see p. 248).
15 **ut . . . fingās**: indirect command with the present subjunctive.
corōnās et unguenta: wreaths and perfumes for use in banquets.
16 **Petraitis**: Trimalchio wants representations of all Petraites' fights
carved on his funerary monument; gladiatorial combats were often carved on funerary reliefs to perpetuate the tradition of funerary games held in honor of deceased noblemen in early times.
ut mihi contingat: purpose clause with present subjunctive.
tuō beneficiō: ablative of cause.
17 **ut sint**: indirect command resumed, dependent on **tē rogō** (14–15).
18 **in agrum**: i.e., from the roadside into the land behind = *in depth.*
While a plot about twenty by thirty feet was usual, Horace has
the narrator of *Satire* 1.8 mention a plot **mīlle pedēs in fronte,**
trecentōs . . . in agrum (line 12), which would dwarf that of
Trimalchio.

19   ***genus, generis,** n., *kind.*
      pōmum, -ī, n., *fruit, fruit-tree.*
      ****circā,** prep. +acc., *around, about.*
      cinis, cineris, m., *ash;* pl., *ashes* (of a corpse that has been cremated).
20   **vīnea, -ae,** f., *vineyard, vine.*
      largiter, adv., *in abundance, plentifully.*
      ***validē,** adv., *strongly, mightily, very.*
      valdē, syncopated variant (see p. 241).
      falsus, -a, -um, *false, wrong.*
      ***vīvus, -a, -um,** *alive, living.*
21   **cultus, -a, -um,** *adorned, elegant, well cared for.*
      ***cūrō, -āre, -āvī, -ātus,** *to care (for).*
      ***diūtius,** compar. adv., *longer.*
      ****habitō, -āre, -āvī, -ātus,** *to live.*
22   ***ideō,** adv., *for that/this reason, therefore.*
      ante, prep. + acc., *before.*
      adiciō [ad- + iaciō, *to throw*], **adicere, adiēcī, adiectus,** *to throw/place near, add.*
      ****monumentum [monimentum], -ī,** n., *funerary monument, tomb.*
      ***hērēs, hērēdis,** m./f., *heir/heiress.*
      ***sequor, sequī, secūtus sum,** *to follow.*
23   **cūra, -ae,** f., *care.*
      ***testāmentum, -ī,** n., *will, testament.*
      ***caveō, cavēre, cāvī, cautus,** *to beware.*
24   **iniūria, -ae,** f., *injury.*
      praepōnō, praepōnere, praeposuī, praepositus, *to put/set before.*
      ***lībertus, -ī,** m., *freedman.*
25   **sepulcrum, -ī,** n., *tomb.*
      custōdia, -ae, f., *guarding, protection.*
      causā + gen., *for the sake of.*
      ***monumentum [monimentum], -ī,** n., *funerary monument, tomb.*
      ***populus, -ī,** m., *people.*
26   **cacō, -āre, -āvī, -ātus,** *to relieve oneself.*
      ***currō, currere, cucurrī, cursūrus,** *to run.*

"Omne genus enim pōma volō sint circā cinerēs meōs, et 19
vīneārum largiter. Valdē enim falsum est vīvō quidem domōs 20
cultās esse, nōn cūrārī eās, ubi diūtius nōbīs habitandum est. Et 21
ideō ante omnia adicī volō: 'Hoc monumentum hērēdem nōn se- 22
quātur.' Cēterum erit mihi cūrae ut testāmentō caveam nē 23
mortuus iniūriam accipiam. Praepōnam enim ūnum ex lībertīs 24
sepulcrō meō custōdiae causā, nē in monumentum meum popu- 25
lus cacātum currat. 26

(paragraph continued on page 159)

19 **Omne genus . . . pōma:** i.e., fruit trees of every kind; **omne genus**
is an adverbial accusative. It was not unusual to have orchards
and vineyards around one's funerary monument, to provide the
resources from which annual offerings and libations to the dead
could be made.
pōma volō sint: volō may be followed by either an infinitive or
subjunctive with or without **ut; pōma** is subject of **sint.**

20 **vīneārum largiter: vīneārum** is partitive genitive dependent on
largiter, which is used substantively, *an abundance of vines.*
Valdē . . . falsum: *It is a very mistaken idea.*
vīvō . . . domōs cultās esse: possessive dative, *that a living* (man's)
homes (should) *be well cared for.*

21 **nōn cūrārī eās:** (but) *that those* (homes). ⋮ . . . (asyndeton, see p. 251).
nōbīs habitandum est: passive periphrastic with a dative of
agency, *living must be done by us = we must live.* The tomb is frequently described as a dwelling place on Roman funerary inscriptions.

22 **'Hoc monumentum hērēdem nōn sequātur': sequātur** is a jussive
subjunctive expressing a command (regularly with **nē** for the
negative instead of **nōn,** which is used incorrectly by Trimalchio
here; see p. 250), *Don't let this monument follow* (i.e., pass to) (my)
heir. This sentiment was often expressed on tombstones, and
was frequently abbreviated as **HMHNS** (see Horace, *Satires*
1.8.13).

23 **erit mihi cūrae:** double dative, *it will be for a care to me = I will take*
care that. . . .
ut . . . caveam: substantive clause of purpose or indirect command
dependent on the phrase **erit mihi cūrae.**
nē . . . accipiam: another substantive clause of purpose or indirect
command with the usual negative **nē.**

24 **ūnum ex lībertīs:** partitive, *one of my freedmen.*

25 **nē . . . currat:** negative purpose clause.

26 **cacātum:** supine (form = perfect passive participle, neuter singular)

expressing purpose after a verb of motion. **nē . . . cacātum cur-**
rat: similar prohibitions are found on ancient funerary monu-
ments.

27   *nāvis, nāvis, nāvium, f., *ship.*
     *vēlum, -ī, n., *sail.*
     euntēs [present participle of **eō, īre, iī, itūrus**, irreg., *to go*], *going;*
        here, *sailing.*
28   *tribūnal, tribūnālis, n., *tribunal* (raised platform on which the
        magistrate's chair was placed).
     praetextātus, -a, -um, *wearing the *toga praetexta* (the toga with
        purple border, worn by magistrates).
     *ānulus, -ī, m., *ring.*
29   ***nummus, -ī, m., *piece of money, coin.*
     pūblicum, -ī, n., *public place.*
     sacculus, -ī, m. [dim. of **saccus, -ī, m.**, *sack*], *little sack.*
     **effundō [ex- + fundō, *to pour*], effundere, effūdī, effūsus, *to
        pour out.*
30   *epulum, -ī, n., *banquet, feast.*
     *bīnī, -ae, -a, *two each.*
     ***dēnārius, -ī, m., *denarius* (a silver coin originally worth ten
        assēs, later sixteen; the **as**, gen. **assis**, m., was the basic unit of
        Roman coinage).
31   suāviter, adv., *sweetly, pleasantly.*
     dextera, -ae, f., *right hand.*
32   columba, -ae, f., *dove.*
33   *catella, -ae, f. [dim. of **catulus, -ī, m.**, *young dog*], *little dog.*
     *cingulum, -ī, n., *belt.*
     alligō [ad- + ligō, *to tie*], -āre, -āvī, -ātus, *to tie.*
     *cicarō, cicarōnis, m. [vulgar word-formation with ending in -ō,
        see p. 244; found only here and at II.2.140, see p. 246], meaning
        uncertain, perhaps *small boy.*
     amphora, -ae, f., *two-handled jug.*
34   cōpiōsē, adv., *abundantly.*
     gypsātus, -a, -um, *sealed with plaster* [**gypsum, -ī**, n., Greek word].
     effluō [ex- + fluō, *to flow*], effluere, effluxī, *to flow out;* here, *to
        allow* (a liquid) *to escape.*
     *licet, -ēre, -uit, impersonal, *it is permitted.*
     *frangō, frangere, frēgī, frāctus, *to break.*
35   sculpō, sculpere, sculpsī, sculptus, *to carve, sculpt.*
     *super, prep. + acc., *above, over.*
     *plōrō, -āre, -āvī, -ātus, *to cry aloud; to lament; to weep.*

"Tē rogō ut nāvēs etiam faciās plēnīs vēlīs euntēs, et mē in 27
tribūnālī sedentem praetextātum cum ānulīs aureīs quīnque et 28
nummōs in pūblicō dē sacculō effundentem; scīs enim quod 29
epulum dedī bīnōs dēnāriōs. Faciātur, sī tibi vidētur, et trīclīnia. 30
Faciās et tōtum populum sibi suāviter facientem. Ad dexteram 31
meam pōnās statuam Fortūnātae meae columbam tenentem: et 32
catellam cingulō alligātam dūcat: et cicarōnem meum, et am- 33
phorās cōpiōsē gypsātās, nē effluant vīnum. Et ūnam licet frāc- 34
tam sculpās, et super eam puerum plōrantem. 35

(paragraph continued on page 161)

---

27 **ut . . . faciās**: indirect command with present subjunctive.
    nāvēs: as symbols of Trimalchio's commercial shipping ventures;
    ships were frequently represented on ancient tombstones.
28 **praetextātum**: Trimalchio wishes to be portrayed in the dress and
    performing the functions of a **sēvir Augustālis** (see note on
    II.1.72).
    cum ānulīs aureīs quīnque: while a **sēvir**, Trimalchio was entitled
    to wear a gold ring; five seem excessive (see note on II.1.124).
29 **in pūblicō**: i.e., to the people.
    scīs . . . quod . . . dedī: vulgar use of **quod**, *that*, and indicative in-
    stead of the normal accusative and infinitive in indirect state-
    ment; cf. the similar use of **quia** in II.2.119–120 and II.2.144 (see
    p. 250).
30 **epulum . . . bīnōs dēnāriōs**: cf. II.2.120.
    Faciātur. . . . Faciās: subjunctives expressing commands or wishes.
    Faciātur: vulgar for **fīat** (see p. 244). **Faciātur . . . trīclīnia**: vul-
    gar first declension feminine instead of second declension neuter
    (see p. 242).
31 **sibi suāviter facientem**: *enjoying themselves.*
32 **Fortūnātae**: Trimalchio's wife.
33 **cicarōnem meum**: for the word, see II.2.140. Trimalchio had no
    son of his own and may be referring here to his pet slave boy
    named Croesus (see II.1.35–37 above and II.5.106–147 below).
34 **nē effluant**: negative purpose clause. Trimalchio presses the usu-
    ally intransitive verb **effluō** into use in place of the transitive **ef-
    fundō**.
    et ūnam: supply **amphoram**.
    licet . . . sculpās: *it is permitteed* (that) *you may carve* = *you may carve.*

36   *hōrologium, -ī, n. [Greek loan word], *sundial, water clock.*
***medium, -ī, n., *middle part, center.*
hōra, -ae, f., *hour.*
**īnspiciō, īnspicere, īnspexī, īnspectus, *to look at.*
37   **nōmen, nōminis, n., *name.*
*legō, legere, lēgī, lēctus, *to read.*
**īnscrīptiō, īnscrīptiōnis, f., *inscription.*
***dīligenter, adv., *carefully, diligently.*
38   *satis, adv., *enough, sufficiently.*
idōneus, -a, -um, *suitable.*
**C., abbrev. of Gaius, *Gaius.*
39   ***hīc, adv., *here.*
requiēscō, requiēscere, requiēvī, requiētūrus, *to rest; to lie.*
sēvirātus, -ūs, m. [word found only here and in inscriptions, see
    p. 246], *office of a sēvir* (a member of a board of six men; in
    provincial towns, sēvir Augustālis, a citizen annually
    appointed to maintain the worship of the cult of Rome and
    Augustus).
absēns, absentis, absent.
dēcernō, dēcernere, dēcrēvī, dēcrētus, *to decide, determine; to de-
    cree.*
40   **decuria, -ae, f., *group of ten; association, club* (of scribes, lictors,
    errand-runners, public criers, and auctioneers, who were orga-
    nized into decuriae and attached to the various magistrates).
Rōma, -ae, f., *Rome.*
pius, -a, -um, *pious, dutiful.*
41   **fortis, -is, -e, *brave, strong.*
fidēlis, -is, -e, *faithful.*
**sēstertius, -ī, m., *sesterce* (small silver coin).
    sēstertium, gen. pl.
*trecentiēs, adv., *three hundred times.*
    trecentiēs (centēna mīlia), *30,000,000.*
42   philosophus, -ī, m. [Greek loan word], *philosopher.*
*valeō, -ēre, -uī, *to be strong, be well.*
    valē, *farewell!*

"Hōrologium in mediō, ut quisquis hōrās īnspiciet, velit nōlit,   36
nōmen meum legat. Īnscrīptiō quoque vidē dīligenter sī haec   37
satis idōnea tibi vidētur: 'C. Pompēius Trimalchiō Maecē-   38
nātiānus hīc requiēscit. Huic sēvirātus absentī dēcrētus est.   39
Cum posset in omnibus decuriīs Rōmae esse, tamen nōluit. Pius,   40
fortis, fidēlis, ex parvō crēvit; sēstertium relīquit trecentiēs, nec   41
umquam philosophum audīvit. Valē! Et tū!'"   42

---

36   **hōrologium**: compare II.1.6.
     ut . . . legat: purpose clause with present subjunctive.
     velit nōlit: asyndeton in a colloquial phrase (see p. 251); cf. our "willy nilly."
37   **vidē . . . sī . . . vidētur**: parataxis of conditional clause with the indicative instead of the normal subordination with the subjunctive introduced by **num**, *whether* (see p. 249).
     haec: modifying **īnscrīptiō**.
38   **C. Pompeius Trimalchiō Maecenātiānus**: see note on II.1.6. Trimalchio's funerary inscription may be compared with funerary inscriptions found throughout the Roman world. One quoted by Sedgwick is given at the bottom of the next page.
39   **absentī**: concessive participle, *although he was out of town at the time*; Trimalchio's pretentious mention of being chosen **sēvir** in absentia recalls instances of high magistrates in Rome occasionally being elected in absentia, such as Scipio Aemilianus, elected to his second consulship in absentia, as reported by Cicero in *The Republic* 6.11.
40   **Cum posset . . . esse**: *Although he could have beeen. . . .*
     in omnibus decuriīs Rōmae: memberships in the **decuriae** were bought, and Trimalchio is here boasting that he could have afforded to have been a member of all the clubs.
     Pius, fortis, fidēlis: asyndeton and alliteration (see p. 251).
42   **Valē! Et tū!**: dialogue. The tombstone inscription communicates Trimalchio's farewell (**Valē!**) to passers-by who stop to read it; as they read the final words (**Et tū!**; supply **valē**), they willy-nilly return the farewell. Dialogue of this sort is frequently incorporated into Roman funerary inscriptions.

43　**fleō, flēre, flēvī, flētus,** *to weep, cry.*
　　ūbertim, adv., *plentifully, abundantly, copiously.*
44　**dēnique,** adv., *finally.*
45　***fūnus, fūneris,** n., *funeral.*
　　lāmentātiō, lāmentātiōnis, f., *wailing, weeping, lamentation.*
　　impleō [in- + pleō, *to fill*], **implēre, implēvī, implētus,** *to fill.*
46　****plōrō, -āre, -āvī, -ātus,** *to cry aloud; to lament; to weep.*
47　****morior, morī, mortuus sum,** *to die.*
　　moritūrōs esse, future active infinitive.
　　***quārē,** interrog. adv., *why?*
　　***fēlīx, fēlīcis,** *fortunate, prosperous, happy.*
48　**perīculum, -ī,** n., *danger.*
　　paenitet, -ēre, -uit, impersonal, *it causes dissatisfaction, gives reason for complaint/regret.*
49　**caleō, -ēre, -uī,** *to be hot.*
　　furnus, -ī, m., *furnace.*
50　***nūdus, -a, -um,** *bare.*
　　cōnsurgō, cōnsurgere, cōnsurrēxī, cōnsurrēctūrus, *to rise, stand up.*
51　***gaudeō, gaudēre, gavīsus sum,** *to rejoice; to be glad/joyful/happy.*
　　subsequor, subsequī, subsecūtus sum, *to follow.*

Pūblius Decimus Pūblī lībertus Erōs Merula, medicus, clīnicus, chīrurgus, oculārius, VIvir. Hic prō lībertāte dedit HS (L mīlia): hic prō sēvirātū in rem pūblicam dedit HS (II mīlia); hic in statuās pōnendās in aedem Herculis dedit HS (XXX mīlia); hic in viās sternendās in pūblicum dedit HS (XXXVII mīlia). Hic prīdiē quam mortuus est relīquit patrimōniī HS mīlia quīngenta vīgintī.

　　lībertus, -ī, m., *freedman.*
　　clīnicus, -ī, m. [Greek loan word], *a doctor who tends patients in bed.*
　　chīrurgus, -ī, m. [Greek loan word], *surgeon.*
　　oculārius, -ī, m., *eye-doctor.*
　　VIvir, = **sēvir.**
　　HS, = abbreviation of **sēstertium** (gen. pl.).
　　sēvirātus, -ūs, m., *the office of a sēvir.*
　　rēs pūblica, reī pūblicae, f., *republic, state.*
　　aedēs, aedis, aedium, f., *temple.*
　　sternō, sternere, strāvī, strātus, *to pave.*
　　in pūblicum, *for the public welfare.*
　　prīdiē, adv. + **quam,** *on the day before.*
　　patrimōnium, -ī, n., *personal possessions, fortune, estate.*

Tears and funeral lamentation are dispelled by the suggestion that everyone take a bath.

Haec ut dīxit Trimalchiō, flēre coepit ūbertim. Flēbat et 43
Fortūnāta, flēbat et Habinnās, tōta dēnique familia, tamquam in 44
fūnus rogāta, lāmentātiōne trīclīnium implēvit. Immō iam coe- 45
peram etiam ego plōrāre, cum Trimalchiō, "Ergō," inquit, "cum 46
sciāmus nōs moritūrōs esse, quārē nōn vīvāmus? Sīc vōs fēlīcēs 47
videam, coniciāmus nōs in balneum, meō perīculō, nōn pae- 48
nitēbit. Sīc calet tamquam furnus." "Vērō, vērō," inquit 49
Habinnās, "dē ūnā diē duās facere, nihil mālō," nūdīsque cōn- 50
surrēxit pedibus et Trimalchiōnem gaudentem subsequī coepit. 51

---

43 **Flēbat . . . flēbat**: anaphora (see p. 251).
46 **cum Trimalchiō . . . inquit**: for the **cum inversum** construction, see the note on II.1.12.
cum sciāmus: *since. . . .*
47 **nōs moritūrōs esse**: *that we are about. . . .*
quārē nōn vīvāmus?: deliberative subjunctive, *why don't we live it up?*
Sīc vōs fēlīcēs videam: subjunctive expressing a wish, *So may I see you happy* (cf. II.4.3–4, see p. 252; the wish is expressed for the purpose of warding off any evil consequences of the proposal to go and take a bath in the middle of the meal.
48 **coniciāmus nōs**: hortatory subjunctive, *let's. . . .*
meō perīculō: ablative absolute, *the danger being mine* = *at my risk*.
nōn paenitēbit: supply **vōs**, *it won't cause you regret* = *you won't regret it*.
For breaking up a long dinner with a bath, see Suetonius, *Nero* 27, where Nero is said to have stretched out his dinners from midday to midnight and to have refreshed himself rather often with hot baths or, in summer, with baths chilled with snow. Juvenal (1.140–146) satirizes the luxurious but dangerous practice of bathing after a big dinner—sudden death awaits the extravagant diner who goes into the bath with his stomach full of undigested boar and peacock. See also Persius 3.97–106 for the deadly results of a bath after an extravagant dinner.
49 **"Vērō, vērō"**: *Certainly*; note the colloquial repetition of words (see p. 251).
50 **dē ūnā diē duās facere, nihil mālō**: = **nihil aliud mālō quam facere dē ūnā diē duās**; note the feminine gender of **diēs** here.

52 cōgitō, -āre, -āvī, -ātus, *to think.*

53 expīrō [ex- + spīrō, *to breathe*], -āre, -āvī, -ātus, *to breathe out; to expire, die.*

assentor [ad- + sentiō, *to perceive*], -ārī, -ātus sum, *to assent, agree.*

54 *petō, petere, petiī, petītus, *to beg, ask; to seek.*

**turba, -ae, f., *crowd.*

***exeō, exīre, exiī, exitus, irreg., *to go out, depart.*

55 **porticus, -ūs, f., *porticus* (walkway covered by a roof supported by columns).

*iānua, -ae, f., *door.*

56 catēnārius, -a, -um [rare word, see pp. 244, 246], *fastened by a chain* [catēna, -ae, f.].

*tantus, -a, -um, *of such a size, so great, such a great.*

tumultus, -ūs, m., *uproar, bustle, commotion.*

***excipiō [ex- + capiō], excipere, excēpī, exceptus, *to take up, catch, receive.*

57 piscīna, -ae, f. [piscis, piscis, piscium, m., *fish*], *fish-pool* (large basin of water, usually called **impluvium**, in the atrium).

*cadō, cadere, cecidī, casūrus, *to fall, fall down.*

ēbrius, -a, -um, *drunk.*

58 natō, -āre, -āvī, -ātūrus, *to swim.*

ops, opis, f., *aid, help.*

gurges, gurgitis, m., *whirlpool; sea; water.*

trahō, trahere, trāxī, tractus, *to draw, drag, pull.*

Encolpius, Ascyltos, and Giton try to escape, and Ascyltos and Encolpius fall into the fish-pool.

Ego respiciēns ad Ascylton, "Quid cōgitās?" inquam. "Ego   52
enim sī vīderō balneum, statim expīrābō." "Assentēmur," ait   53
ille, "et dum illī balneum petunt, nōs in turbā exeāmus." Cum   54
haec placuissent, dūcente per porticum Gītōne ad iānuam vēn-   55
imus, ubi canis catēnārius tantō nōs tumultū excēpit, ut Ascyltos   56
etiam in piscīnam ceciderit. Nec nōn ego quoque ēbrius, dum   57
natantī opem ferō, in eundem gurgitem tractus sum.   58

---

53 **sī vīderō . . . expīrābō:** future more vivid condition with future
perfect and future indicatives.
assentēmur: hortatory subjunctive, *let's agree* (to go to the bath
with the rest).
54 **exeāmus:** hortatory subjunctive, *let's leave* (i.e., escape).
55 **placuissent:** pluperfect subjunctive in a circumstantial clause in
secondary sequence, *when these things had pleased* (us) = *when we
had agreed upon this* (course of action).
dūcente . . . Gītōne: ablative absolute. Giton had to lead the way
because Encolpius and Ascyltos were drunk (see line 85).
per porticum: apparently different from the one mentioned in
II.1.57.
56 **canis catēnārius:** compare II.1.47–50, where Encolpius is bowled
over by the mere picture of a dog at the entrance to the house.
ut . . . ceciderit: perfect subjunctive in a result clause in secondary
sequence; use of the perfect rather than the imperfect subjunctive
in result clauses in secondary sequence emphasizes the actuality
of the result.
57 **Nec nōn:** = *Also*, redundant with **quoque.**
58 **natantī:** i.e., Ascyltos.

59 ***servō, -āre, -āvī, -ātus, *to save.*
*ātriēnsis, ātriēnsis, ātriēnsium, m., *overseer of the* ātrium (the main room in a Roman house), *steward.*
interventus, -ūs, m., *coming up, appearance, intervention.*
60 plācō, -āre, -āvī, -ātus, *to placate, appease.*
tremō, tremere, tremuī, *to quiver, tremble, shiver.*
extrahō, extrahere, extrāxī, extractus, *to draw, drag, pull out.*
siccum, -ī, n., *dry land, dry place.*
61 *dūdum, adv., *a short time ago, formerly.*
*iam dūdum, *some while ago now, long since, long before.*
*ratiō, ratiōnis, f., *account, reckoning; manner, method, plan.*
acūtus, -a, -um, *sharp, clever.*
redimō [re-/red- + emō, *to buy*], redimere, redēmī, redēmptus, *to buy back; to release, set free.*
62 lātrō, -āre, -āvī, -ātūrus, *to bark.*
*spargō, spargere, sparsī, sparsus, *to sprinkle, scatter.*
**at, conj., *but.*
āvocō [ab- + vocō], -āre, -āvī, -ātus, *to call off/away.*
63 cibus, -ī, m., *food.*
furor, furōris, m., *rage, fury.*
supprimō [sub- + premō, *to press*], supprimere, suppressī, suppressus, *to press down, hold back, restrain, stop.*
algeō, algēre, alsī, *to feel cold, be chilled.*
*ūdus, -a, -um, *wet.*
**petō, petere, petiī, petītus, *to beg, ask; to seek.*
64 **ātriēnsis, ātriēnsis, ātriēnsium, m., *overseer of the* ātrium (the main room in a Roman house), *steward.*
*extrā, prep. + acc., *out, outside of.*
**iānua, -ae, f., *door.*
ēmittō [ex- + mittō], ēmittere, ēmīsī, ēmissus, *to send out, let out.*
*errō, -āre, -āvī, -ātūrus, *to wander; to be mistaken.*
65 ***convīva, -ae, m., *guest.*
66 ***iānua, -ae, f., *door.*
*ēmittō [ex- + mittō], ēmittere, ēmīsī, ēmissus, *to send out, let out.*

Saved from the pool, but denied escape

Servāvit nōs tamen ātriēnsis, quī interventū suō et canem 59
plācāvit et nōs trementēs extrāxit in siccum. Et Gītōn quidem 60
iam dūdum sē ratiōne acūtissimā redēmerat ā cane; quicquid 61
enim ā nōbīs accēperat dē cēnā, lātrantī sparserat, at ille āvocātus 62
cibō furōrem suppresserat. Cēterum cum algentēs ūdīque petis- 63
sēmus ab ātriēnse ut nōs extrā iānuam ēmitteret, "Errās," inquit, 64
"sī putās tē exīre hāc posse quā vēnistī. Nēmō umquam con- 65
vīvārum per eandem iānuam ēmissus est; aliā intrant, aliā exe- 66
unt." 67

---

59 **ātriēnsis**: perhaps the same man mentioned in II.1.65.

62 **lātrantī sparserat**: supply **canī**; Giton's action is a comic parody of Vergil's *Aeneid* 6.417–425, where the Sibyl throws a sop to Cerberus.

ille: i.e., the dog.

63 **cum . . . petissēmus**: pluperfect subjunctive in a circumstantial clause.

64 **ut . . . ēmitteret**: indirect command with imperfect subjunctive.

65 **hāc . . . quā**: supply **viā** or **iānuā**, *by this* (same) (way/door) *by which*.

convīvārum: partitive genitive with **nēmō** = *no guest*.

66 **aliā . . . aliā**: supply **viā** or **iānuā**, *by one* (way/door) . . . *by another* (way/door).

68 miser, misera, miserum, *wretched, miserable.*
    labyrinthus, -ī, m. [Greek loan word], *labyrinth.*
69 inclūdō [in- + claudō, *to shut*], inclūdere, inclūsī, inclūsus, *to shut in, enclose, imprison.*
    lavārī, passive used reflexively, *to bathe.*
    *vōtum, -ī, n., *wish, desire; prayer.*
    ultrō, adv., *voluntarily, of one's own accord.*
70 **prōiciō [prō- + iaciō, *to throw*], prōicere, prōiēcī, prōiectus, *to throw off.*
71 *aditus, -ūs, m., *entrance, doorway.*
    siccō, -āre, -āvī, -ātus, *to dry.*
    cisterna, -ae, f., *cistern* (reservoir for water).
72 frīgidārius, -a, -um, *of/for cold water.*
    similis, -is, -e + gen. or dat., *like, similar* (to).
    **rēctus, -a, -um, *upright, straight.*
73 pūtidus, -a, -um, *rotten, stinking, disgusting.*
    iactātiō, iactātiōnis, f., *tossing to and fro; bragging, boasting.*
    **licet, -ēre, -uit, impersonal, *it is permitted.*
    effugiō [ex- + fugiō], effugere, effūgī, *to flee from, escape.*
74 ***turba, -ae, f., *crowd, mob.*
    *aliquandō, adv., *once, formerly.*
75 pīstrīnum, -ī, n., *mill, bakery; place in a house where slaves turned the flour-mill* (a task inflicted upon slaves as a punishment).

Nothing to do but to go to the bath with the other guests

Quid faciāmus hominēs miserrimī et novī generis labyrinthō   68
inclūsī, quibus lavārī iam coeperat vōtum esse?   Ultrō ergō   69
rogāvimus ut nōs ad balneum dūceret, prōiectīsque vestīmentīs,   70
quae Gītōn in aditū siccāre coepit, balneum intrāvimus, cisternae   71
frīgidāriae simile, in quō Trimalchiō rēctus stābat. Ac nē sīc qui-   72
dem pūtidissimam eius iactātiōnem licuit effugere; nam nihil   73
melius esse dīcēbat quam sine turbā lavārī, et eō ipsō locō ali-   74
quandō pīstrīnum fuisse.   75

---

68 **Quid faciāmus**: deliberative subjunctive with the present tense
   (*What are we to do?*) instead of the imperfect, which would be
   normal in narrative (**Quid facerēmus?** *What were we to do?*).
   novī generis: genitive of description with **labyrinthō**, = *a new kind
   of labyrinth.*
69 **quibus lavārī iam coeperat vōtum esse**: *for whom to bathe had now
   become* (our) *wish.*
70 **ut . . . dūceret**: indirect command with imperfect subjunctive.
   prōiectīs . . . vestīmentīs: ablative absolute.
71 **balneum**: i.e., the hot bath.
   cisternae frīgidāriae simile: *like* (i.e., as big as) *a cold-water reser-
   voir*; this would be unusually large for the hot-bath chamber.
72 **nē sīc quidem**: *not even so* = *not even here.*

76   lassō, -āre, -āvī, -ātus, *to tire, weary.*
      cōnsīdō, cōnsīdere, cōnsēdī, *to sit down.*
      *invītō, -āre, -āvī, -ātus, *to invite;* here, *to attract.*
      sonus, -ī, m., *sound; resonance.*
      dīdūcō [dis- + dūcō], dīdūcere, dīdūxī, dīductus, *to draw apart,*
      open up.
77   usque, adv., *continuously.*
      usque ad + acc., *clear up to.*
      *camera, -ae, f., *arched/vaulted ceiling.*
      *ōs, ōris, n., *mouth; voice.*
      *ēbrius, -a, -um, *drunk.*
      Menecratēs, Menecratis, m. [Greek name, meaning "abiding in
      strength"], *Menecrates* (the name of a famous musician of Nero's
      time; see Suetonius, *Nero* 30).
      *canticum, -ī, n., *song.*
      lacerō, -āre, -āvī, -ātus, *to tear, mangle, lacerate.*
78   *sīcut, adv., *as, just as.*
      *lingua, -ae, f., *tongue; language.*
      *intellegō, intellegere, intellēxī, intellēctus, *to understand.*
      cēterī, -ae, -a, *the other, the rest.*
79   ***circā, prep. + acc., *around, about.*
      lābrum [= lavābrum from lavō, -āre, -āvī, -ātus, *to wash*], -ī, n.,
      tub, basin (for bathing)
      nectō, nectere, nexuī, nexus, to join.
      **currō, currere, cucurrī, cursūrus, *to run.*
      gingiliphō [word found only here, see p. 246], abl., origin and
      meaning uncertain, perhaps *pealing laughter,* from a Greek word
      meaning "tickling."
80   *clāmor, clāmōris, m., *shouting.*
      exsonō, exsonāre, exsonuī, *to make a loud noise, resound.*
      restringō, restringere, restrīnxī, restrictus, *to draw back, bind back,*
      fasten back.
      **ānulus, -ī, m., *ring.*
81   pavīmentum, -ī, n., *floor.*
      *cōnor, -ārī, -ātus sum, *to attempt, try.*
      genū, -ūs, n., *knee.*
      *cervīx, cervīcis, f., *neck.*
      **post, prep. + acc., *after, behind.*
82   tergum, -ī, n., *back.*
      flectō, flectere, flexī, flexus, *to bend.*
      **extrēmus, -a, -um, *outermost, farthest, last; the end(s) of.*
      *pollex, pollicis, m., *thumb; big toe.*
      ***tangō, tangere, tetigī, tāctus, *to touch.*

Singing, exercise, and tricks in the bath

Deinde ut lassātus cōnsēdit, invītātus balneī sonō dīdūxit   76
usque ad cameram ōs ēbrium et coepit Menecratis cantica la-   77
cerāre, sīcut illī dīcēbant quī linguam eius intellegēbant. Cēterī   78
convīvae circā lābrum manibus nexīs currēbant et gingiliphō in- 79
gentī clāmōre exsonābant. Aliī autem restrictīs manibus ānulōs   80
dē pavīmentō cōnābantur tollere aut positō genū cervīcēs post   81
terga flectere et pedum extrēmōs pollicēs tangere. Nōs, dum illī 82
sibi lūdōs faciunt, in solium, quod Trimalchiōnī servābātur, dēs- 83
cendimus.   84

---

83 **lūdus, -ī**, m., *game, play.*
    solium, -ī, n., *seat; throne; small bathtub* (for an individual bather).
    ***dēscendō, dēscendere, dēscendī, dēscēnsūrus**, *to go down, de-*
    scend.

---

76 **balneī sonō**: i.e., by the echo from the vaulted ceiling of the bath.
    Horace (*Satires* 1.4.75–76) comments on poets who recite their
    poems in the baths, so that the vaulted ceiling echoes their voice;
    Martial satirizes a poet who never ceases reciting his verses, even
    at the baths (3.44.12–13); and Seneca comments on a bather in the
    bath-house below his apartment who likes to hear his own voice
    in the bath (*Epistulae morales* 56.2).
79 **lābrum**: a large shallow basin set on the floor at the curved end of
    the hot bath chamber, with space around it.
    manibus nexīs: ablative absolute.
    ingentī clāmōre: perhaps a scribe's addition to explain the mean-
    ing of **gingiliphō**.
80 **restrictīs manibus**: ablative absolute.
81 **tollere**: perhaps with their mouths.
    positō genū: ablative absolute, i.e., kneeling.

85   ēbrietās, ēbrietātis, f., *drunkenness*.
**discutiō [dis- + quatiō, *to shake; to strike*], discutere, discussī, discussus, *to strike apart, shatter; to dispel.*
dēdūcō, dēdūcere, dēdūxī, dēductus, *to lead down/away/off.*

86   dispōnō, dispōnere, disposuī, dispositus, *to set in order, arrange.*
**lautitia, -ae, f., *extravagance, elegance, splendor.*
**lucerna, -ae, f., *oil-lamp.*
aēneolus, -a, -um [dim. of aēneus, -a, -um, *made of bronze*], *made of bronze.*

87   piscātor, piscātōris, m., *fisherman.*
calix, calicis, m., *cup, goblet.*
circā, adv., *all around.*

88   fictilis, -is, -e, *made of clay.*
inaurātus, -a, -um, *gilded.*
*cōnspectus, -ūs, m., *sight, view.*
saccus, -ī, m., *sack, bag; bag for straining wine.*
dēfluō, dēfluere, dēfluxī, dēfluxūrus, *to flow down.*

89   barbātōria, -ae, f. [word found only here, see p. 245], *the ceremony of the first shaving of the beard* [barba, -ae, f.].
barbātōriam facere, *to shave the beard for the first time.*

90   praefiscinī, adv. [prae-, *before, in front* + fascinum, -ī, n., *witchcraft*, originally used of security against magic, i.e., preventing the evil eye, and then generalized], *with no evil, without offense, so help me.*
frūgī, indecl. adj. [from frūx, frūgis, f., *fruit; result, success, value*: frūgī is dative of purpose], *useful, fit, honest, virtuous.*
mīcārius, -a, -um [vulgar, found only here, see pp. 244, 246], *careful to pick up crumbs* [mīca, -ae, f.], *thrifty.*
tangomenās [vulgar, found only here and one other place in Petronius, see p. 247], meaning uncertain; see note under text.

91   *usque, adv., *continuously.*
usque in + acc., *clear up to.*
*lūx, lūcis, f., *light; dawn.*

Return to the dinner in a second dining room.

Ergō ēbrietāte discussā in aliud trīclīnium dēductī sumus,   85
ubi Fortūnāta disposuerat lautitiās suās. Lucernās aēneolōsque   86
piscātōrēs notāvimus et mēnsās tōtās argenteās calicēsque circā   87
fictilēs inaurātōs et vīnum in cōnspectū saccō dēfluēns. Tum   88
Trimalchiō, "Amīcī," inquit, "hodiē servus meus barbātōriam   89
fēcit, homō praefiscinī frūgī et mīcārius. Itaque tangomenās   90
faciāmus et usque in lūcem cēnēmus."   91

---

85   **ēbrietāta discussā**: ablative absolute.
86   **suās**: perhaps *in her own way*.
88   **vīnum . . . saccō dēfluēns**: the wine is being strained by being poured through a cloth bag (see Horace, *Satires* 2.4.53–54).
    in cōnspectū: i.e., under our very eyes.
89   **barbātōriam**: compare II.1.63–64, where the box containing the first clippings of Trimalchio's beard is mentioned.
90   **praefiscinī**: superstitious; spoken with the hope that the compliment he is about to pay the slave will have no evil consequences.
    tangomenās faciāmus: a vulgar phrase of uncertain meaning; **tangomenās** may be a passive participle of the Greek verb *tengo*, "to wet, moisten, soak" (confused with Latin **tangō, tangere,** *to touch*), perhaps modifying an implied **epulās,** *feast*, or **pōtiōnēs,** *drinks*, and the Latin phrase may mean *let's make our feast/drinks soaked*, i.e., let's get drunk.
91   **faciāmus . . . cēnēmus**: hortatory subjunctives.

92　***gallus gallīnāceus, -ī, m., *poultry cock.*
　　***cantō, -āre, -āvī, -ātus, *to sing; to crow.*
　　**vōx, vōcis, f., *voice, sound.*
　　cōnfundō, cōnfundere, cōnfūdī, cōnfūsus, *to pour together, confuse, disturb.*
93　*sub, prep. + abl., *under.*
　　***effundō [ex- + fundō, *to pour*], effundere, effūsī, effūsus, *to pour out.*
　　***lucerna, -ae, f., *oil-lamp.*
94　merum, -ī, n., *pure, unmixed wine.*
　　**spargō, spargere, sparsī, sparsus, *to sprinkle.*
　　***ānulus, -ī, m., *ring.*
　　**trāiciō [trāns- + iaciō, *to throw*], trāicere, trāiēcī, trāiectus, *to pierce, stab; to throw across; to transfer.*
95　būcinus, -ī, m. [found only here = būcinātor, būcinātōris, m., *trumpeter*], *trumpeter* [būcina, -ae, f., *trumpet*].
　　***signum, -ī, n., *sign, signal.*
96　incendium, -ī, n., *fire.*
　　fīat: present subjunctive of fīō.
　　vīcīnia, -ae, f., *neighborhood, vicinity.*
　　***anima, -ae, f., *breath; spirit; breath of life.*
　　abiciō [ab- + iaciō, *to throw*], abicere, abiēcī, abiectus, *to cast away, give up.*
97　index, indicis, m./f., *one who points/reveals; informer* (here the cock).
　　corollārium, -ī, n., *money paid for a garland of flowers* [corolla, -ae, f.]; *gift, present, reward, tip.*
98　**dictum, -ī, n., *saying, word.*
　　citius, compar. adv., *more quickly.*
99　*aēnum, -ī, n., *bronze vessel.*
　　*coquō, coquere, coxī, coctus, *to cook.*
　　*lacerō, -āre, -āvī, -ātus, *to tear, mangle, lacerate.*
　　igitur, conj., *therefore.*
　　*doctus, -a, -um [doceō, docēre, docuī, doctus, *to teach*], *learned, scholarly; skilled.*
100　caccabus, -ī, m. [Greek loan word], *cooking-pot.*
　　Daedalus, -ī, m. [Greek name], *Daedalus* (name of the cook, who is named after the mythical Athenian architect who built the labyrinth at Cnossos in Crete).
　　**pōtiō, pōtiōnis, f., *drink;* here, *broth, sauce.*
101　fervēns, ferventis, *boiling-hot.*
　　hauriō, haurīre, hausī, haustus, *to scoop up, draw* (water, etc.); *to drink.*
　　mola, -ae, f., *millstone; mill;* here, *small hand-mill.*
　　buxeus, -a, -um, *made of boxwood.*

Tranquillity disturbed by the crowing of a cock

Haec dīcente eō gallus gallīnāceus cantāvit. Quā vōce cōnfū- 92
sus Trimalchiō vīnum sub mēnsā iussit effundī lucernamque 93
etiam merō spargī. Immō ānulum trāiēcit in dexteram manum 94
et, "Nōn sine causā," inquit, "hic būcinus signum dedit; nam aut 95
incendium oportet fīat, aut aliquis in vīcīniā animam abiciet. 96
Longē ā nōbīs. Itaque quisquis hunc indicem attulerit, corol- 97
lārium accipiet." Dictō citius gallus allātus est, quem Trimalchiō 98
iussit ut aēnō coctus fieret. Lacerātus igitur ab illō doctissimō 99
cocō in caccabum est cōniectus. Dumque Daedalus pōtiōnem 100
ferventissimam haurit, Fortūnāta molā buxeā piper trīvit. 101

---

piper, piperis, n., *pepper.*
terō, terere, trīvī, trītus, *to grind.*

---

92 **Haec dīcente eō**: ablative absolute.
gallus . . . cantāvit: Pliny extols cocks for their regular crowing just before sunrise (mankind's alarm clock), for their crowing at set intervals during the day, and especially for their giving favorable or unfavorable omens not only during the day but also at evening and on one occasion by crowing all night long as a presage to the Boeotians of victory over the Spartans (*Natural History* 10.46–49). Here Trimalchio interprets the untimely crowing of the cock as an ill omen.

93 **effundī . . . spargī**: present passive infinitives.
lucernam . . . merō spargī: the flame's sputtering when sprinkled with wine was thought to be a good omen.

94 **ānulum**: with Trimalchio's changing of his ring from one hand to the other in order to avert an ill omen, compare Pliny's comment that many people recommend changing the ring from the left hand to the right and plunging the hands into hot water to rid themselves of sneezing and hiccoughs (*Natural History* 28.57).

96 **oportet fīat**: *there ought to be/will be.*

97 **Longē ā nōbīs**: supply **absit,** *May it be far from us.*
quisquis . . . attulerit . . . accipiet: = **sī quis attulerit. . . . ,** a future more vivid condition with future perfect and future indicatives.

98 **Dictō**: ablative of comparison with **citius,** i.e., before the words were out of his mouth; for the phrase **dictō citius,** see Vergil, *Aeneid* 1.142. *(notes continued on next page)*

99 **coctus fieret**: = **coquerētur**, subjunctive in indirect command, instead of the usual accusative and infinitive with **iubeō**.

100 **Dum . . . haurit**: **dum** regularly, as here, takes the present indicative when the main verb is perfect, *While he was*. . . .

pōtiōnem ferventissimam haurit: i.e., the cook was dipping up (**haurit**) the hot sauce (**pōtiōnem ferventissimam**) from the bottom of the cooking pot and pouring it over the parts of the bird that were not submerged in the sauce. Alternatively, the words could mean that the cook was drinking the scalding sauce in which the cock was being cooked.

102 **sūmō, sūmere, sūmpsī, sūmptus**, *to take, take up* (e.g., food).

mattea, -ae, f. [Greek loan word], *dainty dish, delicacy*.

familia, -ae, f., *family; the slaves of the household as a group*.

103 **cēnāstis**, = **cēnāvistis**.

***abeō, abīre, abiī, abitūrus**, irreg., *to go away, depart*.

104 **subeō, subīre, subiī, subitus**, irreg., *to come/go under; to succeed, take someone else's place*.

classis, classis, classium, f., *class, division*.

****exclāmō, -āre, -āvī, -ātus**, *to shout out*.

exclāmāvēre, = **exclāmāvērunt**.

105 ****valeō, -ēre, -uī**, *to be strong, be well*.

***valē**, *farewell! goodbye!*

aveō, avēre, *to be/fare well*.

avē, *hail!*

*****hinc**, adv., *from here, next*.

***prīmum**, adv., *first*.

***hilaritās, hilaritātis**, f., *cheerfulness, gaiety, merriment*.

106 **turbō, -āre, -āvī, -ātus**, *to disturb*.

īnspeciōsus, -a, -um [found only here], *not beautiful, ugly*.

107 **intrāsset**, = **intrāvisset**.

minister, ministrī, m., *attendant, servant*.

***invādō, invādere, invāsī, invāsus**, *to attack, rush upon, seize*.

***ōsculor, -ārī, -ātus sum**, *to kiss*.

108 ****diūtius**, compar. adv., *longer, for a rather long time*.

aequum, -ī, n., *what is fair; justice*.

ex aequō, *with justice, on equal terms*.

*****iūs, iūris**, n., *law; right*.

firmus, -a, -um, *firm, strong*.

approbō [ad- + **probō**, *to approve of*], **-āre, -āvī, -ātus**, *to approve, favor; to prove, demonstrate, establish*.

109 **maledīcō, maledīcere, maledīxī, maledictūrus** + dat., *to curse*.

pūrgāmentum, -ī, n., *what is swept/washed off* [**pūrgō, -āre, -āvī, -ātus**, *to clean*], *filth, dirt*.

A second shift of slaves to wait on the table; a beautiful slave boy; Fortunata's jealousy

Sūmptīs igitur matteīs respiciēns ad familiam Trimalchiō, 102
"Quid vōs," inquit, "adhūc nōn cēnāstis? Abīte, ut aliī veniant 103
ad officium." Subiit igitur alia classis, et illī quidem ex- 104
clāmāvēre: "Valē, Gaī," hī autem: "Avē, Gaī." Hinc prīmum hi- 105
laritās nostra turbāta est; nam cum puer nōn īnspeciōsus inter 106
novōs intrāsset ministrōs, invāsit eum Trimalchiō et ōsculārī 107
diūtius coepit. Itaque Fortūnāta, ut ex aequō iūs firmum ap- 108
probāret, maledīcere Trimalchiōnī coepit et pūrgāmentum dēde- 109
cusque praedicāre, quī nōn continēret libīdinem suam. Ultimō 110
etiam adiēcit: "Canis!" 111

---

dēdecus, dēdecoris, n., *disgrace, shame.*
110 praedicō [prae- + dicō, -āre, *to show*], -āre, -āvī, -ātus, *to announce, declare; to proclaim* (to be), *describe* (as).
continēō [con- + teneō], continēre, continuī, contentus, *to hold back.*
libīdō, libīdinis, f., *pleasure; desire, passion, lust.*
ultimō, adv., *finally.*
111 *adiciō [ad- + iaciō, *to throw*], adicere, adiēcī, adiectus, *to throw/place near, add.*

---

102 Sūmptīs . . . matteīs: ablative absolute, *after these delicacies had been taken up* (= *consumed*); the reference is to the freshly cooked and well-seasoned cock.
103 ut . . . veniant: purpose clause.
104 alia classis: cf. decuria (II.3.12 and note); Trimalchio has so many slaves that they have to be organized by divisions or squads.
106 nōn īnspeciōsus: litotes, = speciōsus.
107 intrāsset: pluperfect subjunctive in a temporal clause.
108 ut ex aequō . . . approbāret: purpose clause, *in order to . . . on equal terms* (with her husband).
109 pūrgāmentum dēdecusque praedicāre: *to describe* (him) *as. . . .*
110 quī . . . continēret: relative clause of characteristic.
111 "Canis!": a general term of abuse, with reference to shamelessness, recklessness, biting, or snarling, but here perhaps with a more specifically sexual reference to the male sexual organ.

112   **contrā, adv., *on the other hand.*
offendō, offendere, offendī, offēnsus, *to hit against, shock; to displease, offend.*
convīcium, -ī, n., *abuse, insult.*
*calix, calicis, m., *cup, goblet.*
*faciēs, faciēī, f., *face.*

113   *immittō [in- + mittō], immittere, immīsī, immissus, *to throw at.*
***exclāmō, -āre, -āvī, -ātus, *to shout out.*

114   *tremō, tremere, tremuī, *to quiver, tremble.*
**faciēs, faciēī, f., *face.*
admoveō, admovēre, admōvī, admōtus, *to move to.*
cōnsternō, cōnsternere, cōnstrāvī, cōnstrātus, *to stretch upon the ground; to terrify, dismay.*

115   Scintilla, -ae, f., *Scintilla* (wife of Habinnas; see line 13; the common noun scintilla, -ae, f., means *spark of fire*).
**trepidō, -āre, -āvī, -ātus, *to tremble; to be nervous/anxious.*
*sinus, -ūs, m., *curve; bosom, lap.*
**tegō, tegere, tēxī, tēctus, *to cover, hide; to protect.*

116   officiōsus, -a, -um, *dutiful, obliging, ready to serve.*
urceolus, -ī, m. [dim. of urceus, -ī, m., *pitcher, pot*], *little pitcher, water-pot.*
frīgidus, -a, -um, *cold.*
māla, -ae, f., *cheek.*
*admoveō, admovēre, admōvī, admōtus, *to move to, apply to.*

117   incumbō, incumbere, incubuī, *to lean/recline (upon).*
gemō, gemere, gemuī, gemitus, *to sigh, groan; to groan/grieve for, lament.*
*fleō, flēre, flēvī, flētus, *to weep, cry.*

118   ***contrā, adv., *on the other hand.*
ambūbaia, -ae, f. [from a Syrian word meaning "flute"], *flute-girl* (one of a class of Syrian girls who lived as prostitutes in Rome and played the flute at parties; see Horace, *Satires* 1.2.1–3 and Juvenal 3.60–66).

119   ***meminī, meminisse [perfect forms with present sense], *to remember.*
māchina, -ae, f. [Greek loan word], *machine* (e.g., engine, frame, scaffolding, staging, military machine); *platform* (on which slaves were offered for sale, usually called catasta, -ae, f., Greek loan word).

120   īnflō, -āre, -āvī, -ātus, *to blow into, inflate.*
rāna, -ae, f., *frog.*
**sinus, -ūs, m., *bosom.*
cōnspuō, cōnspuere, cōnspuī, cōnspūtus, *to spit.*

A family quarrel

Trimalchiō contrā offēnsus convīciō calicem in faciem   112
Fortūnātae immīsit. Illa tamquam oculum perdidisset ex-   113
clāmāvit manūsque trementēs ad faciem suam admōvit. Cōn-   114
sternāta est etiam Scintilla trepidantemque sinū suō tēxit. Immō   115
puer quoque officiōsus urceolum frīgidum ad mālam eius ad-   116
mōvit, super quem incumbēns Fortūnāta gemere ac flēre coepit.   117
Contrā Trimalchiō, "Quid enim?" inquit. "Ambūbaiam nōn   118
meminisse! Dē māchinā illam sustulī, hominem inter hominēs   119
fēcī. At īnflat sē tamquam rāna, et in sinum suum cōnspuit,   120
cōdex, nōn mulier. Sed hic quī in pergulā nātus est aedēs nōn   121
somniātur.   122

---

121 **caudex, caudicis,** m., *trunk of a tree, block of wood; dolt, blockhead.*
    cōdex, vulgar for **caudex** (see p. 240).
    pergula, -ae, f., *booth, shop* (in front of a house); *brothel; hut, hovel.*
    **nāscor, nāscī, nātus sum, *to be born.*
    aedēs [aedis], aedis, aedium, f., *building; temple; house.*
122 **somniō, -āre, -āvī, -ātus,** *to dream (of).*
    somniātur, vulgar, affected use of deponent for active (see p. 244).

---

112 **calicem . . . immīsit:** for drinking vessels used as weapons in drunken brawls, see Horace, *Odes* 1.27.1, Ovid, *Metamorphoses* 12.242–244 (battle of Lapiths and Centaurs), and Juvenal 5.24–29.
113 **tamquam (sī) . . . perdidisset:** pluperfect subjunctive expressing a past contrary-to-fact idea.
115 **trepidantem:** supply **Fortūnātam.**
116 **puer:** i.e., a slave boy.
117 **super quem:** the antecedent is **urceolum,** not **puer.**
118 **Quid enim?:** *What then? How then? There you are!*
    Ambūbaiam nōn meminisse!: exclamatory infinitive with accusative subject.
119 **hominem inter hominēs:** note the repetition of words (see p. 251).
120 **in sinum suum cōnspuit:** proverbial of a boastful person; spitting on one's breast was thought to avert divine anger at one's presumptuous hopes (Pliny, *Natural History* 28.36) or at one's boasting (Juvenal 7.112).

(notes continued on next page)

121   cōdex, nōn mulier: cf. piper, nōn homō, II.2.64.
      hic quī . . . nātus est. . . . : a proverb and therefore expressed in
      the masculine, though referring to Fortunata: *he who is born in a*
      hut doesn't dream of a palace, i.e., you cannot expect better behav-
      ior from a woman of such humble birth as Fortunata.

123   *genius, -ī, m., *genius* (tutelar deity of a person, one's guardian
      spirit/angel).
      propitius, -a, -um, *well-disposed, propitious.*
      ***cūrō, -āre, -āvī, -ātus, *to care (for),* look after; *to see to it* (that) +
      ut + subjn. or subjn. only.
      domō, domāre, domuī, domitus, *to tame, break, subdue.*
      domāta, vulgar for domita (see p. 244).

124   Cassandra, -ae, f. [Greek name], *Cassandra* (daughter of Priam,
      king of Troy; she kept predicting the doom of the city, but no
      one listened to her).
      caligārius, -a, -um [see p. 244], *wearing soldier's boots* [caliga, -ae,
      f.].
      dipundiārius, -a, -um [see p. 244], *worth two asses* [the as, gen.,
      assis, m., was the basic unit of Roman coinage].
      ***sēstertius, -ī, m., *sesterce* (small silver coin).
      sēstertium, gen. pl.

125   centiēs, adv., *a hundred times.*
      sēstertium centiēs, = sēstertium centiēs centēna mīlia,
      10,000,000.
      ***mentior, -īrī, -ītus sum, *to lie.*
      Agathō [Greek name, related to the Greek word for "good"], m.,
      Agathon.
      unguentārius, -ī, m., *perfume seller.*

126   proximē, adv., *shortly before, recently.*
      *sēdūcō, sēdūcere, sēdūxī, sēductus, *to lead away, draw aside.*
      suādeō, suādēre, suāsī, suāsus, *to advise, urge.*
      patior, patī, passus sum, *to suffer, bear; to allow, permit.*

127   ***genus, generis, n., *race, stock, family.*
      intereō, interīre, interiī, interitūrus, irreg., *to perish, die.*
      bonātus, -a, -um [word found only here, see p. 245; bonus, -a,
      -um, *good*], *good-natured.*

128   *levis, -is, -e, *light; unreliable, irresponsible; fickle.*
      ascia, -ae, f., *ax.*
      *crūs, crūris, n., *leg.*
      **impingō [in- + pangō, *to fix*], impingere, impēgī, impactus,
      to fix on; to push, thrust at/upon; to strike/drive into.
      *rēctē, adv., *rightly, correctly;* here introducing a threat, *all right*
      then!
      *unguis, unguis, unguium, m., *fingernail.*

Trimalchio's wrath

"Ita genium meum propitium habeam, cūrābō domāta sit   123
Cassandra caligāria. Et ego, homō dipundiārius, sēstertium   124
centiēs accipere potuī. Scīs tū mē nōn mentīrī. Agathō unguen-   125
tārius proximē sēdūxit mē et, 'Suādeō,' inquit, 'nōn patiāris   126
genus tuum interīre.' At ego dum bonātus agō et nōlō viderī   127
levis, ipse mihi asciam in crūs impēgī. Rēctē, cūrābō mē un-   128
guibus quaerās. Et ut dēpraesentiārum intellegās quid tibi   129
fēceris: Habinna, nōlō statuam eius in monumentō meō pōnās,   130
nē mortuus quidem lītēs habeam. Immō, ut sciat mē posse   131
malum dare, nōlō mē mortuum bāsiet."   132

---

129   **quaerō, quaerere, quaesīvī** or **quaesiī, quaesītus,** *to seek, seek*
        out.
        dēpraesentiārum, adv. [word found only here and at one other
        place in Petronius, see p. 246], *at present, here and now.*
        **intellegō, intellegere, intellēxī, intellēctus, *to understand.*
131   ****līs, lītis,** f., *quarrel, dispute, lawsuit.*
132   **malum dare,** *to punish, mete out punishment.*
        bāsiō, -āre, -āvī, -ātus, *to kiss.*

---

123   **Ita genium meum propitium habeam:** *So may I have.* . . . ; the
        wish expressed with the subjunctive adds determination to the
        main statement, **cūrābō domāta sit.** . . . (cf. II.2.84–85; II.4.3–4;
        and II.5.47–49) (see p. 252). We might say, "May I not have . . .
        if I don't see to it that. . . ."
        cūrābō (ut) domāta sit: substantive clause of result dependent
        on a verb of effort, *I'll see to it that.* . . . **domāta sit:** here for
        domētur.
124   **Cassandra caligāria:** Trimalchio labels Fortunata a Cassandra
        because of her sulkiness and her ravings. The epithet **caligāria**
        imputes to her a militant aggressiveness. With this description
        of Fortunata, compare Cicero's description of Clodia as a
        Palātīna Mēdēa, *Medea of the Palatine Hill* (*Pro Caelio* 18), and
        Caligula's description of his greatgrandmother Livia Augusta
        as a **Ulixēs stolātus,** a *Ulysses in Petticoats* (Suetonius, *Caligula*
        23.2).
        homō dipundiārius: i.e., worthless fool that I was.
125   **accipere potuī:** *I could have received,* i.e., as a dowry if I had mar-
        ried another woman.
        Scīs tū: addressed to his wife.   (notes continued on next page)

126 **Suādeō (ut)** . . . **nōn patiāris**: indirect command with colloquial omission of **ut** (see p. 251); introduced wrongly by **(ut) nōn** instead of **nē** (see p. 250), *I urge you not to allow.* . . .

128 **asciam in crūs impēgī**: proverbial.

cūrābō mē . . . **quaerās**: substantive clause of result dependent on a verb of effort, *I'll see to it that you want to seek me out* (i.e., dig me up from my grave) *with your fingernails.*

130 **nōlō** . . . **pōnās**: **nōlō** may be followed by either an infinitive or a subjunctive with or without **ut**.

131 **nē**: introducing a negative purpose clause, *so that I won't.* . . .

mortuus quidem: *even when* (I am) *dead.*

133 *****post**, prep. + acc., *after.*

fulmen, fulminis, n., *thunderbolt.*

dēsinō, dēsinere, dēsiī, dēsitus, *to cease, stop* + infin.

134 ***īrāscor, īrāscī, īrātus sum**, *to be angry.*

*****nostrum**: gen. of **nōs**.

****peccō, -āre, -āvī, -ātūrus**, *to commit a fault, offend, sin.*

135 ****fleō, flēre, flēvī, flētus**, *to weep, cry.*

****genius, -ī**, m., *genius* (tutelar deity of a person, one's guardian spirit/angel).

136 ***appellō** [**ad-** + **pellō**, *to strike*], **-āre, -āvī, -ātus**, *to call* (someone by name), *address.*

****frangō, frangere, frēgī, frāctus**, *to break; to move; to soften.*

sē frangere, *to relent, give way.*

ultrā, adv., *farther, longer, more.*

137 **lacrima, -ae**, f., *tear.*

138 **pecūlium, -ī**, n., *money, property* (usually that acquired and saved by a slave without legal ownership).

****fruor, fruī, frūctus sum** + abl., *to enjoy.*

****frūnīscor, frūnīscī, frūnītus sum** [archaic and vulgar variant of **fruor**, see p. 247], + acc. or abl., *to enjoy* (cf. II.2.44 and II.2.84).

perperam, adv., *wrongly.*

*****faciēs, faciēī**, f., *face.*

139 **īnspuō, īnspuere, īnspuī, īnspūtus**, *to spit on.*

The guests intercede on behalf of Fortunata; Trimalchio defends himself.

Post hoc fulmen Habinnās rogāre coepit ut iam dēsineret   133
īrāscī et, "Nēmō," inquit, "nostrum nōn peccat. Hominēs   134
sumus, nōn deī." Idem et Scintilla flēns dīxit ac per genium eius   135
Gaium appellandō rogāre coepit ut sē frangeret. Nōn tenuit ul-   136
trā lacrimās Trimalchiō et, "Rogō," inquit, "Habinnā, sīc   137
pecūlium tuum frūnīscāris: sī quid perperam fēcī, in faciem   138
meam īnspue.   139

(paragraph continued on page 185)

---

133 **ut . . . dēsineret**: indirect command.
134 **īrāscī**: infinitive, *to be angry.*
     Nēmō . . . nostrum: *No one of us.*
     Hominēs sumus, nōn deī: proverbial.
136 **Gaium appellandō**: gerund, ablative of means, *by calling him Gaius*, i.e., by appealing to him with his **praenōmen** in as personal a manner as possible.
     ut sē frangeret: indirect command.
137 **Habinnā**: vocative.
     sīc pecūlium tuum frūnīscāris: the wish expressed with the subjunctive adds force to the thought that follows, *so may you enjoy your wealth*. . . . (cf. II.5.123–124) (see p. 252).

140   ***bāsiō, -āre, -āvī, -ātus**, *to kiss.*
     frūgālis, -is, -e, *thrifty, frugal.*
     **propter, prep. + acc., *because of, on account of.*
     fōrma, -ae, f., *beauty.*
141   ***frūgī**, indecl. adj. [from **frūx, frūgis**, f., *fruit; result, success, value*:
     frūgī is dative of purpose], *useful, fit, honest, virtuous.*
     *liber, librī, m., *book.*
     **legō, legere, lēgī, lēctus, *to read.*
     thraecium, -ī, n., *Thracian gladiator's suit* (for Thracian gladiators,
     see II.2.128).
142   **diārium, -ī**, n., *diary;* pl., *daily allowance of food* (for slaves; see
     Cato, *On Agriculture* 56).
     arcisellium, -ī, n. [vulgar, found only here, see p. 245; **arcus, -ūs**,
     m., *arch* + **sella, -ae**, f., *chair*], *round-back chair.*
     parō, -āre, -āvī, -ātus, *to prepare, make.*
     trulla, -ae, f., *dipper, scoop* (for dipping wine from the mixing
     bowl into drinking cups).
143   ****dignus, -a, -um**, *worthy.*
     in oculīs ferre, *to keep ever in one's thoughts, to hold as the apple of
     one's eye.*
     vetō, -āre, -āvī, -ātus, *to forbid.*
144   **fulcipedia, -ae**, f. [vulgar, found only here, see p. 246; **fulciō,
     -īre**, *to prop up* + **pēs, pedis**, m., *foot*], meaning uncertain,
     perhaps *high-heeled, high-stepper.*
     *suādeō, suādēre, suāsī, suāsus, *to advise, urge.*
     concoquō, concoquere, concoxī, concoctus, *to cook together; to
     digest; to endure, suffer, put up with; to think upon, weigh, consider
     well.*
     *mīlva, -ae, f. [word found only here; term of abuse; feminine
     form of **mīlvus, -ī**, m., *kite*, a rapacious bird of prey], *she-kite.*
145   **ringor, ringī, rictus sum**, *to open the mouth and show the teeth; to be
     angry, snarl.*
     amāsiuncula, -ae, f. [word found only here, but cf. II.2.110; dim.
     of **amāsiō, amāsiōnis**, m., *lover*], *little darling.*
     aliōquīn, adv., *otherwise.*
     *experior, experīrī, expertus sum, *to try, prove, put to the test; to
     undergo, experience.*
     *cerebrum, -ī, n., *brain; temper, anger.*
146   **nōstī**, = **nōvistī**, from **nōscō**.
     **semel, adv., *once.*
     ***dēstinō, -āre, -āvī, -ātus, *to fix, resolve, intend; to fix upon.*
     clāvus, -ī, m., *nail.*
     trabālis, -is, -e, *of/for a beam* [**trabs, trabis**, f.].
         clāvus trabālis, *spike.*
147   ****fīgō, fīgere, fīxī, fīxus**, *to fix, fasten.*

"Puerum bāsiāvī frūgālissimum, nōn propter fōrmam, sed quia   140
frūgī est: decem partēs dīcit, librum ab oculō legit, thraecium sibi   141
dē diāriīs fēcit, arcisellium dē suō parāvit et duās trullās. Nōn   142
est dignus quem in oculīs feram? Sed Fortūnāta vetat. Ita tibi   143
vidētur, fulcipedia? Suādeō bonum tuum concoquās, mīlva, et   144
mē nōn faciās ringentem, amāsiuncula: aliōquīn experiēris cere-   145
brum meum. Nōstī mē: quod semel dēstināvī, clāvō trabālī   146
fīxum est.   147

---

141   **decem partēs**: his table of tens; cf. II.2.141.
       ab oculō: *at sight.*
       thraecium: from his daily allowance the boy has made or bought
       a toy gladiator's suit to play the Roman equivalent of Cowboys
       and Indians.
142   **dē suō**: *from his own* (resources). The lad is creative!
143   **dignus quem . . . feram**: **dignus** is regularly followed by a rela-
       tive clause in the subjunctive (cf. II.2.113–114), *worth keeping my
       eyes on.*
144   **fulcipedia**: if the adjective here refers to Fortunata's high-heeled
       shoes, it may also be a stab at her pride and self-assurance.
       Suādeō (ut) . . . concoquās: indirect command. **bonum tuum**:
       what's good for you.
       mīlva: cf. II.2.23–24, **mulier quae mulier mīlvīnum genus.**
145   **nōn faciās**: a second indirect command dependent on **suādeō**,
       which would regularly take **nē** instead of **nōn.**
       experiēris: future indicative.
146   **clāvō trabālī**: nails were used in several primitive Roman rituals,
       being driven into the wall of a temple to avert pestilence and to
       mark the number of years (Livy 7.3). Horace describes the
       goddess Necessity as carrying **clāvōs trabālēs** (*Odes* 1.35.17–
       18) as symbols of fixity. To fix something with a **clāvus tra-
       bālis** became proverbial for nailing it down for good (see
       Cicero, *Against Verres* 5.53).

148   **vīvus, -a, -um, *alive, living.*
149   *suāviter, adv., *sweetly, pleasantly.*
     suāviter est + dat., (one) *is having a good time.*
     tam . . . quam, = **tālis . . . quālēs,** *such as.*
     *virtūs, virtūtis, f., *excellence; bravery; manliness; ability.*
150   corcillum, -ī, n. [word found only here, see pp. 245, 246, =
     corculum, -ī, n.; dim. of **cor, cordis,** n., *heart*], *(little) heart* (as
     the seat of intelligence); *brains, intellect.*
     *cēterī, -ae, -a, *the other, the rest.*
     cētera, *all other things, all else.*
151   quisquiliae, -ārum, f. pl., *waste, refuse; sweepings, rubbish, trash.*
     quisquilia, vulgar, affected n. pl. instead of f. pl. (see p. 243).
152   fēlīcitās, fēlīcitātis, f., *happiness, good-fortune.*
     *dissiliō [dis- + saliō, *to jump*], dissilīre, dissiluī, *to leap/burst
     asunder, fly apart.*
     sterteia, -ae, f. [word found only here], *one who snores* [**stertō,**
     stertere].
     *etiamnum, particle, *yet, still, even now.*
     ***plōrō, -āre, -āvī, -ātus, *to cry aloud; to lament; to weep.*
153   **fātum, -ī, n., *fate.*
154   **fortūna, -ae, f., *fortune, good luck.*
     frūgālitās, frūgālitātis, f., *frugality.*
     perdūcō, perdūcere, perdūxī, perductus, *to lead.*

155   tam . . . quam, *as . . . as.*
     candēlābrum, -ī, n., *candelabrum* (stand for holding burning can-
     dles or lamps).
        candēlābrus, vulgar m. for n. (see p. 242).
     ***ad summam, *in short, to be brief.*
156   mētior, metīrī, mēnsus sum, *to measure.*
     celerius, compar. adv., *more swiftly.*
157   rōstrum, -ī, n., *bill, beak, snout, muzzle;* colloquial, *the parts of the
     face around the mouth.*
     barbātus, -a, -um, *bearded.*
     *labrum, -ī, n., *lip.*
     ungō, ungere, ūnxī, ūnctus, *to smear, besmear, anoint.*
158   *dēliciae, -ārum, f. pl., *beloved, favorite, pet.*
     *ipsimus, -ī, m. [superlative of **ipse,** which may be used to mean
     master = *the man himself*], *master.*
     quottuordecim, indecl. adj., *fourteen.*
     *turpis, -is, -e, *ugly, base.*
159   **ipsima, -ae, f., *mistress* (see note above, line 158).
     satis faciō, facere, fēcī, factus + dat., *to give satisfaction, satisfy.*

Change of topic: Trimalchio's career from slavery to riches

"Sed vīvōrum meminerimus. Vōs rogō, amīcī, ut vōbīs   148
suāviter sit. Nam ego quoque tam fuī quam vōs estis, sed virtūte   149
meā ad hoc pervēnī. Corcillum est quod hominēs facit, cētera   150
quisquilia omnia. 'Bene emō, bene vēndō'; alius alia vōbīs dīcet.   151
Fēlīcitāte dissiliō. Tū autem, sterteia, etiamnum plōrās? Iam   152
cūrābō fātum tuum plōrēs. Sed, ut coeperam dīcere, ad hanc mē   153
fortūnam frūgālitās mea perdūxit.   154

---

148   **vīvōrum meminerimus**: see II.2.27.
      ut vōbīs suāviater sit: indirect command, *to have a good time.*
151   **alius alia vōbīs dīcet**: *some people will tell you some things, others*
      other things, implying that some people might attribute his suc-
      cess to factors other than his simply buying well and selling
      well.
152   **Fēlīcitāte dissiliō**: cf. **gaudimōniō dissiliō** (II.4.5).
      Tū: addressed to Fortunata.
153   **cūrābō (ut) . . . plōrēs**: substantive clause of result dependent on
      a verb of effort.

Trimalchio's youth: sex with his master and his master's wife

"Tam magnus ex Asiā vēnī quam hic candēlābrus est. Ad   155
summam, quōtīdiē mē solēbam ad illum mētīrī, et ut celerius   156
rōstrum barbātum habērem, labra dē lucernā ungēbam. Tamen   157
ad dēliciās ipsimī annōs quattuordecim fuī. Nec turpe est quod   158
dominus iubet. Ego tamen et ipsimae satis faciēbam. Scītis quid   159
dīcam: taceō, quia nōn sum dē glōriōsīs.   160

---

160   ****taceō, tacēre, tacuī**, *to be silent.*
      glōriōsus, -a, -um, *bragging, boastful.*

---

156   **ut celerius . . . habērem**: purpose clauses that contain a compar-
      ative adverb are usually introduced by **quō** instead of **ut**.
157   **dē lucernā**: i.e., with oil from the lamp.
158   **ad dēliciās . . . fuī**: **ad** here expresses purpose; he served as the
      sexual pet of his master.
      Nec turpe est quod dominus iubet: cf. Seneca, *Controversiae* 4
      (pref. 10): **Inpudīcitia in ingenuō crīmen est, in servō**

necessitās, in lībertō officium.

159　satis faciēbam: *I satisfied.* . . . , a euphemism.

quid dīcam: indirect question with the subjunctive.

160　dē glōriōsīs: partitive, (one) *of the boastful* (people) = *I'm not boastful.*

162　*ecce, interj., *behold!*

capiō, capere, cēpī, captus, *to take, get.*

***ipsimus, -ī, m., *master* (see note above, line 158).

cerebellum, -ī, n. [dim. of cerebrum, -ī, n., *brain*], *(small) brain.*

cohērēs, cohērēdis, m./f., *co-heir.*

163　Caesar, Caesaris, m., *Caesar* (i.e., the emperor).

*lāticlāvius, -a, -um, *having a broad purple stripe* [lātus clāvus, -ī, m.]; *senatorial* (the tunic with a broad purple stripe was worn by senators).

164　**satis, adv. or substantive, *enough.*

concupīscō, concupīscere, concupīvī or concupiī, concupītus, *to desire strongly.*

*negōtior, -ārī, -atus sum, *to do/engage in business* (especially wholesale or banking ventures).

165　*moror, -ārī, -ātus sum, *to delay.*

**nāvis, nāvis, nāvium, f., *ship.*

*aedificō, -āre, -āvī, -ātus, *to build.*

*onerō, -āre, -āvī, -ātus, *to burden, load.*

166　*contrā, prep. + acc., *against.*

contrā aurum, *worth its weight in gold.*

Sex pays off; Trimalchio inherits a fortune and goes into business.

"Cēterum, quemadmodum dī volunt, dominus in domō fac- 161
tus sum, et ecce cēpī ipsimī cerebellum. Quid multa? Cohē- 162
rēdem mē Caesarī fēcit, et accēpī patrimōnium lāticlāvium. 163
Nēminī tamen nihil satis est. Concupīvī negōtiārī. Nē multīs 164
vōs morer, quīnque nāvēs aedificāvī, onerāvī vīnum—et tunc 165
erat contrā aurum—mīsī Rōmam. 166

---

162   **cerebellum**: the diminutive may express affection. **cēpī ipsimī cerebellum**: i.e., my dear master thought only about me, I took his fancy.

     Quid multa: *What more need I say?*

     Cohērēdem mē Caesarī: it was usual to name the emperor as a legatee in one's will in order to prevent him from annulling the will and taking the whole estate himself; Nero was guilty of the latter (Suetonius, *Nero* 32.2).

163   **lāticlāvium**: i.e., sufficient to make him eligible for the senate as far as money was concerned.

164   **Nēminī . . . nihil**: vulgar pleonastic double negative, translate *for anyone* (cf. II.2.24) (see p. 250).

     Nē multīs (verbīs) vōs morer: negative purpose clause.

165   **aedificāvī, onerāvī . . . mīsī**: asyndeton in rapid, excited narrative (see p. 251).

167 ***nāvis, nāvis, nāvium, f., *ship.*
naufragō [nāvis + frangō, *to break*], -āre, -āvī, *to suffer ship-wreck.*
naufragārunt, = naufragāvērunt.
*factum, -ī, n., *happening, event.*
168 ***fābula, -ae, f., *story, tale.*
Neptūnus, -ī, m., *Neptune* (god of the sea).
**trecentiēs sēstertium, = trecentiēs centēna mīlia sēstertium, *30,000,000 sesterces.*
*dēvorō, -āre, -āvī, -ātus, *to swallow, gobble up, devour.*
169 **dēficiō [dē- + faciō], dēficere, dēfēcī, dēfectus, *to leave, cease, fail, end.*
*mī, = mihi.
**iactūra, -ae, f., *a throwing away; loss.*
gustus, -ūs, m., *tasting (of food), taste.*
gustī, gen. sing.; vulgar second declension form instead of fourth (see p. 243).
170 **factum, -ī, n., *happening, event.*
**fēlīx, fēlīcis, *fortunate, prosperous.*
171 ***fortis, -is, -e, *brave, strong, courageous.*
172 fortitūdō, fortitūdinis, f., *bravery, strength, courage.*
**onerō, -āre, -āvī, -ātus, *to burden, load.*
rūrsus [rūrsum], adv., *again.*
lāridum, -ī, n., *lard.*
lārdum, -ī, n., syncopated colloquial variant (see p. 241).
173 faba, -ae, f., *bean.*
sēplasium, -ī, n. [word found only here], *perfume* (named after the via Seplasia in Capua where perfumes were sold).
mancipium, -ī, n., *slave.*

Disaster followed by a second try

"Putārēs mē hoc iussisse: omnēs nāvēs naufragārunt, factum 167
nōn fābula. Ūnō diē Neptūnus trecentiēs sēstertium dēvorāvit. 168
Putātis mē dēfēcisse? Nōn meherculēs mī haec iactūra gustī fuit, 169
tamquam nihil factī. Alterās fēcī maiōrēs et meliōrēs et fēlī- 170
ciōrēs, ut nēmō nōn mē virum fortem dīceret. Scītis, magna 171
nāvis magnam fortitūdinem habet. Onerāvī rūrsus vīnum, lar- 172
dum, fabam, sēplasium, mancipia. 173

---

167 **Putārēs**: potential subjunctive, *You would have thought.*
  mē hoc iussisse: i.e., that the ships should be wrecked. Trimalchio could be thought to have ordered the ships to be
  wrecked because of the immense profit he made in his second
  mercantile venture that was prompted by his loss in his first
  venture.
  factum nōn fābula: alliteration (see p. 251).
169 **Nōn . . . mī haec iactūra gustī fuit**: **gustī** is genitive of indefinite
  value, *the loss wasn't worth a mouthful to me*, i.e., I didn't mind it
  at all.
170 **tamquam nihil factī**: **factī** is partitive genitive with **nihil**, *as if
  nothing at all* (had happened).
  Alterās: colloquial for **aliās** (see p. 245); supply **nāvēs**.
  maiōrēs . . . meliōrēs: alliteration (see p. 251).
171 **ut . . . nōn . . . dīceret**: result clause.
  Scītis, magna nāvis . . . habet: colloquial parataxis instead of
  subordination as indirect statement (see p. 249).

174   *pius, -a, -um, *pious, dutiful, loyal.*
      *aurum, -ī, n., *gold.*
175   **mī, = mihi.
      **aureus, -ī, m., *gold coin.*
176   *pecūlium, -ī, n., *money, property* (usually that acquired by a
      slave without legal ownership).
      fermentum, -ī, n., *leaven, yeast.*
      ***citō, adv., *quickly.*
177   *cursus, -ūs, m., *course; way; voyage.*
      *centiēs, adv., *a hundred times.*
      centiēs sēstertium, = centiēs centēna mīlia sēstertium,
          10,000,000 *sesterces*
      corrotundō [con- + rotundō, *to make round*], -āre, -āvī, -ātus, *to
          make round, round off;* slang, *to make a sum of money.*
      *redimō [re-/red- + emō, *to buy*], redimere, redēmī, redēmp-
          tus, *to buy back, repurchase, buy up.*
178   *fundus, -ī, m., *farm, estate.*
      patrōnus, -ī, m., *patron.*
      **aedificō [aedēs, aedis, aedium, f., *house* + faciō], -āre, -āvī,
          -ātus, *to build.*
      comparō [con- + parō, *to prepare*], -āre, -āvī, -ātus, *to prepare; to
          purchase, buy.*
179   vēnālīcia, -ōrum, n. pl., *young slaves.*
      coemō [con- + emō, *to buy*], coemere, coēmī, coēmptus, *to pur-
          chase together, buy up.*
      iūmentum, -ī, n., *beast of burden, horse, mule, ass.*
180   *favus, -ī, m., *honeycomb.*

Fortunata sacrifices all to help her husband: success!

"Hōc locō Fortūnāta rem piam fēcit; omne enim aurum   174
suum, omnia vestīmenta vēndidit et mī centum aureōs in manū   175
posuit. Hoc fuit pecūliī meī fermentum. Citō fit quod dī volunt.   176
Ūnō cursū centiēs sēstertium corrotundāvī. Statim redēmī   177
fundōs omnēs, quī patrōnī meī fuerant. Aedificō domum, com-   178
parō vēnālicia, coemō iūmenta; quicquid tangēbam, crēscēbat   179
tamquam favus.   180

---

176   **Citō fit quod dī volunt**: proverbial.
178   **quī patrōnī meī**: genitive of possession, *that belonged to my pa-*
       tron, i.e., to C. Pompeius (see note on II.1.6).
       Aedificō . . . comparō . . . coemō: asyndeton (see p. 252).
180   **tamquam favus**: for the comparison, see II.2.31.

181 *plūs, plūris, n., *more.*
     *patria, -ae, f., *fatherland, home-town.*
182 ***tabula, -ae, f., *board; waxed writing-tablet.*
     negōtiātiō, negōtiātiōnis, f., *wholesale business.*
183 **lībertus, -ī, m., *freedman.*
     faenerō, -āre, -āvī, -ātus, *to lend on interest.*
     *sānē, adv., *soundly, truly, really.*
     negōtium, -ī, n., *business.*
184 exhortor, -ārī, -ātus sum, *to urge, exhort.*
     exhortāvit, vulgar active for deponent (see p. 243).
     mathēmaticus, -ī, m., [Greek loan word], *mathematician; as-*
     trologer (usually Chaldaeans; here apparently an Egyptian).
     **forte, adv., *by chance* [fors, fortis, f.].
     **colōnia, -ae, f., *colony.*
185 Graeculiō, Graeculiōnis, m. [vulgar word-formation with end-
     ing in -ō, see p. 244; word found only here; dim. of Graecus, -ī,
     m., *a Greek*], *a Greekling.*
     Serāpa, -ae, m. [Egyptian name], *Serapa.*
     ***nōmen, nōminis, n., *name.*
     cōnsiliātor, cōnsiliātōris, m., *counsellor; sharer in the counsels* (of).
186 acia, -ae, f. [rare word, see p. 245], *thread* (for sewing).
     acus, -ūs, f., *needle.*
     ***mī, = mihi.
     *expōnō, expōnere, exposuī, expositus, *to put forth, expound.*
     *intestīna, -ōrum, n. pl., *guts, intestines.*
     intestīnās, vulgar f. for n. (see p. 242).
187 ***tantum, adv., *only.*
     *prīdiē, adv., *on the day before.*
188 putāssēs, = putāvissēs.
     *semper, adv., *always.*
     *mēcum, = cum mē.
     ***habitō, -āre, -āvī, -ātus, *to live.*
     habitāsse, = habitāvisse.
189 intersum, interesse, interfuī, interfutūrus, irreg., *to be among, be*
     present.

Trimalchio retires from shipping, goes into usury, and is advised by a soothsayer.

"Postquam coepī plūs habēre quam tōta patria mea habet,   181
manum dē tabulā: sustulī mē dē negōtiātiōne et coepī per   182
lībertōs faenerāre. Et sānē nōlentem mē negōtium meum agere   183
exhortāvit mathēmaticus, quī vēnerat forte in colōniam nostram,   184
Graeculiō, Serāpa nōmine, cōnsiliātor deōrum. Hic mihi dīxit   185
etiam ea quae oblītus eram; ab aciā et acū mī omnia exposuit; in-   186
testīnās meās nōverat; tantum quod mihi nōn dīxerat quid prīdiē   187
cēnāveram. Putāssēs illum semper mēcum habitāsse. Rogō,   188
Habinnā—putō, interfuistī—:   189

(paragraph continued on page 197)

182   **manum dē tabulā**: apparently originally a school teacher's
      phrase, *Hands off your tablet!* (Cicero, *Letters to His Friends*
      7.25.1) = *Stop scribbling!* or *Stop writing* (and let me see what
      you've done so far)! Here, perhaps supply **sustulī**, *I took my
      hand off the tablet*, i.e., I stopped my commercial ventures.
183   **nōlentem mē negōtium meum agere exhortāvit**: i.e., the as-
      trologer encouraged the reluctant Trimalchio to continue his
      business ventures.
185   **nōmine**: ablative of respect, *by name.*
      cōnsiliātor deōrum: i.e., a man privy to the counsels of the gods.
186   **etiam ea quae oblītus eram**: *even those things* (about myself) *that
      I had* (long since) *forgotten.*
      ab aciā et acū: proverbial, from A to Z.
187   **tantum quod . . . nōn**: i.e., almost.
      quid . . . cēnāveram: indirect question here with the indicative
      (vulgar) instead of the subjunctive, **cēnāvissem** (see p. 249).
188   **Putāssēs**: pluperfect subjunctive expressing what might have
      happened (past potentiality), *You would have. . . .*

For passages from ancient sources on trade by sea in the ancient
Mediterranean and on moneylending, see Jo-Ann Shelton, *As the
Romans Did*, pp. 139–141.

190　*domina, -ae, f., *mistress.*

　　　parum, adv., *too little, not enough.*

　　　***fēlīx, fēlīcis, *fortunate, prosperous, happy.*

191　*pār, paris, *equal.*

　　　**grātia, -ae, f., *favor; thanks.*

　　　*referō, referre, retulī, relātus, irreg., *to bear/carry/bring back; to repay.*

　　　lātifundium, -ī, n. [lātus, -a, -um, *wide* + fundus, -ī, m., *farm*], *large estate/farm.*

192　*possideō, possidēre, possēdī, possessus, *to hold, possess.*

　　　vīpera, -ae, f., *viper, snake, serpent.*

　　　**sub, prep. + abl., *under.*

　　　*āla, -ae, f., *wing; armpit.*

　　　nūtrīcō, -āre, -āvī, -ātus, *to nourish.*

193　restō, restāre, restitī, *to remain.*

　　　trīgintā, indecl. adj., *thirty.*

　　　mēnsis, mēnsis, m., *month.*

194　**praetereā, adv., *besides, moreover.*

　　　*hērēditās, hērēditātis, f., *inheritance.*

195　***fātum, -ī, n., *fate.*

　　　fātus, vulgar m. for n. (see p. 242).

　　　**contingō [con- + tangō, *to touch*], contingere, contigī, contāctus, *to touch;* + dat., *to happen* (to one), *befall.*

　　　**fundus, -ī, m., *farm, estate.*

　　　Āpūlia, -ae, f., *Apulia* (a province of south-east Italy).

　　　iungō, iungere, iūnxī, iūnctus, *to join* + acc. and dat. (something to something).

196　***satis, adv., *enough, sufficiently.*

　　　***vīvus, -a, -um, *alive, living.*

"'Tū dominam tuam dē rēbus illīs fēcistī. Tū parum fēlīx in   190
amīcīs es. Nēmō umquam tibi parem grātiam refert. Tū lātifun-   191
dia possidēs. Tū vīperam sub ālā nūtrīcās,' et, quod vōbīs nōn   192
dīxerim, etiam nunc mī restāre vītae annōs trīgintā et mēnsēs   193
quattuor et diēs duōs. Praetereā citō accipiam hērēditātem. Hoc   194
mihi dīcit fātus meus. Quod sī contigerit fundōs Āpūliae iun-   195
gere, satis vīvus pervēnerō.   196

---

190   **'Tū dominam tuam . . . fēcistī':** direct quotation of the soothsayer's words to Trimalchio; deliberately vague, perhaps, *You
made your mistress* (i.e., your wife) (what she is) *from those things*
(i.e., from your wealth).
in amīcīs: *in the case of your friends.*

192   **quod vōbīs nōn dīxerim:** potential subjunctive in a cautious as-
sertion, *what I should hardly tell you.*

194   **citō:** = mox.

195   **fātus meus:** perhaps referring to the astrologer Serapa, perhaps
simply to his horoscope.
sī contigerit . . . pervēnerō: future more vivid condition with future perfect indicative in both clauses. **contigerit:** supply
mihi.

196   **satis vīvus pervēnerō:** *I shall have arrived* (done) *well enough*
(**satis**) *while alive.*

197 **vigilō, -āre, -āvī, -ātūrus,** *to be awake.*
  *****aedificō, -āre, -āvī, -ātus,** *to build.*
198 **cusuc,** word of uncertain origin and meaning, perhaps *hut, shanty.*
  templum, -ī, n., *temple.*
  cēnātiō, cēnātiōnis, f., *dining room.*
199 ***cubiculum, -ī,** n., *bedroom.*
  vīgintī, indecl. adj., *twenty.*
  *****porticus, -ūs,** f., *porticus* (walkway covered by a roof supported by columns).
    porticūs, vulgar m. for f. (see p. 242).
  marmorātus, -a, -um, *covered with marble* [**marmor, marmoris,** n.].
  *sūrsum, adv., *up, upward; upstairs.*
    sūsum, vulgar variant (see p. 242).
  cellātiō, cellātiōnis, f. [vulgar word-formation with ending in -ō, see p. 244; word found only here], *series of store-rooms* [**cella, -ae,** f.].
200 ****cubiculum, -ī,** n., *bedroom.*
  dormiō, -īre, -īvī, -ītūrus, *to sleep.*
  *vīpera, -ae, f., *viper, snake, serpent.*
  sessōrium, -ī, n. [word found only here, see p. 246; **sedeō, sedēre, sēdī, sessūrus,** *to sit*], *sitting room.*
  ōstiārius, -ī, m., *door-keeper* (who guards the **ōstium, -ī, n., *doorway,* and was often referred to as the **iānitor**).
201 ***cella, -ae,** f., *room.*
  perbonus, -a, -um, *very good/fine.*
  hospitium, -ī, n., *guest-chamber; guest-house.*
  *hospes, hospitis, m., *guest.*
  C. = centum, *one hundred.*
202 **Scaurus, -ī,** m., *Scaurus* (a member of a famous noble Roman family).
  hūc, adv., *to here, here.*
  nusquam, adv., *nowhere.*
  māvoluit, vulgar for **māluit,** as if the verb were **māvolō, māvolere, māvoluī,** instead of the irregular **mālō, mālle, māluī** (see p. 244).
  hospitor, -ārī, -ātus sum, *to be a guest, put up, lodge.*
203 **mare, maris, marium,** n., *sea.*
  paternus, -a, -um, *belonging to one's father, paternal.*
  *hospitium, -ī, n., *guest-chamber; guest-house.*
204 ***ostendō, ostendere, ostendī, ostentus** or **ostēnsus,** *to show.*
  *****valeō, -ēre, -uī,** *to be strong.*
205 ***rāna, -ae,** f., *frog.*
  rēx, rēgis, m., *king.*

Trimalchio describes his palace.

"Interim dum Mercurius vigilat, aedificāvī hanc domum. Ut 197
scītis, cusuc erat; nunc templum est. Habet quattuor cēnātiōnēs, 198
cubicula vīgintī, porticūs marmorātōs duōs, sūsum cellātiōnem, 199
cubiculum in quō ipse dormiō, vīperae huius sessōrium, ōstiāriī 200
cellam perbonam; hospitium hospitēs C. capit. Ad summam, 201
Scaurus cum hūc vēnit, nusquam māvoluit hospitārī, et habet ad 202
mare paternum hospitium. Et multa alia sunt, quae statim vōbīs 203
ostendam. Crēdite mihi: assem habeās, assem valeās; habēs, 204
habēberis. Sīc amīcus vester, quī fuit rāna, nunc est rēx. 205

---

197 **Mercurius vigilat**: i.e., while Mercury was looking out for my
interests. For Mercury as the patron god of businessmen and
Trimalchio's favorite deity, see II.1.58.

200 **ōstiāriī cellam**: compare II.1.48–49.

204 **assem habeās** (jussive subjunctive, *have an as*), **assem valeās**
(potential subjunctive, *you would be worth an as*): parataxis
instead of subordination of the first clause as the protasis of a
future less vivid condition, **sī assem habeās** (see p. 249).
Proverbial wisdom: "Money makes the man."

habēs, habēberis: parataxis again (see p. 249), with play on the
two senses of the verb **habeō**, (if) *you have, you will be considered*
= you're thought to be worth only as much as you have.

205 **amīcus vester**: i.e., Trimalchio himself.

206   **Stichus, -ī, m.,** *Stichus* (a common slave's name; here one of Trimalchio's slaves).
     prōferō, prōferre, prōtulī, prōlātus, irreg., *to bring out.*
     vītālia, vītālium, n. pl. [a euphemism for **fūnebria, fūnebrium,** n. pl.], *grave-clothes.*
     ***efferō [ex- + ferō], efferre, extulī, ēlātus,** irreg., *to carry out* (for burial).
207   ***prōferō, prōferre, prōtulī, prōlātus,** irreg., *to bring out.*
     ****unguentum, -ī,** n., *ointment, perfume.*
     ***amphora, -ae,** f., *two-handled jug.*
     ***gustus, -ūs,** m., *tasting* (of food), *taste;* here, *draught of perfume* (from the **amphora**).
208   **os, ossis,** n., *bone.*
     ****moror, -ārī, -ātus sum,** *to delay.*
     ***strāgula, -ae,** f., *pall* (covering for a corpse).
     *****albus, -a, -um,** *white.*
209   **praetexta, -ae,** f., *toga with purple stripe* (worn by higher magistrates).
     ****temptō, -āre, -āvī, -ātus,** *to handle, feel, test.*
     ****an,** particle, *whether.*
210   ***lāna, -ae,** f., *wool.*
     cōnficiō [con- + faciō], cōnficere, cōnfēcī, cōnfectus, *to make.*
     subrīdeō, subrīdēre, subrīsī, *to smile.*
211   ***mūs, mūris,** m./f., *mouse.*
     tinea, -ae, f., *gnawing worm, moth.*
     ***aliōquīn,** adv., *otherwise.*
     combūrō [con- + ūrō, *to burn***], combūrere, combussī, combustus,** *to burn up.*
212   ***glōriōsus, -a, -um,** *bragging, boastful; full of glory, in splendor.*
     ****efferō [ex- + ferō], efferre, extulī, ēlātus,** irreg., *to carry out* (for burial).
213   **imprecor [in- + precor,** *to pray for***], -ārī, -ātus sum** + dat., *to call down/invoke upon;* with **bene,** *to bless.*
     ***ampulla, -ae,** f. [dim. of **amphora,** Greek loan word, *large, two-handled earthenware jar for holding wine*], *bottle, flask.*
     nardus, -ī, f., or **nardum, -ī,** n. [Greek loan word], *nard.*
     aperiō, aperīre, aperuī, apertus, *to open.*
214   ***ungō, ungere, ūnxī, ūnctus,** *to smear, besmear, anoint.*
     spērō, -āre, -āvī, -ātus, *to hope.*
     ***aequē,** adv., *equally.*
     iuvō, iuvāre, iūvī, iūtus, *to help; to please, delight.*
215   **vīnārium, -ī,** n., *wine-jug.*
     ***īnfundō, īnfundere, īnfūdī, īnfūsus,** *to pour in.*

Trimalchio displays his funerary vestments and stages his own funeral.

"Interim, Stiche, prōfer vītālia, in quibus volō mē efferrī. 206
Prōfer et unguentum et ex illā amphorā gustum, ex quā iubeō 207
lavārī ossa mea." Nōn est morātus Stichus, sed et strāgulam al- 208
bam et praetextam in trīclīnium attulit iussitque nōs temptāre an 209
bonīs lānīs essent cōnfecta. Tum subrīdēns, "Vidē tū," inquit, 210
"Stiche, nē ista mūrēs tangant aut tineae; aliōquīn tē vīvum com- 211
būram. Ego glōriōsus volō efferrī, ut tōtus mihi populus bene 212
imprecētur." Statim ampullam nardī aperuit omnēsque nōs 213
ūnxit et, "Spērō," inquit, "futūrum ut aequē mē mortuum iuvet 214
tamquam vīvum." Nam vīnum quidem in vīnārium iussit īn- 215
fundī et, "Putāte vōs," ait, "ad parentālia mea invītātōs esse." 216

---

216 **parentālia, parentālium,** n. pl., *parentalia* (annual commemora-
     tion of dead relatives).
     **invītō, -āre, -āvī, -ātus, *to invite.*

---

206 **Interim . . . prōfer vītālia:** with Trimalchio's staging of his own
     funeral, compare Seneca's description of a certain Pacuvius,
     who was governor of Syria early in the first century A.D.:
     "Pacuvius . . . used to perform the rites of the dead for himself
     with wine and the usual funerary banquets; he was carried
     from dinner into his bedroom accompanied by the applause of
     his male whores while the following was sung [in Greek] to
     musical accompaniment, 'He has lived his life, he has lived his
     life.' No day passed that he didn't carry himself out for burial"
     (Seneca, *Epistulae morales* 12.8–9).
209 **praetextam:** the toga with purple border that Trimalchio wore
     when serving as **sēvīr Augustālis.**
     an . . . essent cōnfecta: indirect question, *whether they had
     been. . . .*
211 **nē . . . tangant:** indirect command dependent on **Vidē** (210).
212 **ut . . . imprecētur:** purpose clause.
214 **Spērō . . . futūrum (esse) ut . . . mē . . . iuvet: futūrum esse ut** +
     subjunctive may be used instead of the future infinitive, *I hope
     that it will happen that it* (i.e., the nard) *pleases me. . . .* = *I hope
     that it will please me. . . .*

217   **summus, -a, -um**, superl. adj., *highest.*
      nausea, -ae, f., *nausea.*
      *****ēbrietās, ēbrietātis**, f., *drunkenness.*
218   ******turpis, -is, -e**, *ugly, base.*
      gravis, -is, -e, *heavy; drunk.*
      acroāma, acroāmatis, n. [Greek loan word], *something heard with pleasure; a pleasant sound; a dinner-table entertainer, buffoon; buffoonery.*
      cornicen, cornicinis, m., *horn-blower* [**cornū, -ūs**, *horn* + **canō, canere, cecinī**, *to sing; to play*, on musical instruments].
219   ******addūcō, addūcere, addūxī, adductus**, *to bring (in).*
      fulciō, fulcīre, fulsī, fultus, *to prop up.*
      *****cervīcal, cervīcālis, cervīcālium**, n., *pillow.*
      *****extendō, extendere, extendī, extentus**, *to stretch out, extend.*
      ******suprā**, prep. + acc., *above.*
      torus, -ī, m., *couch.*
      *******extrēmus, -a, -um**, *outermost, farthest, last; the end/edge of.*
220   *****fingō, fingere, fīnxī, fictus**, *to form, fashion, make; to imagine, suppose, think.*
221   *****bellus, -a, -um**, *beautiful; fine.*
      cōnsonō, cōnsonāre, cōnsonuī, *to sound together.*
       cōnsonuēre, = **cōnsonuērunt.**
      *****cornicen, cornicinis**, m., *horn-blower* [**cornū, -ūs**, *horn* + **canō, canere, cecinī**, *to sing; to play*, on musical instruments].
      fūnebris, -is, -e, *funereal.*
      strepitus, -ūs, m., *noise, sound.*
      *****praecipuē**, adv., *chiefly, most of all, especially.*
222   **libitīnārius, -ī**, m., *undertaker.*
      honestus, -a, -um, *regarded with honor/respect.*
223   **intonō, intonāre, intonuī**, *to make a noise, resound.*
      concitō, -āre, -āvī, -ātus, *to move violently, shake, stir up, arouse.*
      *****vīcīnia, -ae**, f., *neighborhood, vicinity.*

The blast of a funeral trumpet rouses the whole neighborhood.

Ībat rēs ad summam nauseam, cum Trimalchiō ēbrietāte   217
turpissimā gravis novum acroāma, cornicinēs, in trīclīnium iussit   218
addūcī, fultusque cervīcālibus multīs extendit sē suprā torum ex-   219
trēmum et, "Fingite mē," inquit, "mortuum esse. Dīcite aliquid   220
bellī." Cōnsonuēre cornicinēs fūnebrī strepitū. Ūnus praecipuē   221
servus libitīnāriī illīus, quī inter hōs honestissimus erat, tam   222
valdē intonuit, ut tōtam concitāret vīcīniam.   223

---

217 **ēbrietāte turpissimā**: ablative with **gravis**.
220 **Dīcite aliquid bellī**: addressed to the **cornicinēs**. **Dīcite**: =
     Canite, *Play*. **aliquid bellī**: = *something nice.*
222 **libitīnāriī illīus**: one of the other freedmen at the dinner, C.
     Julius Proculus.
223 **ut . . . concitāret**: result clause.

224   **vigil, vigilis,** m., *watchman, fireman.*
       reor, rērī, ratus sum, *to believe, think, suppose.*
       ardeō, ardēre, arsī, *to burn.*
       effringō [ex- + frangō, *to break*], **effringere, effrēgī, effractus,** *to break off, break open.*
225   ***secūris, secūris, secūrium,** f., *ax.*
       tumultuor, -ārī, -ātus sum, *to make a disturbance, raise a tumult.*
226   ****occāsiō, occāsiōnis,** f., *opportunity, occasion.*
       ***opportūnus, -a, -um,** *convenient, timely.*
       *****nancīscor, nancīscī, nactus sum,** *to obtain, receive, get; to seize.*
227   **verba dare** + dat., *to deceive, cheat* (someone); *give* (someone) *the slip.*
       ***raptim,** adv., *by snatching/ hurrying away; speedily, suddenly.*
       ***tam . . . quam,** *as . . . as.*
       ***incendium, -ī,** n., *fire.*

Firemen rush in; Encolpius, Ascyltos, and Giton finally escape.

Itaque vigilēs ratī ardēre Trimalchiōnis domum effrēgērunt 224
iānuam subitō et cum aquā secūribusque tumultuārī suō iūre 225
coepērunt. Nōs occāsiōnem opportūnissimam nactī Agamem- 226
nonī verba dedimus raptimque tam plānē quam ex incendiō 227
fūgimus. 228

---

224 **ratī**: *thinking, supposing;* the past participle of deponent verbs is passive in form but active in meaning, and may often be translated as a present.
225 **suō iūre**: *according to their rights, legitimately.*
226 **occāsiōnem opportūnissimam**: object of **nactī**.
227 **tam plānē quam**: = **plānē tamquam,** *exactly as if.*
228 **fūgimus**: the ending of the narrator's account of Trimalchio's dinner may owe something to the ending of Horace's satire on Nasidienus' dinner, from which Fundanius and his companions fled (**fūgimus**), taking their revenge on their host by tasting nothing (*Satires* 2.8.93–94).

More Roman Banquets

Horace, *Satires* 2.8, the dinner party of Nasidienus.
Seneca, *Epistulae morales*, 95.22–29, condemnation of lavish banquets
Martial 3.82, the dinner party of a thoroughly disgusting man named Malchio.
Pliny, *Letters* 2.6, how wine is served by a stingy host.
Pliny, *Letters* 3.1.8–9, Spurinna's moderate style of bathing and dining.
Juvenal, *Satire 5*, how grand patrons entertain their clients.

1 **mātrōna, -ae,** f., *matron* (married woman).
******quīdam, quaedam, quoddam,** indef. adj., *a certain*.
Ephesus, -ī, f., *Ephesus* (city on the west coast of Asia Minor).
nōtus, -a, -um, *known, well-known*.
pudīcitia, -ae, f., *modesty, chastity, virtue*.
2 **vīcīnus, -a, -um,** *neighboring*.
gēns, gentis, gentium, f., *nation, people*.
*spectāculum, -ī, n., *spectacle, sight, viewing*.
3 **ēvocō, -āre, -āvī, -ātus,** *to call out, call forth, summon*.
*****efferō [ex- + ferō], efferre, extulī, ēlātus,** irreg., *to carry out*
(for burial).
*contentus, -a, -um, *content, satisfied*.
vulgāris, -is, -e, *common, ordinary, usual*.
4 ****mōs, mōris,** m., *manner, custom, way*.
**fūnus, fūneris, n., *funeral*.
*pandō, pandere, ____, passus, *to spread out*.
passus, -a, -um, *loose, dishevelled* (of hair).
*prōsequor, prōsequī, prōsecūtus sum, *to follow, attend, accompany*.
crīnis, crīnis, crīnium, m., *hair*.
nūdātus, -a, -um, *bared*.
pectus, pectoris, n., *breast*.
**cōnspectus, -ūs, m., *sight, view, presence*.
5 **frequentia, -ae,* f., *crowd, multitude, throng*.
**plangō, plangere, plānxī, plānctus, *to strike the breast; to bewail,
mourn*.
conditōrium, -ī, n., *tomb*.
etiam, particle, *even, actually*.
**prōsequor, prōsequī, prōsecūtus sum, *to follow, attend, accompany*.
6 **dēfūnctus, -ī,** m., *dead man*.
hypogaeum, -ī, n. [Greek loan word], *underground burial vault*.
Graecus, -a, -um, *Greek*.
*****mōs, mōris,** m., *manner, custom, way*.
**corpus, corporis, n., *body*.
7 **custōdiō, -īre, -īvī, -ītus,** *to guard*.
*****fleō, flēre, flēvī, flētus,** *to weep, cry*.
*nox, noctis, noctium, f., *night*.

III.

THE MATRON OF EPHESUS

*Enclopius, Giton, and Eumolpus (a poet who has joined their company)
have unwittingly boarded the ship of an old enemy of Encolpius' named
Lichas. The latter is conveying a libidinous woman named Tryphaena (Greek
for Ms. Wanton) to exile in Tarentum. On some earlier occasion she had been
wronged by Giton. When our three vagrants discover who their host and
hostess are aboard the ship, they attempt to disguise themselves in order to
avoid the wrath of the wronged parties. The disguise fails, however, and there
is a mock battle between the two factions, after which Eumolpus draws up a
treaty and peace ensues. Eumolpus, self-fashioned poet and raconteur, is eager
to sustain the gaiety in the air. Claiming that there is no woman so faithful
and pure as to rebuff the love of even a stranger, he entertains the company
with the following tale.*

*A chaste matron of Ephesus followed her dead husband's body into the
tomb itself.*

[111–112] Mātrōna quaedam Ephesī tam nōtae erat pudīci-   1
tiae, ut vīcīnārum quoque gentium fēminās ad spectāculum suī   2
ēvocāret. Haec ergō cum virum extulisset, nōn contenta vulgārī   3
mōre fūnus passīs prōsequī crīnibus aut nūdātum pectus in cōn-   4
spectū frequentiae plangere, in conditōrium etiam prōsecūta est   5
dēfūnctum, positumque in hypogaeō Graecō mōre corpus   6
custōdīre ac flēre tōtīs noctibus diēbusque coepit.   7

---

1 **tam nōtae . . . pudīcitiae**: genitive of description, *of such. . . .*
2 **vīcīnārum**: modifying **gentium**.
   suī: objective genitive, *of herself.*
3 **vulgārī mōre**: ablative of manner.
4 **passīs . . . crīnibus**: ablative absolute.
7 **tōtīs noctibus diēbusque**: ablative of time within which instead of
   accusative of duration of time, as commonly in colloquial Latin.

8 afflictō [ad- + flīgō, *to strike down*], -āre, -āvī, -ātus, *to trouble, distress, afflict.*

*mors, mortis, mortium, f., *death.*

inedia, -ae, f., *not eating* [edō, esse, ēdī, ēsus], *fasting.*

***persequor, persequī, persecūtus sum, *to follow after, pursue.*

parēns, parentis, parentum or parentium, m./f., *parent.*

9 abdūcō, abdūcere, abdūxī, abductus, *to lead/take away.*

propinquus, -ī, m., *kinsman, relative.*

magistrātus, -ūs, m., *magistrate.*

*ultimō, adv., *finally.*

10 repellō, repellere, reppulī, repulsus, *to drive back, reject, repulse.*

complōrō [con- + plōrō, *to bewail*], -āre, -āvī, -ātus, *to bewail, lament together.*

singulāris, -is, -e, *singular, unique, remarkable.*

exemplum, -ī, n., *example.*

11 *quīntus, -a, -um, *fifth.*

alimentum, -ī, n. [alō, alere, aluī, altus, *to feed*], *nourishment, food.*

*trahō, trahere, trāxī, tractus, *to draw, drag.*

diem trahere, *to spend a day.*

assideō [ad- + sedeō], assidēre, assēdī, assessus + dat., *to sit by/near.*

12 aeger, aegra, aegrum, *sick.*

fīdus, -a, -um, *faithful.*

ancilla, -ae, f., *female slave.*

simul, adv., *at the same time.*

*lacrima, -ae, f., *tear.*

commodō, -āre, -āvī, -ātus, *to give, bestow, lend.*

lūgeō, lūgēre, lūxī, lūctus, *to mourn, lament.*

13 quotiēns, adv., *as often as, whenever.*

***dēficiō [dē- + faciō], dēficere, dēfēcī, dēfectus, *to leave, cease, fail, end, expire.*

lūmen, lūminis, n., *light.*

renovō, -āre, -āvī, -ātus, *to renew.*

No one could dissuade the chaste matron from her intention of dying over the body of her husband.

Sīc afflictantem sē ac mortem inediā persequentem nōn pa-   8
rentēs potuērunt abdūcere, nōn propinquī; magistrātūs ultimō   9
repulsī abiērunt, complōrātaque singulāris exemplī fēmina ab   10
omnibus quīntum iam diem sine alimentō trahēbat. Assidēbat   11
aegrae fīdissima ancilla, simulque et lacrimās commodābat lū-   12
gentī et quotiēns dēfēcerat positum in monumentō lūmen re-   13
novābat.   14

---

8   **inediā**: ablative of means with **mortem . . . persequentem**.
9   **nōn propinquī**: supply **potuērunt abdūcere**.
10   **complōrāta . . . ab omnibus**: *lamented by all.*
     singulāris exemplī: genitive of description with **fēmina**; she was an unusual and exemplary woman.
12   **aegrae**: supply **mātrōnae**, dative with **assidēbat**.
     lūgentī: *to the mourning* (woman).
13   **renovābat**: supply **id**; i.e., as often as the light went out, the **ancilla** renewed it.

15   *igitur, conj., *therefore.*
cīvitās, cīvitātis, f., *the citizens that make up a city/state; a city/state.*
affulgeō [ad- + fulgeō, *to shine*], affulgēre, affulsī, *to shine, appear.*

16   *vērus, -a, -um, *true.*
*pudīcitia, -ae, f., *modesty, chastity, virtue.*
*amor, amōris, m., *love.*
*exemplum, -ī, n., *example.*
ōrdō, ōrdinis, m., *order, rank, class.*

17   cōnfiteor [con- + fateor, *to admit*], cōnfitērī, cōnfessus sum, *to confess, own, acknowledge.*
imperātor, imperātōris, m., *commander; governor.*
prōvincia, -ae, f., *province.*
*latrō, latrōnis, m., *thief.*

18   crux, crucis, f., *cross.*
affīgō [ad- + fīgō, *to drive/fix in*], affīgere, affīxī, affīxus, *to fix/fasten on, attach to.*
**secundum, prep. + acc., *by, next to.*
**casula, -ae, f. [dim. of casa, -ae, f., *cottage*], *little/humble cottage; here, tomb.*
recēns, recentis, *fresh, recent.*
cadāver, cadāveris, n., *corpse.*

19   *mātrōna, -ae, f., *matron* (married woman).
dēfleō, dēflēre, dēflēvī, dēflētus, *to weep over, lament.*
proximus, -a, -um, *next.*
**nox, noctis, noctium, f., *night.*
**mīles, mīlitis, m., *soldier.*
*crux, crucis, f., *cross.*

20   asservō [ad- + servō, *to watch; to save*], -āre, -āvī, -ātus, *to guard.*
sepultūra, -ae, f., *burial.*
***corpus, corporis, n., *body.*
*dētrahō, dētrahere, dētrāxī, dētractus, *to draw off; to take down.*
notāsset, = notāvisset.

21   *lūmen, lūminis, n., *light.*
clārius, compar. adv., *rather brightly.*
fulgeō, fulgēre, fulsī, *to gleam, shine.*
*gemitus, -ūs, m., *sigh, groan, lamentation.*
*lūgeō, lūgēre, lūxī, lūctus, *to mourn, lament.*

22   audīsset, = audīvisset.
vitium, -ī, n., *vice, fault, failing.*
*gēns, gentis, gentium, f., *nation, people.*
hūmānus, -a, -um, *human.*
  gēns hūmāna, *the human race.*
concupīscō, concupīscere, concupīvī or concupiī, concupītus, *to desire strongly.*

In the meantime, the governor of the province orders certain thieves to be cru-
cified near the tomb, and the soldier stationed to guard the bodies on the
crosses becomes curious about the light in the tomb.

Ūna igitur in tōtā cīvitāte fābula erat, sōlum illud affulsisse 15
vērum pudīcitiae amōrisque exemplum omnis ōrdinis hominēs 16
cōnfitēbantur, cum interim imperātor prōvinciae latrōnēs iussit 17
crucibus affīgī secundum illam casulam, in quā recēns cadāver 18
mātrōna dēflēbat. Proximā ergō nocte cum mīles, quī crucēs as- 19
servābat nē quis ad sepultūram corpus dētraheret, notāsset sibi 20
lūmen inter monumenta clārius fulgēns et gemitum lūgentis 21
audīsset, vitiō gentis hūmānae concupiit scīre quis aut quid fac- 22
eret. 23

---

15 **Ūna . . . fābula erat:** (There was) *one* (and only one) *story* (i.e.,
subject of gossip).
sōlum illud affulsisse vērum . . . exemplum . . . hominēs cōn-
fitēbantur: *men acknowledged that only that* (**illud**) *had shown*
forth/appeared (**affulsisse**) (as) *a true example. . . .*
16 **omnis ōrdinis:** genitive of description with **hominēs**, *men of every*
social order.
17 **cum . . . iussit:** the **cum inversum** construction; see note on II.1.12.
18 **recēns cadāver:** accusative object of **dēflēbat.**
19 **Proximā . . . nocte:** ablative of time when.
20 **ad sepultūram:** **ad** + accusative to express purpose. Part of the
punishment of the crucified thieves is denial of burial; Vergil,
Aeneid 6.325–330, has the Sibyl explain to Aeneas that the souls of
the unburied dead are not allowed to cross the river Styx until
they have fluttered about on the shore for a hundred years.

24 **dēscendō, dēscendere, dēscendī, dēscēnsūrus, *to go down, descend.*
    **igitur, conj., *therefore.*
    *conditōrium, -ī, n., *tomb.*
    pulcher, pulchra, pulchrum, *beautiful.*
        pulcherrimus, -a, -um, superlative.
25 prīmō, adv., *at first.*
    **quasi, conj., *as if.*
    mōnstrum, -ī, n., *monster, wonder, marvel.*
    īnfernus, -a, -um, *belonging to the lower world, infernal.*
    *imāgō, imāginis, f., *image; ghost.*
26 *turbō, -āre, -āvī, -ātus, *to disturb.*
    subsistō, subsistere, substitī, *to stop, halt.*
    **iaceō, iacēre, iacuī, iacitūrus, *to lie.*
    *cōnspiciō [con- + speciō, *to see*], cōnspicere, cōnspexī, cōnspectus, *to catch sight of, see.*
27 **lacrima, -ae, f., *tear.*
    **cōnsīderō, -āre, -āvī, -ātus, *to look at, inspect, consider.*
    **unguis, unguis, unguium, m., *fingernail.*
    **secō, secāre, secuī, sectus, *to cut.*
    *reor, rērī, ratus sum, *to believe, think, suppose.*
    **scīlicet, particle, *of course, certainly, evidently.*
28 dēsīderium, -ī, n., *desire.*
    extīnctus, -ī, m., *dead man.*
    *patior, patī, passus sum, *to suffer, bear, endure.*
29 cēnula, -ae, f. [dim. of cēna, -ae, f., *dinner*], *little dinner.*
    hortor, -ārī, -ātus sum, *to encourage.*
    **lūgeō, lūgēre, lūxī, lūctus, *to mourn, lament.*
30 **persevērō, -āre, -āvī, -ātūrus, *to continue, persist, persevere.*
    dolor, dolōris, m., *grief, sorrow.*
    supervacuus, -a, -um, *useless, unnecessary.*
    prōsum, prōdesse, prōfuī, irreg., *to be of use, benefit, profit.*
        prōfutūrus, future active participle, *that will be of use.*
    **gemitus, -ūs, m., *sigh, groan, lamentation.*
31 *pectus, pectoris, n., *breast.*
    *dīdūcō [dis- + dūcō], dīdūcere, dīdūxī, dīductus, *to draw apart, open up, split.*
    *exitus, -ūs, m., *outcome, end; departure, death.*
    domicilium, -ī, n., *dwelling, home.*
32 **cēterī, -ae, -a, *the other, the rest.*
    exulcerō, -āre, -āvī, -ātus, *to make sore.*
    *mēns, mentis, mentium, f., *mind.*
    sānitās, sānitātis, f., *health.*
    revocō, -āre, -āvī, -ātus, *to call back.*

The soldier tries to console the matron.

Dēscendit igitur in conditōrium, vīsāque pulcherrimā 24
muliere prīmō quasi quōdam mōnstrō īnfernīsque imāginibus 25
turbātus substitit. Deinde ut et corpus iacentis cōnspexit et 26
lacrimās cōnsīderāvit faciemque unguibus sectam, ratus scīlicet 27
id quod erat, dēsīderium extīnctī nōn posse fēminam patī, attulit 28
in monumentum cēnulam suam coepitque hortārī lūgentem nē 29
persevērāret in dolōre supervacuō ac nihil prōfutūrō gemitū 30
pectus dīdūceret: omnium eundem esse exitum et idem domicil- 31
ium, et cētera quibus exulcerātae mentēs ad sānitātem revocan- 32
tur. 33

24 **vīsā . . . pulcherrimā muliere**: ablative absolute.
25 **quōdam mōnstrō īnfernīsque imāginibus**: ablative of means or
     instrument with **turbātus**.
26 **iacentis**: i.e., of the dead man.
27 **ratus**: *thinking, supposing;* the past participle of deponent verbs is
     passive in form but active in meaning, and may often be trans-
     lated as a present.
28 **dēsīderium . . . nōn posse fēminam patī**: indirect statement in
     apposition to **id quod erat**, translate, *namely that. . . .*
29 **nē persevērāret . . . dīdūceret**: indirect commands dependent on
     hortārī.
30 **nihil prōfutūrō gemitū**: *with useless lamentation.*
31 **omnium eundem esse exitum. . . . :** indirect statement dependent
     on an implied verb of saying; supply *saying that. . . .*
32 **exulcerātae**: *made sore* (with grief).

34 ***at, conj., *but.*

ignōtus, -a, -um, *unknown, unfamiliar, strange; lacking fame/honor;* sometimes = ignōbilis, -is, -e, *unknown; of low birth; inglorious, base, mean.*

*cōnsōlātiō, cōnsōlātiōnis, f., *consolation, comfort.*

percutiō [per- + quatiō, *to shake; to strike*], percutere, percussī, percussus, *to strike through and through;* of emotions, *to affect deeply, stir.*

**lacerō, -āre, -āvī, -ātus, *to tear, mangle, lacerate.*

vehementius, compar. adv., *more violently.*

35 **pectus, pectoris, n., *breast.*

rumpō, rumpere, rūpī, ruptus, *to break; to tear.*

*crīnis, crīnis, crīnium, m., *hair.*

***iaceō, iacēre, iacuī, iacitūrus, *to lie.*

*impōnō [in- + pōnō], impōnere, imposuī, impositus, *to place upon.*

recēdō, recēdere, recessī, recessūrus, *to go back, withdraw.*

36 ***mīles, mīlitis, m., *soldier.*

exhortātiō, exhortātiōnis, f., *exhortation.*

***temptō, -āre, -āvī, -ātus, *to test, try.*

37 *muliercula, -ae, f. [dim. of mulier, mulieris, f., *woman*], *little woman* (the ancilla).

*cibus, -ī, m., *food.*

*dōnec, conj., *until.*

*ancilla, -ae, f., *female slave.*

odor, odōris, m., *smell, odor.*

corrumpō [con- + rumpō, *to break*], corrumpere, corrūpī, corruptus, *to corrupt; to entice, seduce.*

**prīmum, adv., *first.*

38 porrigō [por-, *forth* + regō, *to direct*], porrigere, porrēxī, porrēctus, *to stretch out, reach out, extend.*

*hūmānitās, hūmānitātis, f., *humanity; kindness.*

***invītō, -āre, -āvī, -ātus, *to invite.*

**vincō, vincere, vīcī, victus, *to conquer, overcome.*

39 *reficiō [re- + faciō], reficere, refēcī, refectus, *to make again; to make strong again, revive.*

***pōtiō, pōtiōnis, f., *drink.*

**cibus, -ī, m., *food.*

expugnō, -āre, -āvī, -ātus, *to attack.*

**domina, -ae, f., *mistress.*

pertinācia, -ae, f., *constancy, obstinacy, pertinacity.*

But to no avail. Ignored by the matron, the soldier wins over her maid, who then launches her own attack upon the matron.

At illa ignōtā cōnsōlātiōne percussa lacerāvit vehementius 34
pectus ruptōsque crīnēs super corpus iacentis imposuit. Nōn re- 35
cessit tamen mīles, sed eādem exhortātiōne temptāvit dare 36
mulierculae cibum, dōnec ancilla vīnī odōre corrupta prīmum 37
ipsa porrēxit ad hūmānitātem invītantis victam manum, deinde 38
refecta pōtiōne et cibō expugnāre dominae pertināciam coepit 39

(paragraph continued on page 217)

34 **ignōtā cōnsōlātiōne** (abl. of means or instrument) **percussa** (nom.,
modifying the subject of the sentence): *stirred by this base* (attempt
at) *consolation.* To the matron, the soldier's attempt to console her
is **ignōta**, *unfamiliar, lacking honor, inglorious,* or *base,* because if
she accepted it she would not maintain her noble image as *a true
example of chastity and love* (line 16). By the soldier's attempt at
consolation, the matron is only stirred (**percussa**) to beat her
breast more violently.
38 **ad hūmānitātem invītantis**: *to the kindness of the* (man who was)
inviting (her).
39 **pōtiōne et cibō**: ablative of means with **refecta**.

40   *prōsum prōdesse, prōfuī, irreg. + dat., *to be of use, benefit, profit.*
     solvō, solvere, solvī, solūtus, *to loose, release, dissolve, destroy.*
     *inedia, -ae, f., *not eating* [edō, esse, ēdī ēsus, *to eat*], *fasting.*

41   sepeliō, sepelīre, sepelīvī or sepeliī, sepultus, *to bury.*
     antequam, conj., *before.*
     ***poscō, poscere, poposcī, *to ask, demand.*
     indemnātus, -a, -um, *uncondemned, unsentenced.*
     *spīritus, -ūs, m., *air; breath* (of life).

43   *cinis, cineris, m., *ash; ashes* (of a corpse that has been cremated).
     mānēs, mānium, m. pl., *shade, ghost.*
     *sentiō, sentīre, sēnsī, sēnsus, *to feel, perceive, notice.*
     *sepeliō, sepelīre, sepelīvī or sepeliī, sepultus, *to bury.*

44   revīvīscō, revīvīscere, revīxī, *to come to life again.*
     ***discutiō [dis- + quatiō, *to shake; to strike*], discutere, dis-
     cussī, discussus, *to strike apart, shatter; to dispel.*
     muliebris, -is, -e, *of/belonging to a woman* [mulier, mulieris, f.].
     error, errōris, m., *mistake, error.*
     **quam diū, *as long as.*

45   ***licet, -ēre, -uit, impersonal, *it is permitted.*
     **lūx, lūcis, f., *light.*
     commodum, -ī, n., *convenience, advantage, profit; a useful thing, a
     good.*
     ***fruor, fruī, frūctus sum + abl., *to enjoy.*
     *admoneō, -ēre, -uī, -itus + gen., *to remind* (of); *to advise, urge.*

et, "Quid prōderit," inquit, "hoc tibi, sī solūta inediā fueris, sī tē 40
vīvam sepelieris, sī antequam fāta poscant, indemnātum spīri- 41
tum effūderis? 42

Id cinerem aut mānēs crēdis sentīre sepultōs? 43

Vīs tū revīvīscere? Vīs discussō muliebrī errōre, quam diū 44
licuerit, lūcis commodīs fruī? Ipsum tē iacentis corpus admonēre 45
dēbet ut vīvās." 46

---

40 **Quid prōderit . . . hoc tibi**: *What benefit will this be to you?*
solūta . . . fueris: future perfect passive, *you will have been destroyed.*
inediā: ablative of means.
41 **antequam**: with the subjunctive when its clause refers to an un-
completed future action.
43 **Id . . . sepultōs**: a quotation from Vergil's *Aeneid* 4.34, from a
speech in which Dido's nurse, Anna, tries to persuade her to forget her allegiance to her dead husband, Sychaeus, and to yield to
her newly felt love for Aeneas. **Id**: this pronoun, object of the infinitive **sentīre**, refers to Dido's newly felt love for Aeneas and
the prospect of marriage to him and of children born of that marriage. **cinerem et manēs . . . sepultōs**: subject of the infinitive
sentīre and referring to Sychaeus' ashes and shade.
44 **discussō muliebrī errōre**: ablative absolute, *having dispelled this
womanly error* (i.e., the mistake of thinking one must remain faithful to a dead husband).
45 **lūcis commodīs**: ablative with **fruī**, *to enjoy the good things of the
light* (i.e., of life).
46 **ut vīvās**: indirect command.

47   invītus, -a, -um, *unwilling(ly)*.
    *cōgō, cōgere, coēgī, coāctus, *to force, compel.*
    ***cibus, -ī, m., *food.*
    *sūmō, sūmere, sūmpsī, sūmptus, *to take, take up.*
48   ***aliquot, indecl. adj., *several, some.*
    abstinentia, -ae, f., *abstinence.*
    siccus, -a, -um, *dry.*
    **patior, patī, passus sum, *to suffer, bear, endure; to allow, permit.*
49   ***frangō, frangere, frēgī, fractus, *to break; to move; to soften.*
    *pertinācia, -ae, f., *constancy, obstinacy, pertinacity.*
    **minus, compar. adv., *less.*
    avidē, adv., *greedily.*
    *repleō, replēre, replēvī, replētus, *to fill up.*
50   **ancilla, -ae, f., *female slave.*
    prior, prior, prius, priōris, compar. adj., *former, previous, first.*
    ***vincō, vincere, vīcī, victus, *to conquer, overcome.*
    plērumque, adv., *for the most part, commonly, very frequently.*
51   ***temptō, -āre, -āvī, -ātus, *to try, attempt; to make an attempt on.*
    *hūmānus, -a, -um, *human.*
    satietās, satietātis, f., *satiety.*
    blanditiae, -ārum, f. pl., *flatteries, blandishments, allurements.*
    impetrō, -āre, -āvī, -ātus, *to accomplish, bring it about that* + ut + subjn.
52   **mātrōna, -ae, f., *matron* (married woman).
    **pudīcitia, -ae, f., *modesty, chastity, virtue.*
53   aggredior [ad- + gradior, *to step, walk*], aggredī, aggressus sum, *to attack.*
    *dēfōrmis, -is, -e, *ugly.*
    īnfācundus, -a, -um, *ineloquent.*
    iuvenis, iuvenis, m., *young man.*
    castus, -a, -um, *chaste.*
54   conciliō, -āre, -āvī, -ātus, *to bring together, gain, win.*
    ***grātia, -ae, f., *favor.*
    ***ancilla, -ae, f., *female slave.*
    **subinde, adv., *thereupon, promptly; repeatedly, constantly.*
55   placitus, -a, -um, *pleasing, agreeable.*
    *pugnō, -āre, -āvī, -ātūrus + dat., *to fight (against), resist.*
    **amor, amōris, m., *love.*
56   **mēns, mentis, mentium, f., *mind.*
    *cōnsīdō, cōnsīdere, cōnsēdī, *to sit down, settle, make one's home.*
    arvum, -ī, n., *cultivated field.*

The matron yields first to her maid and then to the soldier.

Nēmō invītus audit, cum cōgitur aut cibum sūmere aut vī- 47
vere. Itaque mulier aliquot diērum abstinentiā sicca passa est 48
frangī pertināciam suam, nec minus avidē replēvit sē cibō quam 49
ancilla quae prior victa est. Cēterum scītis quid plērumque 50
soleat temptāre hūmānam satietātem. Quibus blanditiīs im- 51
petrāverat mīles ut mātrōna vellet vīvere, īsdem etiam pudīcitam 52
eius aggressus est. Nec dēfōrmis aut īnfācundus iuvenis castae 53
vidēbātur, conciliante grātiam ancillā ac subinde dīcente: 54

"Placitōne etiam pugnābis amōrī? 55
Nec venit in mentem, quōrum cōnsēderis arvīs?" 56

---

48 **aliquot diērum abstinentiā**: ablative of means with **sicca**, *dry
    from*. . . .
    passa est: perfect, *she allowed*.
51 **Quibus blanditiīs . . . , īsdem**: *With the blandishments by which . . . ,
    with the same* (ones) = *With the same blandishments by which*.
53 **iuvenis**: nominative.
    castae: dative, *to the chaste* (woman).
54 **conciliante . . . ancillā ac . . . dīcente**: ablative absolute, *while her
    maid was joining favor . . . and saying*, i.e., trying to make the ma-
    tron favor the soldier.
55 **Placitōne . . . arvīs**: another quotation from the speech of Anna to
    Dido in the fourth book of the *Aeneid* (38–39). **Placitō . . . amōrī**:
    the pleasing love is the love Dido has begun to feel for Aeneas.
56 **quōrum cōnsēderis arvīs**: Dido, fleeing from her home in Tyre,
    had settled on the shore of North Africa and founded Carthage.
    She was surrounded by potentially dangerous African tribes, and
    Anna is suggesting that she should ally herself with Aeneas and
    his Trojans for safety. The matron of Ephesus has settled in an
    even more inauspicious land (i.e., of the dead), and she should
    keep this in mind and ally herself with the soldier as a way back
    to life. This line of the quotation from Vergil thus serves the
    purposes of the **ancilla** exceedingly well. It does not, however,
    appear in some of the manuscripts of Petronius, and it is possible
    that it was added by a later copyist.

57   ***diūtius, compar. adv., *longer*.

    ***moror, -ārī, -ātus sum, *to delay*.

    abstineō [ab- + teneō], abstinēre, abstinuī, abstentus, *to hold back, be abstinent.*

58   victor, victōris, m., *victor*.

    **persuādeō, persuādēre, persuāsī, persuāsus, *to persuade, prevail upon;* + acc., *to succeed in urging a course of action, succeed in recommending.*

    ūnā, adv., *together*.

59   nōn tantum . . . sed . . . etiam, *not only . . . but also.*

    ***nox, noctis, noctium, f., *night*.

    nūptiae, -ārum, f. pl., *marriage*.

    *posterus, -a, -um, *next, following.*

60   **tertius, -a, -um, *third*.

    *praeclūdō [prae- + claudō, *to shut*], praeclūdere, praeclūsī, praeclūsus, *to shut, close.*

    vidēlicet, adv., *it is easy to see, clearly, of course.*

    **conditōrium, -ī, n., *tomb*.

    *forēs, forium, f. pl., *two leaves of a door.*

61   *nōtus, -a, -um, *known.*

    *ignōtus, -a, -um, *unknown.*

    *expīrō [ex- + spīrō, *to breathe*], -āre, -āvī, -ātus, *to breathe out; to expire, die.*

      expīrāsse, = expīrāvisse.

62   pudīcus, -a, -um, *modest, chaste, virtuous.*

    **uxor, uxōris, f., *wife*.

    **dēlectō, -āre, -āvī, -ātus, *to please, delight.*

63   *fōrma, -ae, f., *beauty*.

    sēcrētum, -ī, n., *solitude, retreat, secrecy.*

    facultās, facultātis, f., *capability, power, means.*

64   *coemō [con- + emō, *to buy*], coemere, coēmī, coēmptus, *to buy up.*

Honeymoon in the tomb

Quid diūtius moror? Nē in hanc quidem partem mulier ab- 57
stinuit, victorque mīles utrumque persuāsit. Iacuērunt ergō ūnā 58
nōn tantum illā nocte quā nūptiās fēcērunt, sed posterō etiam ac 59
tertiō diē, praeclūsīs vidēlicet conditōriī foribus, ut quisquis ex 60
nōtīs ignōtīsque ad monumentum vēnisset, putāret expīrāsse 61
super corpus virī pudīcissimam uxōrem. Cēterum dēlectātus 62
mīles et fōrmā mulieris et sēcrētō, quicquid bonī per facultātēs 63
poterat coemēbat et prīmā statim nocte in monumentum ferēbat. 64

---

57 Nē . . . quidem: *Not even.*
    in hanc . . . partem: *in this direction/matter.*
58 utrumque: i.e., both to eat and to make love.
60 praeclūsīs . . . conditōriī foribus: ablative absolute.
    ex nōtīs ignōtīsque: partitive with quisquis, *whatever known or
    unknown people.*
63 fōrmā . . . sēcrētō: ablative of means with dēlectātus (62).
    per facultātēs: *within his means.*

65   cruciārius, -ī, m., *man who has been crucified.*
*parēns, parentis, parentum or parentium, m./f., *parent.*
laxō, -āre, -āvī, -ātus, *to slacken, relax.*
*custōdia, -ae, f., *guarding, protection.*
66   **dētrahō, dētrahere, dētrāxī, dētractus, *to draw/pull off, take down.*
dētrāxēre, = dētrāxērunt.
*suprēmus, -a, -um, superl. adj., *highest, last, final.*
suprēmum officium, -ī, n., *burial.*
mandō, -āre, -āvī, -ātus, *to commit, consign.*
67   circumscrībō, circumscrībere, circumscrīpsī, circumscrīptus, *to enclose in a circle, entrap, snare.*
dēsideō [dē- + sedeō], dēsidēre, dēsēdī, *to sit idle, be inactive.*
**posterus, -a, -um, *next, following.*
68   *cadāver, cadāveris, n., *corpse.*
**crux, crucis, f., *cross.*
vereor, -ērī, -itus sum, *to fear.*
supplicium, -ī, n., *punishment.*
69   accidō [ad- + cadō, *to fall*], accidere, accidī, *to fall out, happen, occur.*
**expōnō, expōnere, exposuī, expositus, *to put forth, explain.*
*expectō [ex- + spectō, *to look at*], -āre, -āvī, -ātus, *to await, wait for.*
*iūdex, iūdicis, m., *judge.*
sententia, -ae, f., *sentence.*
70   **gladius, -ī, m., *sword.*
iūs dīcere, *to pronounce/administer judgment.*
ignāvia, -ae, f., *laziness, idleness, inactivity.*
*commodō, -āre, -āvī, -ātus, *to give, bestow, lend.*
***modo, adv., *only provided that* +subjn.
*pereō, perīre, periī, peritūrus, irreg., *to pass away, die.*
71   fātālis, -is, -e, *fated* [fātum, -ī, n., *fate*].
***conditōrium, -ī, n., *tomb.*
familiāris, familiāris, familiārium, m./f., *intimate friend.*

An unexpected complication arises.

Itaque ūnīus cruciāriī parentēs ut vīdērunt laxātam custō- 65
diam, dētrāxēre nocte pendentem suprēmōque mandāvērunt of- 66
ficiō. At mīles circumscrīptus dum dēsidet, ut posterō diē vīdit 67
ūnam sine cadāvere crucem, veritus supplicium, mulierī quid 68
accidisset expōnit: nec sē expectātūrum iūdicis sententiam, sed 69
gladiō iūs dictūrum ignāviae suae. Commodāret modo illa peri- 70
tūrō locum et fātāle conditōrium familiārī ac virō faceret. 71

---

65 **ut vīdērunt: ut** + indicative = *when.*
67 **dum dēsidet:** i.e., while he wasn't attending to his duty.
68 **veritus:** *fearing.*
    mulierī quid accidisset expōnit: = **mulierī expōnit quid accidis-
    set**, subjunctive in indirect question.
69 **nec sē expectātūrum (esse):** indirect statement depending on an
    implied verb of saying.
70 **ignāviae suae:** genitive of the charge for which he is condemned,
    for his laziness (= his neglect of duty).
    Commodāret modo. . . faceret: clauses of proviso, *Only provided
    that. . . .*
71 **fātāle conditōrium . . . faceret:** *that she make* (it) *the fated tomb. . . .*

72 ***minus, compar. adv., *less.*
misericors, misericordis, *compassionate, merciful.*
*pudīcus, -a, -um, *modest, chaste, virtuous.*
73 sinō, sinere, sīvī, situs, *to allow, permit.*
***cārus, -a, -um, *dear.*
74 ***fūnus, fūneris, n., *funeral.*
spectō, -āre, -āvī, -ātus, *to see.*
impendō [in- + pendō, pendere, *to place in the scales, weigh*],
impendere, impendī, impēnsus, *to weigh out; to pay out; to expend, devote* (to a particular purpose).
75 ***secundum, prep. + acc., *by, next to; in accordance with.*
ōrātiō, ōrātiōnis, f., *speech.*
arca, -ae, f., *box, chest; coffin.*
76 marītus, -ī, m., *husband.*
*vacō, -āre, -āvī, -ātūrus, *to be empty.*
***crux, crucis, f., *cross.*
*affīgō [ad- + fīgō, *to drive/fix in*], affīgere, affīxī, affīxus, *to fix/
fasten on, attach to.*
*ūtor, ūtī, ūsus sum + abl., *to use, make use of; to take advantage of.*
77 ingenium, -ī, n., *innate quality, nature; cleverness.*
prūdēns, prūdentis, *foreseeing; knowing; wise; clever.*
***posterus, -a, -um, *next, following.*
78 **ratiō, ratiōnis, f., *account; reckoning; manner; way.*
īsset, plpf. subjn. of eō, īre, iī, itūrus, irreg., *to go.*

The matron again chooses life over death.

Mulier nōn minus misericors quam pudīca, "Nec istud," in-   72
quit, "diī sinant, ut eōdem tempore duōrum mihi cārissimōrum   73
hominum duo fūnera spectem. Mālō mortuum impendere   74
quam vīvum occīdere." Secundum hanc ōrātiōnem iubet ex arcā   75
corpus marītī suī tollī atque illī quae vacābat crucī affīgī. Ūsus   76
est mīles ingeniō prūdentissimae fēminae, posterōque diē popu-   77
lus mīrātus est quā ratiōne mortuus īsset in crucem.   78

---

72 Nec . . . diī sinant: subjunctive of wish, *May the gods not allow.* . . .
74 mortuum impendere quam vīvum occīdere: mortuum and
    vīvum are objects of the infinitives, *I prefer to expend a dead man
    rather than to kill a living man.* impendere: the third conjugation
    verb, but possibly with a play on the meaning of the second
    conjugation verb pendeō, pendēre, pependī, *to be suspended,
    hang.*
76 corpus . . . tollī: *the body to be lifted up.*
    illī . . . crucī: dative with affīgī, *to be fixed onto.*
78 quā ratiōne . . . īsset: indirect question with pluperfect subjunc-
    tive.

The story of the matron of Ephesus as Eumolpus tells it is subject to
a variety of interpretations. It is introduced by Eumolpus as a tale il-
lustrating the fickleness of women (muliebrem levitātem)—how easily they fall in love, how quickly they forget even their own sons, and
how there is no woman so chaste as not to be driven to madness with
lust for a foreigner. The people on the ship react to the story in different ways. We are told that when Eumolpus finished the story the
sailors received it with laughter, Tryphaena blushed deeply as she
placed her head lovingly on Giton's shoulder (having now forgiven
whatever offense he had committed against her in the past), but Lichas
in anger shook his head and said that if the governor has been just he
ought to have brought the body back into the tomb and strung the
woman up on the cross.

A simpler version of the story is contained in the appendix to the
collection of Phaedrus' fables (first half of the first century A.D.). It is
number 15 in Perotti's Appendix to Phaedrus (found in the Loeb
Classical Library edition of Babrius and Phaedrus, translated by B. E.
Perry).

Eumolpus' version of the story is told with great economy and pre-
cision, and the quotations from Vergil contained in it invite the reader
to compare the story of Dido, her sister Anna, Sychaeus, and Aeneas

with the story of the matron, her **ancilla**, her husband, and the soldier. The former story ends with Dido's tragic death, while Eumolpus' story is a celebration of the choice of life over death, brought about by the matron's **misericordia** (72) and **prūdentia** (77). The ultimate meaning of the story may be as elusive as everything else in Petronius, but in responding to it we need not be limited by the intentions of Eumolpus in telling the story or by the reactions of its audience on board the ship.

1 *repente, adv., *suddenly.*
  **hūmānus, -a, -um, *human.*
  circumagō, circumagere, circumēgī, circumāctus, *to drive in a circle, turn around.*
  **levis, -is, -e, *light; swift.*
2 vertex, verticis, m., *whirl, eddy, whirlpool* (here of the swirling motion of the waves on the seashore.).
  lītus, lītoris, n., *shore.*
  *dēferō, dēferre, dētulī, dēlātus, irreg., *to carry, bring (down).*

3 *subsistō, subsistere, substitī, *to stop, halt; to remain in a place.*
  *trīstis, -is, -e, *sad.*
  ūmeō, -ēre, *to be moist, damp, wet.*
  *mare, maris, marium, n., *sea.*
4 ***īnspiciō [in- + speciō, *to see*], īnspicere, īnspexī, īnspectus, *to look at, examine; to contemplate.*
  forsitan, adv., *perhaps.*
  **prōclāmō, -āre, -āvī, -ātus, *to cry out, shout.*
5 sēcūrus, -a, -um, *without care* [cūra, -ae, f.], *untroubled, fearless.*
  **expectō [ex- + spectō, *to look at*], -āre, -āvī, -ātus, *to await, wait for.*
  ***uxor, uxōris, f., *wife.*
  *forsitan, adv., *perhaps.*
  ignārus, -a, -um + gen., *ignorant (of).*
  *tempestās, tempestātis, f., *weather; storm.*
6 **utīque, adv., *in any case, certainly.*
  proficīscor, proficīscī, profectus sum, *to set out.*
  ōsculum, -ī, n., *kiss.*
7 cōnsilium, -ī, n., *plan, purpose, intention.*
  mortālis, mortālis, mortālium, m., *a mortal.*
  **vōtum, -ī, n., *wish, desire; prayer.*
  ēn, interj., *behold!*
8 *natō, -āre, -āvī, -ātūrus, *to swim.*

IV.

THE DEATH OF LICHAS

Peace aboard Lichas' ship is short-lived. A storm arises and destroys both ship and passengers, leaving only Encolpius, Giton, and Eumolpus alive and afloat on the sea, to be rescued by a fisherman and brought to shore. The following day Encolpius finds a body being washed ashore by the waves.

[115] Repente videō corpus hūmānum circumāctum levī   1
vertice ad lītus dēferrī.   2

Thinking the body to be that of some unfamiliar passenger from the shipwrecked boat, Encolpius begins a soliloquy on the inopportune timeliness of death.

Substitī ergō trīstis coepīque ūmentibus oculīs maris fidem   3
īnspicere et, "Hunc forsitan," prōclāmō, "in aliquā parte ter-   4
rārum sēcūra expectat uxor, forsitan ignārus tempestātis fīlius,   5
aut patrem aut utīque relīquit aliquem, cui proficīscēns ōsculum   6
dedit. Haec sunt cōnsilia mortālium, haec vōta. Ēn homō quem-   7
admodum natat."   8

---

3 **ūmentibus oculīs**: ablative absolute or ablative of means with **īn-spicere**.
4 **Hunc . . . expectat uxor . . . aut patrem . . . relīquit**: *a wife awaits him or he left behind a father.*
5 **sēcūra**: with **uxor**.
7 **vōta**: supply **mortālium**.

9   **ignōtus, -a, -um, *unknown.*
     *dēfleō, dēflēre, dēflēvī, dēflētus, *to weep over, lament.*
     *inviolātus, -a, -um, *unhurt, undisturbed, unharmed.*
     **ōs, ōris, n., *mouth; face.*
     flūctus, -ūs, m., *wave.*

10 *convertō, convertere, convertī, conversus, *to turn (around), turn back.*
     *agnōscō [ad- + gnōscō, *to become acquainted with*], agnōscere, agnōvī, agnitus, *to recognize.*
     terribilis, -is, -e, *terrible.*
     *paulō, adv., *by a little, a little.*
     **ante, adv., *before.*
     implācābilis, -is, -e, *implacable, unappeasable.*

11 Lichās, -ae, m. [Greek name], *Lichas* (in mythology, the attendant of Hercules who brought him the poisoned robe; here the owner of the ship on which the narrator and his companions were sailing).
     *subiciō [sub- + iaciō, *to throw*], subicere, subiēcī, subiectus, *to put under; to subject to + dat.*

12 ***igitur, conj., *therefore.*
     ***lacrima, -ae, f., *tear.*
     *percutiō [per- + quatiō, *to shake; to strike*], percutere, percussī, percussus, *to strike through and through, beat.*
     ***semel, adv., *once.*
     *iterum, adv., *again, a second time.*

13 ***pectus, pectoris, n., *breast, chest.*
     īrācundia, -ae, f., *anger.*
     impotentia, -ae, f., *lack of power over oneself, violence, fury.*

14 nempe, particle, *indeed, to be sure.*
     *piscis, piscis, piscium, m., *fish.*
     bēlua, -ae, f., *beast, monster.*
     ***expōnō, expōnere, exposuī, expositus, *to put forth, expose.*
     **paulō, adv., *by a little, a little.*

15 ***ante, adv., *before.*
     *iactō, -āre, -āvī, -ātus, *to throw; to boast.*
     vīrēs, vīrium, f. pl., *strength, power.*
     imperium, -ī, n., *command, authority, dominion.*

16 naufragus, -ī, m., *shipwrecked person.*

Suddenly he recognizes the body and expounds on the ironic reversal of fortune.

Adhūc tamquam ignōtum dēflēbam, cum inviolātum ōs flūc-   9
tus convertit in terram, agnōvīque terribilem paulō ante et im-   10
plācābilem Licham pedibus meīs paene subiectum. Nōn tenuī   11
igitur diūtius lacrimās, immō percussī semel iterumque manibus   12
pectus et, "Ubi nunc est," inquam, "īrācundia tua, ubi impoten-   13
tia tua? Nempe piscibus bēluīsque expositus es, et quī paulō   14
ante iactābās vīrēs imperiī tuī, dē tam magnā nāve nē tabulam   15
quidem naufragus habēs.   16

---

9 inviolātum ōs: accusative.

17 īte, imperative of eō, īre, iī, itūrus, irreg., *to go.*
    *mortālis, mortālis, mortālium, m., *a mortal.*
    cōgitātiō, cōgitātiōnis, f., *thinking, thought.*
    *impleō [in- + pleō, *to fill*], implēre, implēvī, implētus, *to fill.*
18 cautus, -a, -um, *careful, cautious, wary.*
    opēs, opum, f. pl., *wealth, riches.*
    fraus, fraudis, f., *cheating, deceit, fraud.*
    *capiō, capere, cēpī, captus, *to take, get, seize.*
    *dispōnō, dispōnere, disposuī, dispositus, *to set in order, arrange;
       to distribute, dispose.*
19 *nempe, particle, *indeed, to be sure.*
    *proximus, -a, -um, *next, nearest, the one just before.*
    ***lūx, lūcis, f., *light; day.*
    ***ratiō, ratiōnis, f., *account; account book.*
    **nempe, particle, *indeed, to be sure.*
20 ventūrus, -a, -um, future active participle.
    **patria, -ae, f., *fatherland, home-town.*
    **animus, -ī, m., *mind.*
    **fingō, fingere, fīnxī, fictus, *to form, fashion.*
    animō fingere, *to imagine.*
21 dea, -ae, f., *goddess.*
    dēstinātiō, dēstinātiōnis, f., *destination.*

22 **mortālis, mortālis, mortālium, m., *a mortal.*
    **mare, maris, marium, n., *sea.*
    praestō, praestāre, praestitī, praestātus, *to stand forth; to make
       available, furnish.*
       fidem praestāre, *to show one's trustworthiness, keep one's word.*
23 bellō, -āre, -āvī, -ātūrus, *to wage war, fight.*
    arma, -ōrum, n. pl., *weapons, arms.*
    dēcipiō [dē- + capiō], dēcipere, dēcēpī, dēceptus, *to deceive.*
    ***vōtum, -ī, n., *wish, desire; prayer; votive offering* (something
       solemnly promised to a divinity).
    Penātēs, Penātium, m. pl., *Penates* (household gods).
24 ruīna, -ae, f., *falling down, fall, collapse.*
    **sepeliō, sepelīre, sepelīvī or sepeliī, sepultus, *to bury.*
    vehiculum, -ī, n., *carriage, vehicle.*
    lābor, lābī, lāpsus sum, *to slip, fall.*
    properō, -āre, -āvī, -ātus, *to hasten, hurry.*
    **spīritus, -ūs, m., *air; breath* (of life).
25 excutiō [ex- + quatiō, *to shake*], excutere, excussī, excussus, *to
       shake off, drive out.*
    avidus, -a, -um, *greedy.*
    *strangulō, -āre, -āvī, -ātus, *to strangle.*

The death of Lichas offers a lesson for all mankind.

"Īte nunc mortālēs, et magnīs cōgitātiōnibus pectora implēte. 17
Īte cautī, et opēs fraudibus captās per mīlle annōs dispōnite. 18
Nempe hic proximā lūce patrimōniī suī ratiōnēs īnspexit, nempe 19
diem etiam, quō ventūrus esset in patriam, animō suō fīnxit. Diī 20
deaeque, quam longē ā dēstinātiōne suā iacet! 21

---

18 **cautī**: addressed to shrewd financiers.
   fraudibus: i.e., by usury.
   per mīlle annōs dispōnite: i.e., in investments that will pay off
   thousands of years from the present.
19 **proximā lūce**: *just yesterday.*

Everywhere danger stalks mankind.

"Sed nōn sōla mortālibus maria hanc fidem praestant. Illum 22
bellantem arma dēcipiunt, illum diīs vōta reddentem Penātium 23
suōrum ruīna sepelit. Ille vehiculō lāpsus properantem spīritum 24
excussit, cibus avidum strangulāvit, abstinentem frūgālitās. Sī 25
bene calculum pōnās, ubīque naufragium est. 26

---

abstineō, abstinēre, abstinuī, abstentus, to hold back, be absti-
   nent, be temperate.
frūgālitās, frūgālitātis, f., *frugality.*
26 *calculus, -ī,* m., *small stone; counter* (used in playing draughts);
   stone (used in reckoning on a counting board).
   calculum pōnere, to reckon.
ubīque, adv., *everywhere.*
naufragium, -ī, n., *shipwreck.*

---

22 **nōn sōla ... maria**: *not only the seas.*
   hanc fidem praestant: sarcastic, = *show this* (un)*trustworthiness.*
   Illum bellantem: a fictitious rhetorical example, *That warrior.*
23 **illum. . . . Ille ... avidum ... abstinentem**: four other examples of
   the irony of life.
25 **cibus avidum ... abstinentem frūgālitās**: chisamus.

27 *flūctus, -ūs, m., *wave.*
    obruō, obruere, obruī, obrutus, *to overwhelm.*
    ***contingō [con- + tangō], contingere, contigī, contāctus, *to touch;* + dat., *to happen* (to one), *befall.*
    *sepultūra, -ae, f., *burial.*
28 interest, interesse, interfuit, impersonal, *it makes a difference, it is of importance.*
    **pereō, perīre, periī, peritūrus, irreg., *to pass away, die.*
    *cōnsūmō, cōnsūmere, cōnsūmpsī, cōnsūmptus, *to eat, devour; to consume, destroy.*
    ignis, ignis, ignium, m., *fire.*
29 ***an, particle, *whether; or.*
    **flūctus, -ūs, m., *wave.*
    ***mora, -ae, f., *delay.*
    eōdem, adv., *to the same place.*
30 fera, -ae, f., *wild beast.*
    ***lacerō, -āre, -āvī, -ātus, *to tear, mangle, lacerate.*
31 *ignis, ignis, ignium, m., *fire.*
    **poena, -ae, f., *punishment.*
    *gravis, -is, -e, *heavy; serious; severe.*
32 **īrāscor, īrāscī, īrātus sum + dat., *to become angry* (at), *be angry* (at).
    dēmentia, -ae, f., *madness.*
33 **sepultūra, -ae, f., *burial.*

34 rogus, -ī, m., *funeral pyre.*
    *inimīcus, -a, -um, *hostile; belonging to an enemy.*
    cōnferō, cōnferre, cōntulī, collātus, irreg., *to bring together, collect.*
    adoleō, adolēre, _____, adultus, *to burn, consume* (by fire).
35 epigramma, epigrammatis, n. [Greek loan word], *epigram.*
36 arcessō, arcessere, arcessīvī, arcessītus, *to summon, fetch, seek.*
    sēnsus, -ūs, m., *feeling, sentiment, emotion.*
    longius, compar. adv., *quite far.*

Death is the same for everyone.

"'At enim flūctibus obrutō nōn contingit sepultūra.'   27
Tamquam intersit, peritūrum corpus quae ratiō cōnsūmat, ignis   28
an flūctus an mora. Quicquid fēceris, omnia haec eōdem ven-   29
tūra sunt. 'Ferae tamen corpus lacerābunt.' Tamquam melius   30
ignis accipiat; immō hanc poenam gravissimam crēdimus, ubi   31
servīs īrāscimur. Quae ergō dēmentia est, omnia facere, nē quid   32
dē nōbīs relinquat sepultūra?"   33

---

27   'At . . . sepultūra': the observation of a fictitious interlocutor.
flūctibus obrutō: obrutō is dative with contingit; flūctibus is ablative of means with obrutō.
28   peritūrum corpus: *a body that is going to perish* (anyway).
cōnsūmat: subjunctive in an indirect question.
29   omnia haec: *all these things* = *everything.*
eōdem ventūra sunt: i.e., will all suffer the final annihilation of
death.
30   'Ferae . . . lacerābunt': a second observation of a fictitious interlocutor.
31   ignis: the reference is to cremation. The sense is: What madness to
worry about whether wild beasts will devour us, as if it were better that the fire of the crematory receive us, especially since we
believe that fire is the harshest punishment for wayward slaves!

The burial of Lichas

Et Licham quidem rogus inimīcīs collātus manibus adolēbat.   34
Eumolpus autem dum epigramma mortuō facit, oculōs ad   35
arcessendōs sēnsūs longius mittit.   36

---

34   inimīcīs . . . manibus: i.e., by the hands of the narrator and his
companions.

1	**lēgātum, -ī**, n., *bequest, legacy.*
  **praeter, prep. + acc., *except for, besides.*
2	*****lībertus, -ī**, m., *freedman.*
  condiciō, condiciōnis, f., *condition.*
  percipiō [**per-** + **capiō**], **percipere, percēpī, perceptus**, *to take possession of.*
3	**concīdō** [**con-** + **caedō**, *to cut*], **concīdere, concīdī, concīsus**, *to cut up.*
  astō [**ad-** + **stō**], **astāre, astitī**, *to stand near.*
  ***comedō [**con-** + **edō**; see p. 246], **comesse, comēdī, comēsus**, *to consume, eat up.*
  ***apud, prep. + acc., *at, in, among.*
4	****gēns, gentis, gentium**, f., *nation, people.*
  *propinquus, -ī, m., *kinsman, relative.*
5	****cōnsūmō, cōnsūmere, cōnsūmpsī, cōnsūmptus**, *to take up, eat, devour.*
  *dēfūnctus, -ī, m., *dead man.*
  *adeō, adv., *indeed; to such a degree.*
  obiurgō, -āre, -āvī, -ātus, *to scold, blame, rebuke.*
  *aeger, aegra, aegrum, *sick.*
6	**frequenter**, adv., *frequently.*
  carō, carnis, carnium, f., *flesh.*
  **admoneō, -ēre, -uī, -itus + gen., *to remind* (of); + acc., *to advise, urge; to warn*
7	**recūsō, -āre, -āvī, -ātus**, *to object to, reject.*
  animī, -ōrum, m. pl., *courage, spirit.*
8	**dēvōveō, dēvōvēre, dēvōvī, dēvōtus**, *to curse.*
  ***spīritus, -ūs, m., *air; breath* (of life); *spirit, soul, one's being.*
  ***cōnsūmō, cōnsūmere, cōnsūmpsī, cōnsūmptus, *to take up, eat, devour.*

V.

EATING HUMAN FLESH FOR MONEY

Our adventurers arrive at Croton, a city full of rapacious legacy-hunters (captātōrēs). *Eumolpus poses as a childless millionaire, and everyone courts his favor. Slowly people grow suspicious of his imaginary fortune, and in order to keep the lid on the cauldron, he decides to compose his long-awaited will—but not without inserting a most distasteful provision. He reads his will to the people:*

[141] "Omnēs quī in testāmentō meō lēgāta habent praeter   1
lībertōs meōs hāc condiciōne percipient quae dedī, sī corpus   2
meum in partēs concīderint et astante populō comēderint. Apud   3
quāsdam gentēs scīmus adhūc lēgem servārī, ut ā propinquīs   4
suīs cōnsūmantur dēfūnctī, adeō quidem ut obiurgentur aegrī   5
frequenter, quod carnem suam faciant peiōrem. Hīs admoneō   6
amīcōs meōs nē recūsent quae iubeō, sed quibus animīs   7
dēvōverint spīritum meum, eīsdem etiam corpus cōnsūmant."   8

---

1 **Omnēs quī . . . lēgāta habent**: i.e., all the people to whom I have bequeathed money in my will.

3 **astante populō**: ablative absolute.

4 **quāsdam gentēs**: such peoples are mentioned by Herodotus (the Callatiae of India, 3.38, and the Issedones, a people living beyond the Scythians, 4.26).

6 **quod . . . faciant**: subjunctive because the reason is given as that of people other than the narrator himself.
Hīs: ablative of cause, *For these reasons.*

7 **quibus animīs . . . eīsdem**: *with the same spirit with which. . . .*

8 **cōnsūmant**: jussive subjunctive, *let them. . . .*

9   excaecō, -āre, -āvī, -ātus, *to make blind.*
     fāma, -ae, f., *report, rumor.*
     ***animus, -ī, m., *mind.*
10 *miser, misera, miserum, *wretched, miserable.*
11 ***parātus, -a, -um, *prepared, ready.*
     exsequor, exsequī, exsecūtus sum, *to pursue, follow up, carry out.*

12 stomachus, -ī, m., *stomach.*
     recūsātiō, recūsātiōnis, f., *objection, rejection, refusal.*
     ***sequor, sequī, secūtus sum, *to follow;* here, *to obey.*
13 *imperium, -ī, n., *command, order.*
     prōmittō, prōmittere, prōmīsī, prōmissus, *to promise.*
     ***prō, prep. + abl., *for, on behalf of; instead of; as a reward for, in
       return for.*
     *hōra, -ae, f., *hour.*
     fastīdium, -ī, n., *loathing, aversion.*
14 *bona, -ōrum, n. pl., *goods, possessions.*
     pēnsātiō, pēnsātiōnis, f., *recompense, compensation.*
     ***operiō, operīre, operuī, opertus, *to cover.*
     ***modo, adv., *only, just.*
     ***fingō, fingere, fīnxī, fictus, *to form, fashion, make; to imagine.*
15 ***hūmānus, -a, -um, *human.*
     viscera, viscerum, n. pl., *inner organs; flesh.*
     **centiēs, adv., *a hundred times.*
       *centiēs sēstertium, = centiēs centēna mīlia sēstertium,
         10,000,000 sesterces.
     accēdit, used impersonally, *there is added.*
16 *hūc, adv., *to here, here; to this.*
     blandīmentum, -ī, n., *blandishment, flattery; charm, delight;* here,
       spices, seasoning (for food).
     sapor, sapōris, m., *flavor.*
17 *mūtō, -āre, -āvī, -ātus, *to change.*
     ūllus, -a, -um, *any.*
     *carō, carnis, carnium, f., *flesh, meat.*
     ars, artis, artium, f., *art, skill.*
18 *corrumpō [con- + rumpō, *to break*], corrumpere, corrūpī, cor-
       ruptus, *to corrupt, spoil, make worse; to adulterate, falsify.*
     *stomachus, -ī, m., *stomach.*
     *conciliō, -āre, -āvī, -ātus, *to bring together, win over, make favorable
       to.*
     āversus, -a, -um, *turned away, opposed, averse.*

At least one Crotonite is ready to carry out the distasteful provsision of the will.

Excaecābat pecūniae ingēns fāma oculōs animōsque mi-   9
serōrum.   10
Gorgiās parātus erat exsequī . . .   11

---

11   The text is fragmentary here.

Eumolpus continues to read his will and suggests ways to make the eating of his flesh more palatable.

"Dē stomachī tuī recūsātiōne nōn habeō quod timeam. Se-   12
quētur imperium, sī prōmīseris illī prō ūnīus hōrae fastīdiō   13
multōrum bonōrum pēnsātiōnem. Operī modo oculōs et finge tē   14
nōn hūmāna viscera sed centiēs sēstertium comesse. Accēdit   15
hūc quod aliqua inveniēmus blandīmenta, quibus sapōrem   16
mūtēmus. Neque enim ūlla carō per sē placet, sed arte quādam   17
corrumpitur et stomachō conciliātur āversō.   18

---

12   **Sequētur imperium**: *It* (your stomach) *will obey* (your) *order/ command.* **Sequētur . . . sī prōmīseris**: future more vivid condition.
13   **illī**: i.e., to your stomach.
14   **Operī**: imperative.
16   **quibus . . . mūtēmus**: relative clause of purpose.

19   **quod sī, *but if.*
**exemplum, -ī, n., *example.*
*probō, -āre, -āvī, -ātus, *to test, examine, judge.*
*cōnsilium, -ī, n., *plan, purpose, intention.*
Saguntīnī, -ōrum, m. pl., *inhabitants of Saguntum* (a town in Hispania Tarraconensis, besieged and captured by Hannibal in 219 B.C., precipitating the Second Punic War).

20   *opprimō [ob- + premō, *to press*], opprimere, oppressī, oppressus, *to press down, overpower, oppress.*
Hannibal, Hannibalis, m., *Hannibal* (Carthaginian general in the Second Punic War, 218–201 B.C.).
edō, esse, ēdī, ēsus, *to eat.*
ēdēre, = ēdērunt.
**carō, carnis, carnium, f., *flesh.*
**hērēditās, hērēditātis, f., *inheritance.*

21   ***expectō [ex- + spectō, *to look at*], -āre, -āvī, -ātus, *to await, wait for, expect.*
Petēlīnī, -ōrum, m. pl., *inhabitants of Petelia* (a town in Bruttium in Italy, besieged by Himilco in 216 B.C.).
ultimus, -a, -um, *last, farthest, extreme.*
*famēs, famis, f., *hunger.*
famē, abl.

22   epulātiō, epulātiōnis, f., *feasting, eating.*
captō, -āre, -āvī, -ātus, *to catch at, chase, seek.*
ēsuriō, ēsurīre, _____, ēsurītūrus, *to be hungry.*

23   Numantia, -ae, f., *Numantia* (a town in Hispania Tarraconensis, besieged and captured by Scipio Aemilianus in 133 B.C.).
**capiō, capere, cēpī, captus, *to take, get, seize, capture.*

24   līberī, -ōrum, m. pl., *children.*
sēmēsus, -a, -um, *half-eaten* [sēmi-, *half* + edō, esse, ēdī, ēsus, *to eat*].
***sinus, -ūs, m., *curve; bosom, lap.*

Others have eaten human flesh—and without even the inducement of a legacy!

"Quod sī exemplīs quoque vīs probārī cōnsilium, Saguntīnī 19
oppressī ab Hannibale hūmānās ēdēre carnēs, nec hērēditātem 20
expectābant. Petēlīnī idem fēcērunt in ultimā famē, nec quic- 21
quam aliud in hāc epulātiōne captābant nisi tantum nē ēsurīrent. 22
Cum esset Numantia ā Scīpīōne capta, inventae sunt mātrēs 23
quae līberōrum suōrum tenērent sēmēsa in sinū corpora." 24

---

19 **vīs probārī cōnsilium:** *you wish my plan to be judged.*
21 **Petēlīnī:** Livy (23.30.1–5) describes how the citizens of Petelia were
reduced to starvation and ate the flesh of four-footed beasts of
usual and unusual sorts and hides, grass, roots, bark, and leaves,
but he does not mention their eating human flesh.

APPENDIX

LANGUAGE AND STYLE

For an introduction to the material presented here, see Introduction, pages iv–viii. Not all examples are cited in the following lists.

I.   Phonology

    A. Vowels and diphthongs

        u instead of *i*

Literary sources have spellings in *i* and *u*, as in **lacrima/ lacruma** and **monumentum/monimentum**. Freedmen use both spellings of the latter word in Petronius:

> **monimenta** (II.4.25, p. 133); **monumentum** (II.5.22, p. 157; II.5.25, p. 157; III.13, p. 209)

The following is an example of the vulgar spelling with *u* instead of *i*:

> **manuciolum** (II.4.72, p. 148), vulgar for unattested **maniceolum**

o instead of *u* and insertion of consonant:

> **plovēbat** (II.2.90, p. 88), vulgar for **pluēbat**

ō instead of *au* (thus the plebeian spelling **Clōdius** instead of **Claudius**):

> **cōda** (II.2.75, p. 84), vulgar for **cauda**
> **plōdō** (II.2.131, p. 100), vulgar for **plaudō**
> **cōpōnis** (II.4.12, p. 128), vulgar for **caupōnis**
> **cōdex** (II.5.121, p. 179), vulgar for **caudex**
> The educated characters in Petronius use **cauda, plaudō,** and **caupō.**

ū instead of *au*:

> **clūsō** (II.4.70, p. 148), for **clausō**
> The educated characters in Petronius use spellings with *au*.

i instead of *e* before another vowel (thus, vulgar **vīnia** instead of **vīnea, -ae**, f., *vineyard*):

240

cauniārum (II.2.76, p. 84), vulgar for cauneārum.
manuciolum (II.4.72, p. 148), vulgar for unattested maniceolum

Elision (dropping) of *u* before another vowel:

cardēlēs (II.2.144, p. 104), vulgar for carduēlēs.

Progressive vowel assimilation (second of two vowels changed to match the first):

percolopābant (II.2.62, p. 80), vulgar formation from colaphus (Greek loan word)

Syncope (dropping of a vowel between two consonants)

The syncopated forms of the first two words given below are found in the language of educated characters in Petronius and are commonly found in colloquial Latin of all periods; the unsyncopated forms are not found in Petronius and would be inappropriate for his conversational narrative style. The syncopated form of the fourth word occurs only here in extant Latin and in the speech of a freedman:

balneum (II.1.10, p. 20), colloquial for balineum.
calda (II.2.6, p. 66), colloquial for calida
calfēcit (II.2.6, p. 66), colloquial for calefēcit
būblum (II.2.74, p. 82), vulgar for būbulum

B. Consonants

c instead of qu

Both forms of the first word given below occur in the speech of freedmen, so that Petronius does not make a clear distinction here between refined and colloquial speech. He uses only the colloquial cōcus and never the literary/urbane coquus:

cōtīdiē (II.2.10, p. 68), colloquial for quōtīdiē (II.2.74, p. 83)
cōcī (II.3.9, p. 112), colloquial for coquī

Loss of aspiration (i.e., Greek *ph* > *p*):

percolopābant (II.2.62, p. 80), vulgar formation from colaphus (Greek loan word)

Reduction of consonant clusters:

Both forms of the following word are used by Trimalchio:

sūsum (II.5.199, p. 199), vulgar for sūrsum (II.4.77, p. 151)

II.   Gender and Declension

A.   Change of gender

The neuter tended to disappear in the popular language and to be absorbed by the masculine; the neuter disappeared in all of the Romance languages except Romanian.

Masculine for neuter, second declension:

balneus (II.2.6, p. 66), vulgar for balneum
vīnus (II.2.7, p. 66), vulgar for vīnum
fātus (II.2.20, p. 70; II.5.3, p. 152), vulgar for fātum
caelus (II.2.97, p. 90), vulgar for caelum
amphitheāter (II.2.104, p. 92), vulgar for amphithe-
    ātrum
candēlābrus (II.5.155, p. 186), vulgar for candēlābrum

Masculine for neuter, third declension:

lactem (II.5.2, p. 152), vulgar for lac.

Masculine for feminine in the fourth declension (due to the similarity of fourth to second declension nouns):

porticūs marmorātōs (II.5.199, p. 198), vulgar for por-
    ticūs marmorātās.

Neuter for masculine (by hypercorrection, i.e., an affected or wrong-headed attempt to be correct by using neuter forms instead of the more natural —and correct!—masculine):

nervia (II.2.127,p. 98), vulgar for nervōs
libra (II.2.151, p. 106), vulgar for librōs
thēsaurum (II.2.161, p. 108), vulgar for thēsaurus

B.   Change of gender and declension:

First declension feminine for neuter of second declension:

trīclīnia, first declension nom. sing. fem. (II.5.30, p. 159),
    vulgar for second declension neuter trīclīnium
intestīnās (II.5.186, p. 194), vulgar for neuter pl. in-
    testīna

Greek loan words of the third declension ending in -ma

(**schēma** and **stigma**) used by the freedmen as first declension feminine nouns:

schēmās (II.2.67, p. 82), vulgar for **schēmata**, third declension neuter plural

stigmam (II.2.118, p. 96), vulgar for **stigma**, third declension neuter singular

Neuter for first declension feminine (hypercorrection or affectation, i.e., a wrong-headed attempt to be correct):

margarītum (II.4.59, p. 144), vulgar for **margarītam**.
quisquilia (II.5.151, p. 186), vulgar for **quisquiliae**

C. Change of declension (simplifying the declensional system by bringing third and fourth declension nouns into the first and second declensions):

Third into first:

strīgae (II.4.61, p. 144), vulgar for **strigēs**

Third into second:

pauperōrum (II.2.135, p. 102), vulgar for **pauperum**.

Fourth into second:

gustī (II.5.169, p. 190), vulgar for **gustūs**

D. Third declension nominative (or accusative) formed from stem found in genitive:

excellente (II.2.99, p. 90), vulgar for **excellēns**
bovis (II.4.49, p. 140), vulgar for **bōs**

E. Confusion of stem in third declension proper names derived from Greek:

Philerōnem (II.2.158, p. 109), vulgar for **Philerōtem**
Nīcerōnem (II.4.55, p. 143), vulgar for **Nīcerōtem**

IV. Verbs

Active forms for deponent verbs (a simplification that eventually led to the disappearance of deponent forms) :

argūtat (II.2.133, p. 102), vulgar for **argūtātur**
loquere (II.2.134, p. 102), vulgar for **loquī**
loquis (II.2.134, p. 102), vulgar for **loqueris**
amplexāret (II.4.71, p. 148), vulgar for **amplexārētur**
exhortāvit (II.5.184, p. 194), vulgar for **exhortātus est**

Deponent for active verbs (hypercorrection or affectation, i.e., a wrong-headed attempt to be correct):

delectārētur (II.2.110, p. 94), vulgar for delectat
fastīdītum (esse) (II.3.27, p. 118), vulgar for fastīdīvisse
somniātur (II.5.122, p. 179), vulgar for somniat

Simplification or regularization of verb forms:

vincitūrus (II.2.122, p. 96), vulgar for victūrus
fefellitus (II.4.17, p. 129), vulgar for falsus
faciātur (II.5.30, p. 159), vulgar for fīat
domāta (II.5.123, p. 180), vulgar for domita
māvoluit (II.5.202, p. 198), vulgar for māluit

V.   Word-Formation

Word-formation (the following tend to be more common in the speech of the freedmen than elsewhere in the *Satyricon*):

Nouns in -mōnium:

gaudimōnium (II.4.5, p. 126), for gaudium
trīstimōnium (II.4.61, p. 144), for trīstitia

Third declension nouns ending in -ō, gen., -ōnis:

cicarō (II.2.140, p. 102, and II.5.33, p. 158)
bārō (II.4.69, p. 148)
vavatō (II.4.74, p. 148)
Graeculiō (II.5.185, p. 194)
cellātiō (II.5.199, p. 198)

Nouns and adjectives in -ārius (a favorite suffix in colloquial/vulgar Latin):

vestiārius (II.2.7, p. 66)
pultārius (II.2.11, p. 68)
ōrāculārius (II.2.41, p. 74)
centōnārius (II.2.93, p. 90)
sēstertiārius (II.2.111, p. 94; II.2.123, p. 98)
catēnārius (II.5.56, p. 164)
mīcārius (II.5.90, p. 172)
caligārius (II.5.124, p. 180)
dipundiārius (II.5.124, p. 180)

Adjectives in -āx:

abstināx (II.2.17, p. 69), for abstinēns

Adjectives in -ōsus:

>   linguōsus (II.2.34, p. 72; II.4.56, p. 142)

Adjectives in -ātus:

>   bonātus (II.5.127, p. 180)

Adjectives in -īvus:

>   absentīvus (II.1.131, p. 60), for absēns

Adjectives in -icius:

>   lanisticius (II.2.100, p. 90)

VI. Lexicon

alter used where alius would be correct:

>   alter (II.2.78, p. 84) and Alterās (II.5.170, p. 191)

Diminutives (found frequently throughout the *Satyricon*; often used in colloquial language without any specifically diminutive force; the following are a few of many examples):

>   casula (II.2.82, p. 85)
>   amāsiunculus (II.2.110, p. 94)
>   audāculus (II.4.64, p. 146)
>   manuciolum (II.4.72, p. 148)
>   amāsiuncula (II.5.145, p. 184)
>   corcillum (II.5.150, p. 186)

Vulgar or colloquial coinages and compounds (many of the compounds are also vulgar or colloquial coinages); many of these words are found only once or twice in Petronius and rarely or nowhere else in extant Latin writing (listed in alphabetical order):

>   absentīvus (II.1.130, p. 60)
>   abstināx (II.2.17, p. 69)
>   acia (II.5.186, p. 194)
>   aginō (II.4.19, p. 130)
>   amasiunculus (II.2.110, p. 94)
>   apocūlāmus (II.4.24, p. 132)
>   arcisellium (II.5.142, p. 184)
>   audāculus (II.4.64, p. 146)
>   bacciballum (II.4.13, p. 128)
>   baliscus (II.2.10, p. 68)
>   barbātōria (II.5.89, p. 172)
>   bisaccium (II.1.112, p. 52)
>   burdubasta (II.2.126, p. 98)
>   caldicerebrius (II.2.101, p. 92)

cantābundus (II.4.26, p. 132)
catēnārius (II.5.56, p. 164)
centōnārius (II.2.93, p. 90)
cerasinus (II.1.44, p. 32)
chīramaxium (II.1.35, p. 30)
cicarō (II.2.140, p. 102; II.5.33, p. 158)
corcillum (II.5.150, p. 186)
dēpraesentiārum (II.5.129, p. 180)
disparpallō (II.2.139, p. 102)
domūsiō (II.2.152, p. 106; II.3.26, p. 118)
ēlēgō (II.2.40, p. 74)
embolum (II.1.71, p. 40)
exopīnissō (II.4.51, p. 140)
fulcipedia (II.5.144, p. 184)
gallicinia (II.4.25, p. 132)
gaudimōnium (II.4.5, p. 126)
gingiliphō (II.5.79, p. 170)
lanisticius (II.2.100, p. 90)
linguōsus (II.2.34, p. 72; II.4.56, p. 142)
lōripēs (II.2.126, p. 98)
manuciolum (II.4.72, p. 148)
matauitatau (II.4.36, p. 136)
matus (II.2.7, p. 66)
mīcārius (II.5.90, p. 172)
mixcix (II.2.103, p. 92)
ōrāculārius (II.2.41, p. 74)
pataracina (II.2.3, p. 66)
plūsscius (II.4.76, p. 150)
poricinō (II.2.37, p. 120)
Prīmigenius (II.2.157, p. 108)
prōmulsidāre (II.1.111, p. 52)
sessōrium (II.5.200, p. 198)
sēstertiārius (II.2.111, p. 94; II.2.123, p. 98)
sēvirātus (II.5.39, p. 160)
stāminātus (II.2.7, p. 66)
subolfaciō (II.2.119, p. 96)
trīstimōnium (II.4.61, p. 144)
urceātim (II.2.89, p. 88)
vavatō (II.4.74, p. 148)
versipellis (II.4.49, p. 140)

Compound instead of simple verb:

comedō, comesse, comēdī, comēsus, *to consume, eat up,* instead of edō, esse, ēdī, ēsus, *to eat* (II.2.33, p. 72, and so forth)

subolfaciō, subolfacere (II.2.119, p. 96), with the same meaning as **olfaciō**

Double prefix:

recorrigō [re- + con- + regō] (II.2.36, p. 74)

Hybrid compounds consisting of Latin and Greek elements:

bilychnis (II.1.74, p. 42)
percolopō (II.2.62, p. 80)
apocūlāmus (II.4.24, p. 132)

Vulgar use of words borrowed from Greek:

propīn (II.1.33, p. 28), Greek infinitive used as a noun
laecasīn (II.2.12, p. 68)
penthiacum (II.3.8, p. 112)
tangomenās (II.5.90, p. 172)

VII. Syntax:

    A. Nouns and Adjectives (Case Usage)

        1. Accusative taking over functions of the other cases (a tendency that accelerated in the development of the Romance languages from vulgar Latin):

Accusative instead of genitive:

    quantum ipse voluit (II.2.37, p. 74), instead of **quantī ipse voluit** (genitive of price)

Accusative instead of dative:

    Aedīlēs male ēveniat (II.2.57, p. 79), instead of **Aedīlibus male ēveniat**
    tē persuādeam (II.2.136, p. 102), instead of **tibi persuādeam**

Accusative instead of ablative:

    meōs frūnīscar (II.2.84, p. 86), instead of **meīs frūnīscar** or **fruor** + abl.
    pecūlium tuum frūnīscāris (II.5.138, p. 182), instead of **pecūliō tuō frūnīscāris** or **fruor** + abl.
    prae litterās (II.2.135, p. 102), instead of **prae litterīs**

Accusative instead of locative:

    forās (II.1.77, p. 42; II.2.81, p. 84), instead of **forīs**

This and the following represent confusions in expression of the ideas of place to which and place where in the popular language.

Locative instead of accusative of place to which:

Capuae (II.4.21, p. 131), instead of **Capuam**

2. Omission of preposition:

cum Āfricam libuerit īre (II.3.23, p. 117), instead of **ad Āfricam**

3. Use of prepositional phrase instead of partitive genitive (as the genitive lost ground in the popular language):

quantum dē vītā (II.1.7–8, p. 21), instead of **quantum vītae.**

4. Use of **ūnus** in a sense approximating an indefinite article (a use that would prevail in the Romance languages):

ūnus servus Agamemnonis (II.1.3–4, p. 19), instead of **ūnus ē servīs Agamemnonis**

B. Tenses of Verbs

Present tense for future (occurring in the speech of both the educated characters and the freedmen):

pōnitis (II.1.23, p. 27), colloquial for **ponētis.**
cēnat (II.1.77, p. 43), colloquial for **cēnābit.**

Future perfect where a simple future would be correct:

sī . . . fueris, dīcēs (II.2.98, p. 91), instead of **sī . . . eris, dīcēs**

Use of the active periphrastic with no special meaning instead of the simple future:

futūrum est (II.2.83, p. 87), instead of **erit**

C. Clauses

1. Parataxis

Positioning of short main clauses with the indicative or imperative side by side (the Greek technical term is *parataxis*) instead of subordinating one clause to the other with a subordinating conjunction and/or the subjunctive mood or the accusative and infinitive construction is typical of the speech of the un- or poorly educated freedmen in Petronius. The following are typical:

Paratactic indirect questions with the indicative instead of the subjunctive:

nēmō cūrat, quid annōna mordet (II.2.54–55, p. 79), instead of nēmō cūrat, quid annōna mordeat
nārrā . . . quam contrōversiam . . . dēclāmāstī (II.3.25–26, p. 119), instead of nārrā . . . quam contrōversiam . . . dēclāmāveris
Rogō . . . numquid . . . tenēs (II.3.35–36, p. 121), instead of Rogō . . . numquid . . . teneās
nōn dīxerat quid prīdiē cēnāveram (II.5.187–188, p. 195), instead of nōn dīxerat quid prīdiē cēnāvissem

Parataxis of a direct command instead of subordination as an indirect command with ut and the subjunctive:

"Ōrō tē, melius loquere" (II.2.93, p. 91), instead of ōrō tē ut melius loquāris
Ōrō tē . . . nārrā illud (II.4.3, p. 127), instead of Ōrō tē . . . ut nārrēs illud

Parataxis of two main clauses instead of subordination of one of the clauses as a condition:

Servā mē, servābō tē (II.2.57–58, p. 79), instead of Sī mē servāveris, servābō tē.
fēcit assem, sēmissem habuī (II.4.15–16, p. 129), instead of sī fēcit assem, sēmissem habuī
assem habeās, assem valeās (II.5.204, p. 199), instead of sī assem habeās, assem valeās

Parataxis of two main clauses instead of subordination of one of the clauses as a temporal clause:

inquit rūsticus; varium porcum perdiderat (II.2.94, p. 91), instead of inquit rūsticus cum varium porcum perdidisset.

Parataxis of a conditional clause with the indicative instead of subordination with the subjunctive introduced by num:

vidē . . . sī . . . vidētur (II.5.37–38, p. 161), instead of vidē . . . num . . . videātur

Parataxis of direct statement instead of subordination:

Scītis, magna nāvis magnam fortitūdinem habet (II.5.171, p. 191), instead of Scītis magnam navem magnam fortitūdinem habēre.

2. Other distinctive syntactical features

Use of subjunctive instead of indicative in subordinate clauses (an affectation or hypercorrection, i.e., a wrong-headed attempt to be correct):

> etiam sī magister . . . sit (II.2.146–147, p. 105), instead of etiam sī magister . . . est
> dōnec . . . pervenīrem (II.4.37, p. 137, instead of dōnec . . . pervēnī
> dum . . . amplexāret (II.4.71, p. 149), instead of dum . . . amplexātur
> etiam sī . . . oppresserit (II.5.2–3, p. 153), instead of etiam sī . . . oppressit

Use of quia or quod, *that*, and the indicative in indirect statements instead of the accusative and infinitive construction (the use of quia and quod to introduce indirect statement is typical of vulgar Latin; quia became the favored conjunction in later Latin):

> subolfaciō quia . . . datūrus est Mammea (II.2.119–120, p. 97), instead of subolfaciō Mammeam . . . datūrum esse
> scīs . . . quod epulum dedī (II.5.29–30, p. 159), instead of scīs mē epulum dedisse

Use of nōn instead of nē in negative clauses:

> 'Hoc monumentum hērēdem nōn sequātur' (II.5.22–23, p. 157), instead of 'Hoc monumentum hērēdem nē sequātur'

Pleonastic double negative, in which the second negative takes the place of a positive and does not cancel the first:

> Nēminem nihil bonī facere oportet (II.2.24, p. 71), meaning *No one ought to do* (them) *any favors.*

Construction according to sense (synesis):

> istī maiōrēs maxillae (II.2.58–59, p. 79)
> larvās . . . istōs (II.2.62, p. 81)

VIII. Style

A. Alliteration (the use of words that begin with the same sound; for further examples, see also Anaphora and Paronomasia):

fortis, fidēlis (II.5.41, p. 161)
factum . . . fābula (II.5.167–168, p. 191)
maiōrēs . . . meliōrēs (II.5.170, p. 191)

B. Anaphora (the repetition of the same word at the beginning of successive clauses):

honestē vīxit, honestē obiit (II.2.28–29, p. 73)
Sed rēctus, sed certus (II.2.64–65, p. 81)
Nēmō . . . nēmō . . . nēmō (II.2.85–86, p. 87)
Modo sīc, modo sīc (II.2.93–94, p. 91)
Nōn . . . nōn . . . nōn (II.4.73, p. 149)
sunt . . . sunt (II.4.76, p. 151)
Flēbat . . . flēbat (II.5.43–44, p. 163)

C. Colloquial repetition of words:

Modo modo (II.2.14, p. 68; II.2.159, p. 109)
amīcus amīcō (II.2.35, p. 75; II.2.65, p. 81)
ōlim ōliōrum (II.2.49, p. 77)
caelum caelum (II.2.85, p. 87)
Modo sīc, modo sīc (II.2.93–94, p. 91)
Glycō, Glycō (II.2.117, p. 97)
mortuus prō mortuō (II.2.126–127, p. 99)
magis magisque (II.3.47, p. 123)
Vocā, vocā (II.3.49, p. 123)
Quid? Quid? (II.3.47–48, p. 125)
Vērō, vērō (II.5.49, p. 163)
hominen inter hominēs (II.5.119, p. 179)

D. Asyndeton (omission of conjunctions or connective particles where they would be expected):

Within sentences:

domī leōnēs, forās vulpēs (II.2.80–81, p. 85), instead of domī leōnēs, sed forās vulpēs
rogāmus, mittās (II.3.55, p. 125), instead of rogāmus ut mittās.
per scūtum per ocream (II.4.19, p. 131)
ēgī agināvī (II.4.19, p. 131)
domōs cultās esse, nōn cūrārī eās (II.5.20–21, p. 157), instead of sed nōn cūrārī eās
velit nōlit (II.5.36, p. 161), instead of utrum velit an nōlit
Pius, fortis, fidēlis (II.5.40–41, p. 161)
Suādeō . . . (ut) nōn patiāris (II.5.126, p. 182)
aedificāvī, onerāvī . . . mīsī (II.5.165–166, p. 189)

Aedificō ... comparō ... coemō (II.5.178–179, p. 193)
Between sentences:

See II.4.24–27, p. 133, for a good example.

E. Oaths or asseverations:

Ita meōs frūnīscar, ut ego putō. ... (II.2.84, p. 87)
sīc fēlīcem mē videās, nārrā. ... (II.4.3, p. 127)
Sīc vōs fēlīcēs videam, coniciāmus. ... (II.5.47–48, p. 163)
Ita genium meum propitium habeam, cūrābō. ... (II.5.123, p. 181)
sīc pecūlium tuum frūnīscāris, ... īnspue (II.5.137–139, p. 183)

F. Proverbs

Proverbs, wise sayings, and old saws are frequently; woven into the language of the freedmen and are identified in the notes accompanying the passagaes.

G. Comparisons

Colorful and highly original similes and metaphors occur frequently in the language of the freedmen and are often identified in the notes.

VOCABULARY

A

ā or **ab**, prep. + abl., *from; by*

abeō, abīre, abiī, abitūrus, irreg., *to go away, depart*

ac, conj., *and, and also, and even*

accēdō, accēdere, accessī, accessus, *to approach*

accipiō, accipere, accēpī, acceptus, *to receive; to deal with, treat*

ad summam, *in short, to be brief*

ad, prep. + acc., *to, toward; at, near*

adhūc, adv., *until now, still, yet*

aedificō, -āre, -āvī, -ātus, *to build*

afferō, afferre, attulī, allātus, irreg. + dat., *to bring (to)*

agō, agere, ēgī, āctus, *to do; to drive*

aiō, defective verb used mainly in present and imperfect indicative, *to say*

albus, -a, -um, *white*

aliquī, aliqua, aliquod, indef. adj., *some, any*

aliquis, aliquis, aliquid, indef. pron., *someone, anything, something, anything*

aliquot, indecl. adj., *several, some*

alius, alia, aliud, *other, another*

alius . . . alius, *one . . . another*

alter, altera, alterum, *the one, the other* (of two)

ambulō, -āre, āvī, -ātūrus, *to walk*

amīcus, -ī, m. or **amīca, -ae**, f., *friend*

amō, -āre, -āvī, -ātus, *to love*

ancilla, -ae, f., *female slave*

anima, -ae, f., *breath; spirit; breath of life*

animus, -ī, m., *mind; soul; spirit*

annus, -ī, m., *year*

ante, adv., *before*

ānulus, -ī, m., *ring*

appāreō, -ēre, -uī, *to appear, come in sight; to be revealed*

apud, prep. + acc., *at, in, among*

aqua, -ae, f., *water*

argenteus, -a, -um, *of silver*

as, assis, m., *as* (small copper coin)

at, conj., *but*

atque, conj., *and, and also, and even*

audiō, -īre, īvī, ītus, *to hear*

aureus, -a, -um, *of gold*

autem, particle, *moreover, furthermore*

B

balineum, -ī, n., *bath; baths* (i.e., a public bathing establishment or a set of rooms for bathing in a private home)

bene, adv., *well*

beneficium, -ī, n., *kindness, favor; benefit, service*

bonus, -a, -um, *good*

C

canis, canis, m./f., *dog*

cantō, -āre, -āvī, -ātus, *to sing; to play; to crow*

caput, capitis, n., *head*

cārus, -a, -um, *dear*

causa, -ae, f., *lawsuit, cause, case*

cēna, -ae, f., *dinner*

cēnō, -āre, -āvī, -ātus, *to dine*

centum, indecl. adj., *a hundred*

cēterum, adv., *for the rest, moreover*

cibus, -ī, m., *food*

circā, prep. + acc., *around, about*

circulus, -ī, m., *circle, group of people*

citō, adv., *quickly; too quickly; speedy, soon*

clāmō, -āre, -āvī, -ātūrus, *to shout*

coepī, coepisse, coeptus [pf. tenses only], *to begin*

comedō, comesse, comēdī, comēsus, *to consume, eat up*

conditōrium, -ī, n., *tomb*

cōniciō, cōnicere, cōniēcī, cōniectus, *to throw, hurl, cast; to throw together, put in, include*

cōnsūmō, cōnsūmere, cōnsūmpsī, cōnsūmptus, *to take up, eat, devour; to destroy*

contingō, contingere, contigī, contāctus, *to touch;* + dat., *to happen* (to one), *befall*

contrā, adv., *on the other hand*

contrōversia, -ae, f., *debate, controversy; matter* (for discussion); *formal debate* (in schools of rhetoric with pupils taking opposite sides); *subject* (of such a debate, usually involving a fictitious situation)

convīva, -ae, m., *guest*

coquus, -ī, m., *cook*

corpus, corporis, n., *body*

cōtīdiē [quōtīdiē], adv., *daily*

crās, adv., *tomorrow*

crēdō, crēdere, crēdidī, crēditus, *to lend* (money); *to trust; to believe; to think*

crēscō, crēscere, crēvī, crētūrus, *to increase, grow*

crux, crucis, f., *cross*

cum, conj. + subjn. or indic., *when; since; although*

cum, prep. + abl., *with*

cūrō, -āre, -āvī, -ātus, *to care (for), look after; to see to it* (that) + **ut** + subjn. or subjn. only

D

dē, prep. + abl., *down from; concerning*

dēbeō, -ēre, -uī, -itus, *to owe; ought, must*

decem, indecl. adj., *ten*

dēficiō, dēficere, dēfēcī, dēfectus, *to leave, cease, fail, end, expire*

deinde, adv., *afterward, then, next*

dēnārius, -ī, m., *denarius* (a silver coin originally worth ten **assēs**, later sixteen; the **as**, gen. **assis**, m., was the basic unit of Roman coinage)

dēns, dentis, m., *tooth*

dēstinō, -āre, -āvī, -ātus, *to fix, resolve, intend; to fix upon*

deus, -ī, m., *god*

dexter, dextra, dextrum, *right*

dīcō, dīcere, dīxī, dictus, *to say, tell*

diēs, diēī, m./f., *day*

digitus, -ī, m., *finger*

dīligenter, adv., *carefully, diligently*

discō, discere, didicī, *to learn*

discutiō, discutere, discussī, discussus, *to strike apart, shatter; to dispel*

dispēnsātor, dispēnsātōris, m., *household superintendent, manager, steward*

diū, adv., *for a long time*

diūtius, compar. adv., *longer*

dō, dare, dedī, datus, *to give*

dominus, -ī, m., *master*

domus, -ūs, f., *house, home*

dūcō, dūcere, dūxī, ductus, *to lead, take, bring*

dum, conj., *while*

duo, duae, duo, *two*

E

ē or **ex**, prep. + abl., *out of, from*

effērō, efferre, extulī, ēlātus, irreg., *to carry out* (for burial)
effundō, effundere, effūdī, effūsus, *to pour out/forth;* pass.
with intransitive active sense,
to flow forth
ego, meī, pron., *I*
emō, emere, ēmī, ēmptus, *to buy*
enim, particle, *for*
eō, īre, iī, itūtus, irreg., *to go*
ergō, particle, *therefore*
et, conj., *and*
et . . . et, conj., *both . . . and*
etiam, particle, *still; also; even;
actually*
etiam sī, *even if, although*
excipiō, excipere, excēpī, exceptus, *to take up, catch, receive*
exclāmō, -āre, -āvī, -ātus, *to
shout out*
exeō, exīre, exiī, exitus, irreg., *to
go out, depart*
exinterō, -āre, -āvī, -ātus, *to gut*
expectō, -āre, -āvī, -ātus, *to await,
wait for, expect*
expōnō, expōnere, exposuī, expositus, *to put forth, explain, expound, expose*
extrēmus, -a, -um, *outermost, farthest, last; the end/edge of*

F
fābula, -ae, f., *story, tale*
faciēs, faciēī, f., *face*
faciō, facere, fēcī, factus, *to make*
familia, -ae, f., *family*
fātum, -ī, n., *fate; luck*
fēlīx, fēlīcis, *fortunate, prosperous,
happy*
fēmina, -ae, f., *woman*
ferō, ferre, tulī, lātus, irreg., *to
bring, carry, bear*
fidēs, fideī, f., *faith; trust; credibility*
fīlia, -ae, f., *daughter*

fīlius, -ī, m., *son*
fingō, fingere, fīnxī, fictus, *to
form, fashion, make; to imagine*
fīō, fierī, factus sum, *to be made;
to become; to happen*
fleō, flēre, flēvī, flētus, *to weep,
cry*
fortis, -is, -e, *brave, strong, courageous*
forum, -ī, n., *marketplace*
frangō, frangere, frēgī, fractus,
to break; to move; to soften
frāter, frātris, m., *brother*
fruor, fruī, frūctus sum + abl., *to
enjoy*
fugiō, fugere, fūgī, *to flee*
fūnus, fūneris, n., *funeral*

G
gallus gallīnāceus, -ī, m., *poultry
cock*
genus, generis, n., *birth; kind,sort,
species; way; race, stock, family*
grātia, -ae, f., *favor; regard;* pl.,
thanks
gustō, -āre, -āvī, -ātus, *to taste*

H
habeō, -ēre, -uī, -itus, *to have,
hold; to consider*
habitō, -āre, -āvī, -ātus, *to live*
hic, haec, hoc, dem. adj. and
pron., *this; he, she, it*
hīc, adv., *here*
hinc, adv., *from here, next*
hodiē, adv., *today*
homō, hominis, m., *man; human
being*
hūmānus, -a, -um, *human*

I
iaceō, iacēre, iacuī, iacitūrus, *to
lie*
iam, adv., *already, now*
iānua, -ae, f., *door*

īdem, eadem, idem, dem. adj.
and pron., *the same*
ideō, adv., *for that/this reason,*
therefore
igitur, conj., *therefore*
ille, illa, illud, dem. adj. and
pron., *that; he, she, it*
immō, particle, *nay, on the con-*
trary, rather
in, prep. + abl., *in; on*
in, prep. + acc., *into, onto*
ingēns, ingentis, *large, huge*
inquit, *(he/she) says, said*
īnspiciō, īnspicere, īnspexī, īnspectus, *to look at, examine; to*
contemplate
inter, prep. + acc., *between; among*
interim, adv., *in the meantime,*
meanwhile
intrō, -āre, -āvī, -ātus, *to enter*
inveniō, invenīre, invēnī, inventus, *to find*
invītō, -āre, -āvī, -ātus, *to invite*
ipse, ipsa, ipsum, intens. adj.
and pron., *himself, herself, itself*
ipsimus, -ī, m., *master*
is, ea, id, dem. adj. and pron.,
this; that; he, she, it
ita, adv., *thus, so*
itaque, adv., *and so, therefore*
iubeō, iubēre, iussī, iussus, *to*
order, command
iūs, iūris, n., *law; right*

L
labōrō, -āre, -āvī, -ātus, *to work;*
to suffer; to suffer from strain, feel
tired
lacerō, -āre, -āvī, -ātus, *to tear,*
mangle, lacerate
lacrima, -ae, f., *tear*
lavō, lavāre, lāvī, lavātus or lautus or lōtus, *to wash;* pass. in
reflexive sense, *to bathe oneself.*
lectus, -ī, m., *bed; couch; bier*

lēx, lēgis, f., *law; custom*
lībertus, -ī, m., *freedman*
licet, -ēre, -uit, impersonal, *it is*
permitted
litterae, -ārum, f. pl., *letter* (i.e.,
an epistle); *literature; learning;*
liberal education
locus, -ī, m., *place*
longē, adv., *far, by far*
longus, -a, -um, *long, tall*
loquor, loquī, locūtus sum, *to*
speak
lucerna, -ae, f., *oil-lamp*
lūx, lūcis, f., *light; day*

M
magis, compar. adv., *more; rather*
magnus, -a, -um, *big, large, great*
maior, maior, maius, maiōris
[compar. of magnus, -a, -um],
bigger, larger, greater
male, adv., *badly*
mālō, mālle, māluī, irreg., *to pre-*
fer
malus, -a, -um, *bad, evil*
manus, -ūs, f., *hand*
māter, mātris, f., *mother*
maximus, -a, -um [superl. of
magnus, -a, -um], *biggest,*
largest, greatest
medium, -ī, n., *middle part, center*
meherculēs, interj., *by Hercules!*
melior, melior, melius, meliōris
[compar. of bonus, -a, -um],
better
meminī, meminisse [perfect
forms with present sense], *to re-*
member
mēnsa, -ae, f., *table*
mentior, -īrī, -ītus sum, *to lie*
meus, -a, -um, *my, mine*
mī, = mihi
mīles, mīlitis, m., *soldier*
mīlle, indecl. adj., *a thousand*
minimus, -a, -um [superl. of

parvus, -a, -um], *smallest, very
small*
minor, minor, minus, minōris
[compar. of parvus, -a, -um],
smaller
minus, compar. adv., *less*
mīror, -ārī, -ātus sum, *to wonder;
to marvel at*
mittō, mittere, mīsī, missus, *to
send*
modo, adv., *only, just; only recently, just now; only provided
that* + subjn.
   modo... modo, *at one
time . . . at another time,
now . . . now;*
monumentum [monimentum],
-ī, n., *funerary monument, tomb*
mora, -ae, f., *delay*
moror, -ārī, -ātus sum, *to delay*
mortuus, -a, -um, *dead*
mōs, mōris, m., *manner, custom,
way*
mulier, mulieris, f., *woman*
multus, -a, -um, *much*
   multī, -ae, -a, *many*

N
nam, particle, *for*
nārrō, -āre, -āvī, -ātus, *to tell, report, relate*
nāvis, nāvis, nāvium, f., *ship*
nē, conj. + subjn., *in order that . . .
not, so that . . . not*
nē . . . quidem, *not even*
nec, conj., *and not, neither*
   nec . . . nec, conj., *neither . . . nor*
nēmō, nēminis, m., *no one*
nihil, n., indecl., *nothing*
nisi, conj., *unless, except*
nōlō, nōlle, nōluī, irreg., *to be
unwilling; to refuse*
nōmen, nōminis, n., *name*
nōn, adv., *not*
nōn tantum . . . sed etiam, *not
only . . . but also*
nōs, nostrī or nostrum, *we, us*
nōscō, nōscere, nōvī, nōtus, *to
become acquainted with; pf., to
know; plpf., knew*
noster, nostra, nostrum, *our,
ours*
notō, -āre, -āvī, -ātus, *to note,
mark; to observe*
novem, indecl. adj., *nine*
novus, -a, -um, *new*
nox, noctis, noctium, f., *night*
nummus, -ī, m., *piece of money,
coin*
numquam, adv., *never*
nunc, adv., *now*

O
ō, interj., *oh!*
oblīvīscor, oblīvīscī, oblītus
sum + gen., *to forget*
occīdō, occīdere, occīdī, occīsus,
to cut down; to kill, slay.
octō, indecl. adj., *eight*
oculus, -ī, m., *eye*
officium, -ī, n., *duty, task*
omnis, -is, -e, *all, the whole, every*
operiō, operīre, operuī, opertus,
to cover; to shut, close
oportet, -ēre, -uit, impersonal +
subjn. without ut, *it is proper/
right; ought*
optimus, -a, -um [superl. of
bonus, -a, -um], *best, very good,
excellent*
ōvum, -ī, n., *egg*

P
paene, adv., *almost*
pallium, -ī, n., *cloak*
pānis, pānis, pānium, m., *bread*
parātus, -a, -um, *prepared, ready*
pars, partis, partium, f., *part, side*
parvus, -a, -um, *small, little*
pater, patris, m., *father*

patrimōnium, -ī, n., *inheritance*
pectus, pectoris, n., *breast, chest*
pecūnia, -ae, f., *money*
peior, peior, peius, peiōris
[compar. of malus, -a, -um],
worse
pendeō, pendēre, pependī, *to
hang, hang down*
perdō, perdere, perdidī, perditus, *to destroy; to kill; to lose*
persequor, persequī, persecūtus
sum, *to follow after, pursue*
perveniō, pervenīre, pervēnī,
perventūrus, *to come to, arrive*
pēs, pedis, m., *foot*
pessimus, -a, -um [superl. of
malus, -a, -um], *worst, very bad*
pictūra, -ae, f., *picture*
pingō, pingere, pīnxī, pictus, *to
paint*
placeō, -ēre, -uī + dat., *to please*
plānē, adv., *clearly, plainly, openly*
plēnus, -a, -um, *full, generous; +
gen. or abl., full (of)*
plōrō, -āre, -āvī, -ātus, *to cry
aloud; to lament; to weep*
plūs . . . quam, *more than*
pōnō, pōnere, posuī, positus, *to
put, place*
populus, -ī, m., *people*
porcus, -ī, m., *pig*
porticus, -ūs, f., *porticus* (walkway covered by a roof supported by columns)
poscō, poscere, poposcī, *to ask,
demand*
possum, posse, potuī, *to be able;
can*
post, prep. + acc., *after, behind*
posterus, -a, -um, *next, following*
postquam, conj., *after*
pōtiō, pōtiōnis, f., *drink*
prīmus, -a, -um, *first*
prō, prep. + abl., *for, on behalf of;
instead of, in place of; as a reward

*for, in return for; in a degree cor-
responding to, in proportion to*
puer, puerī, m., *boy; slave*
pulcher, pulchra, pulchrum,
beautiful
putō, -āre, -āvī, ātus, *to think*

Q

quam, adv., *than*
quattuor, indecl. adj., *four*
-que, enclitic conj., *and*
quemadmodum, adv., *in what
manner, how, just as*
quī, quae, quod, rel. pron., *who,
which, that;* rel. adj., *which;* interrog. adj., *what, which*
quia, conj., *because*
quīdam, quaedam, quoddam,
indef. adj., *a certain*
quidem, particle, *indeed, it is true,
to be sure*
quīnque, indecl. adj., *five*
Quis . . . ? Quid . . . ? interrog.
pron., *Who . . . ? What . . . ?*
quisquis, quisquis, quidquid/
quicquid, indef. pron., *whoever,
whatever*
quod, conj., *because*
quoque, adv., *also*
quōtīdiē [cōtīdiē], adv., *daily*

R

ratiō, ratiōnis, f., *account; account
book*
reddō, reddere, reddidī, redditus, *to give back; to render, represent*
redeō, redīre, rediī, reditūrus,
irreg., *to go/come back, return*
relinquō, relinquere, relīquī,
relictus, *to leave*
rēs, reī, f., *thing; matter*
respiciō, respicere, respexī, respectus, *to look at*
rīdeō, rīdēre, rīsī, rīsus, *to laugh*

(at)
rogō, -āre, -āvī, -ātus, *to ask*
rūsticus, -ī, m., *peasant*

S

satis, adv. or substantive, *enough,*
sufficiently
sciō, scīre, scīvī, scītus, *to know*
scrībō, scrībere, scrīpsī, scrīptus, *to write*
sē, reflex, pron., *himself, herself,*
itself, themselves
secundum, prep. + acc., *by, next*
to; in accordance with
sed, conj., *but*
sedeō, sedēre, sēdī, sessūrus, *to*
sit
semel, adv., *once*
septem, indecl. adj., *seven*
sequor, sequī, secūtus sum, *to*
follow
servō, -āre, -āvī, -ātus, *to serve; to*
save; to preserve, keep
servus, -ī, m., *slave*
sēstertius, -ī, m., *sesterce* (small
silver coin)
sex, indecl. adj., *six*
sī, conj., *if*
sīc, adv., *so, thus*
signum, -ī, n., *sign, signal*
sine, prep. + abl., *without*
sinus, -ūs, m., *curve; bosom, lap*
soleō, solēre, solitus sum + infin., *to be accustomed* (to)
sōlus, -a, -um, *only, alone*
soror, sorōris, f., *sister*
spīritus, -ūs, m., *air; breath* (of
life); *spirit, soul, one's being*
spolium, -ī, n., *booty, spoil*
statim, adv., *immediately*
statua, -ae, f., *statue*
stō, stāre, stetī, statūrus, *to stand*
subitō, adv., *suddenly*
sum, esse, fuī, futūrus, irreg., *to*
be

super, prep. + acc., *above, over, on*
suus, -a, -um, *his own, her own, its*
own, their own

T

tabula, -ae, f., *board; waxed writ-*
ing-tablet
tam, adv., *as, so, such*
tamen, adv., *yet, nevertheless*
tamquam, conj., *just as* (if)
tangō, tangere, tetigī, tāctus, *to*
touch
tantum, adv., *only*
temptō, -āre, -āvī, -ātus, *to han-*
dle, feel, test; to try, attempt; to
make an attempt on
tempus, temporis, n., *time*
teneō, tenēre, tenuī, tentus, *to*
hold
terra, -ae, f., *earth, ground*
testāmentum, -ī, n., *will, testa-*
ment
thēsaurus, -ī, m. [Greek loan
word], *treasure*
timeō, timēre, timuī, *to fear*
tollō, tollere, sustulī, sublātus,
to lift; to pick up; to take away,
remove
tōtus, -a, -um, *all, the whole, the*
entire
trēs, trēs, tria, *three*
trīclīnium, -ī, n., *dining room*
tū, tuī, pron., *you* (sing.)
tunc, adv., *then*
tunica, -ae, f., *tunic*
turba, -ae, f., *crowd, mob*

U

ubi, adv., *where, when*
umquam, adv., *ever*
ūnus, -a, -um, *one, only*
ut, conj. + subjn., *in order to, so*
that; + indic., *as, when*
uterque, utraque utrumque,
each of two, both

uxor, uxōris, f., *wife*

V

valeō, -ēre, -uī, *to be strong, be well*

validē [valdē], adv., *strongly, mightily, very*

vēndō, vēndere, vēndidī, vēnditus, *to sell*

veniō, venīre, vēnī, ventūrus, *to come*

vērō, adv., *but, however, indeed*

vestīmentum, -ī, n., *clothing;* pl., *clothes*

vestis, vestis, vestium, f., *garment*

via, -ae, f., *road*

videō, vidēre, vīdī, vīsus, *to see* videor, vidērī, vīsus sum, *to seem, appear*

vīlla, -ae, f., *country estate*

vincō, vincere, vīcī, victus, *to conquer, overcome; to be victorious, win*

vīnum, -ī, n., *wine*

vir, virī, m., *man; husband*

vīta, -ae, f., *life*

vīvō, vīvere, vīxī, vīctūrus, *to live*

vīvus, -a, -um, *alive, living*

volō, velle, voluī, *to be willing; to wish*

vōs, vostrī *or* vostrum, pron., *you* (pl.)

vōtum, -ī, n., *wish, desire; prayer; votive offering* (something solemnly promised to a divinity)

vultus, -ūs, m., *face; expression*

GILDERSLEEVE'S LATIN GRAMMAR

B. L. Gildersleeve & G. Lodge

New to this edition:
+ Foreword by **Ward W. Briggs, Jr.**
+ Comprehensive bibliography by **William Wycislo.**

The classic Latin grammar favored by many students and teachers.

613 pp. (1895, third ed., reprint with additions 1997) paperback ISBN 0-86516-353-7

"Compare his work with any other treatise hitherto in use, and its superiority will be manifest."
Southern Review

NEW LATIN GRAMMAR

Charles E. Bennett

"Great pleasure attends the reissue of Bennett's *New Latin Grammar* by Bolchazy-Carducci ... Teachers and students alike can rejoice at its reappearance. Bennett's definitions and explanations of the basic grammatical and syntactical points are a paragon of clearness and succinctness. I strongly recommend it for high-school teachers and for undergraduates at all levels; for graduate students and scholars it is ideal for a quick look since the organization is clear and 'user-friendly'."

xvi + 287 pp. (1908, reprint 1995) Paperback ISBN: 0-86516-261-1

Robert I. Curtis, *Univ. of Georgia*

A NEW LATIN SYNTAX

E.C. Woodcock

This book gives a historical account of the chief Latin constructions in twenty-five chapters arranged in such order as to make it useful as a progressive revision course in syntax for Advanced Level and University students.

xxiv + 2687 pp. (1959, reprint 1987) Paperback, ISBN: 0-86516-126-7

Bolchazy-Carducci Publishers, Inc. — www.bolchazy.com

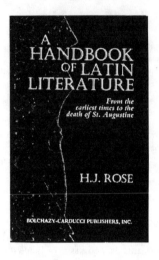

A HANDBOOK
OF LATIN
LITERATURE
*From the earliest times to
the death of St. Augustine*

H. J. Rose

582 pp. (1936, rpt. 1996)
ISBN: 0-86516-317-0
Paperback, $19.00

This reference work offers a matchless overview of
Latin literature from the beginnings to St. Augustine.
First published in 1936, this book is a penetrating
study of Latin literature and includes not only the
classical and post-classical authors, but also a
representative selection of Christian writers. Each
known work is discussed and analyzed in terms of
content, chronology, genre, significance, meaning,
genetic relationship to other works, ancient and
modern scholarship and influence. Also included is
a supplementary bibliography by E. Courtney.

Bolchazy-Carducci Publishers, Inc. — www.bolchazy.com

CICERO & CATULLUS

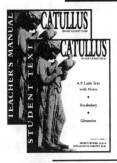

CATULLUS: AP Edition
ed. and trans. by
Henry V. Bender, Ph.D.,
and Phyllis Young Forsyth, Ph.D.

Student text:
105 pp., 8½ x 11"
(1996), Paperback
ISBN: 0-86516-275-1

Teacher's manual:
Reproducible Pages
95 pp., 8½ x 11"
(1996), Paperback
ISBN: 0-86516-276-X

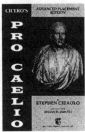

CICERO'S *PRO CAELIO*
AP Edition
ed. by
Stephen Ciraolo

xxxii + 192 pp.
(1997)
Paperback
ISBN: 0-86516-264-6

This edition of one of Cicero's greatest orations provides all the linguistic and background material for the Cicero component of the *Advanced Placement* program in Latin literature.

CICERO'S
FIRST CATILINARIAN
ORATION
Karl Frerichs

80 pp., 8½x11"
(1997)
Paperback
ISBN: 0-86516-341-3

✦ Clear, tripartite page layout for text, vocabulary and notes on facing pages
✦ Running vocabulary separate from notes and complete vocabulary at the end
✦ Introduction and *Glossary of Terms and Figures of Speech* provide basic biographical, historical and rhetorical background
✦ Maps and illustrations

Bolchazy-Carducci Publishers, Inc. — www.bolchazy.com

PLAUTUS' MENAECHMI
Gilbert Lawall

"This new edition is intended for second-year Latinists...it might very well be attractive for the first reading of Plautus...The book is eminently helpful, intelligently presented and reflects the editor's care and understanding."

200 pp. (1978, reprint 1995) Paperback
ISBN: 0-86516-007-4

Malcom Willcock, *JACT*

PLAUTUS' *POENULUS*
John H. Starks, Jr., Matthew D. Panciera, et al

This "audio-lingual-lectographic" package with
✦ **student edition** ✦ **teacher edition** ✦ **video**
is a great pedagogical tool for learning, hearing, & performing Latin.

A brilliant example of the colloquial Latin spoken at the time.

Student edition:	Teacher edition:	Videotape:
✦ text	✦ translation	Live, Latin
✦ introduction	✦ director's notes	performance by
✦ facing vocabulary	✦ information on	graduate students
✦ commentary	Roman theater	at Chapel Hill.
✦ glossary	✦ exercises	ISBN 0-86516-324-3
ISBN 0-86516-323-5	ISBN 0-86516-347-2	

THE PHAEDRA OF SENECA
Gilbert Lawall,
Sarah Lawall, Gerde Kinkel

● Latin Text ● Facing Vocabulary
● Study Questions ● Analysis
● Stage Directions ● Illustrations
● New Translation of the Hippolytus of Euripides

"...though the book was developed with college students in mind, it could probably be used successfully by advanced high school students or by adults who wish to do some independent reading in Latin literature."

Illus., 238 pp.
(1982,reprint 1989)
Paperback
ISBN: 0-86516-016-3

Rudolph Masciantonio, *NECN*

Bolchazy-Carducci Publishers, Inc. — www.bolchazy.com

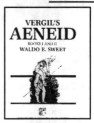